MW00651998

THE SAIGON SISTERS

A volume in the
NIU Southeast Asian Series
Edited by Kenton Clymer

For a list of books in the series, visit our website at cornellpress.cornell.edu.

THE SAIGON SISTERS

Privileged Women in the Resistance

Patricia D. Norland

NORTHERN ILLINOIS UNIVERSITY PRESS

AN IMPRINT OF CORNELL UNIVERSITY PRESS   ITHACA AND LONDON

First published 2020 by Cornell University Press

Printed in the United States of America

Library of Congress Cataloging-in-Publication Data

Names: Norland, Patricia, author.
Title: The Saigon sisters : privileged women in the resistance / Patricia D. Norland.
Description: Ithaca : Northern Illinois University Press, an imprint of Cornell
    University Press, 2020. | Series: NIU series in Southeast Asian studies |
    Includes bibliographical references and index.
Identifiers: LCCN 2019046479 (print) | LCCN 2019046480 (ebook) |
    ISBN 9781501749735 (cloth) | ISBN 9781501749742 (epub) |
    ISBN 9781501749759 (pdf)
Subjects: LCSH: Indochinese War, 1946–1954—Personal narratives, Vietnamese. |
    Indochinese War, 1946–1954—Women—Vietnam—Ho Chi Minh City. |
    Women revolutionaries—Vietnam—Ho Chi Minh City—Biography. |
    Upper class women—Vietnam—Ho Chi Minh City—Biography. |
    Upper class women—Political activity—Vietnam—Ho Chi Minh City. |
    Ho Chi Minh City (Vietnam)—History—20th century.
Classification: LCC DS553.5 .N67 2020 (print) | LCC DS553.5 (ebook) |
    DDC 959.704/1109252095977—dc23
LC record available at https://lccn.loc.gov/2019046479
LC ebook record available at https://lccn.loc.gov/2019046480

To my mother and father,
with eternal gratitude

Contents

Foreword

In 1988, Patricia Norland landed at Tan Son Nhat airport outside of Saigon, now Ho Chi Minh City, as part of a nonprofit organization working to promote better understanding between the United States and the Socialist Republic of Vietnam in the absence of formal diplomatic ties between Washington and Hanoi. During her visit, Norland struck up a friendship with Nguyen Thi Oanh, a former revolutionary during the two wars that tore Vietnam apart between 1945 and 1975, first against the French, then against the Americans. The two women kept in touch, and the friendship between them was such that Oanh introduced Norland to a "band of sisters" with whom she had gone to high school in Saigon in the late 1940s before they joined the resistance war against the French in 1950. The Saigon sisters, as Norland calls them, form the basis of this remarkable book about the trials and tribulations of these women through two decades of war.

Nguyen Thi Oanh and her fellow classmates at a then all-girls elite colonial high school in Saigon, Lycée Marie Curie, were not necessarily destined to become revolutionaries during the First Indochina War, pitting the French against the Vietnam that Ho Chi Minh had declared independent in September 1945. After all, these young women had all grown up in well-off Vietnamese families, spoke French fluently, and followed the latest trends in the films they watched and the clothes they wore. They had little or no contact with the countryside or the majority peasant population living there. Nor did they know much about the finer points of Marxism-Leninism or even the intricacies of French colonial policies in Indochina since 1945. Overall, they enjoyed privileged, rather cloistered lives.

Most of their parents and certainly the French colonial authorities would have preferred that they continue to do so. The reality of their relationship to their upbringing and their milieu, however, would prove to be more complicated. For one, as the war dragged on, these Saigon sisters became politically more active. While some parents kept their heads down and avoided politics in the hope that things would work out, others taught their children of Vietnam's glorious past and filled them in on the major political events missing in their school manuals—Ho Chi Minh's creation of the Indochinese Communist Party in 1930 and, that same year, the French execution of the leader of the Vietnamese Nationalist Party, Nguyen Thai Hoc. One of the sisters had a father who had not only pulled himself out of crushing poverty to become a self-made man in colonial Saigon but had also secretly worked for the resistance and, apparently, had been doing so for a very long time as a Communist agent.

Paradoxically, the colonial classroom probably provided the best space for these privileged Vietnamese teenagers, boys and girls alike, to discover politics and develop a political activism that would push many of them into action and into the maquis. Private French lycées in Saigon like Marie Curie, Chasseloup-Laubat, and Pétrus Ky were not the reactionary bastions of settler society some might think. Nor were they under the control of the colonial security services. At the end of the Second World War, many longtime teachers in these elite schools retired or left their positions to return to France. Administrators in Saigon and elsewhere had to recruit teachers from the metropolis to teach the national curriculum, called the baccalauréat. Many of the new teachers were fresh out of universities in France. Some had experienced the resistance in France, accepted the inevitability of decolonization, and did not necessarily toe the colonial line. (A real hostility existed in postwar colonial society between the "new" and the "old" French, aggravated by the Vichy years of collaboration in France and Indochina.)[1]

In the classrooms, many young Vietnamese thinking in critical ways began to question French colonialism and the legitimacy of the war designed to preserve it. They did so in discussions with Left-leaning French professors sympathetic to Vietnam's independence and in a myriad of exchanges with fellow classmates, Vietnamese and French. It is no accident that Marguerite Duras's *Barrage contre le Pacifique* was an eye-opening read for one Saigon sister. No one had ever told her that colonialism oppressed poor white settlers, *les petits blancs*, as much as the "natives." It was not just a question of race, she realized, but one of class as well. We learn too that Georges Boudarel taught philosophy to some of the Saigon sisters during their time at Marie Curie. He would leave this lycée and cross over to Ho Chi Minh's government in 1950, at the same time as the Saigon sisters.[2]

Gender mattered. Young Vietnamese women were as involved as their male counterparts in the political activism building in the late 1940s. They filled colonial schools like never before after 1945. They also joined a growing number of student associations popping up in schools, much to the dismay of the French authorities. They took part in meetings and debates and rapidly discovered the power of protest inside and outside the classroom. Several of the Saigon sisters dared to hand out subversive tracts and pamphlets in their high school or convince their classmates to wear white as a sign of defiance to the colonial order. Of course, not all privileged urban Vietnamese youth, male or female, were destined to become revolutionaries. Many focused on finishing their studies and getting a job. Others, just as anticolonialist, rejected Ho Chi Minh and the Communist state he hoped to create in favor of a democratic form of government free of the French. However, the political awareness that had spread throughout elite schools in the years after the Second World War ensured that a handful of the best and the brightest of this generation would make choices that would change them and the course of their lives forever, one of the most fascinating themes running through this moving book from start to finish.

In early 1950, several events combined to set the Saigon sisters down radically different paths none of them could have imagined just a few months earlier (except perhaps for the sister whose father was already deeply involved in the resistance and the Communist party at its helm). The choices each made at this time directly impacted her life, those of her immediate family, and her relationships with the other young women. The first event occurred on January 9, 1950, when thousands of middle school and lycée students in Saigon converged in front of the prime minister's palace in downtown Saigon. They were upset with the political course the country had taken under the French and were determined to make their voices heard and to push for change.

Indeed, much had been going on in the preceding months. In mid-1949, the former emperor of Vietnam, Bao Dai, had returned to Vietnam to serve as the head of state of the newly created Associated State of Vietnam, with Tran Van Huu as his prime minister. The French may have grudgingly agreed to allow Bao Dai to unify Vietnam by combining the Cochinchinese colony, southern Vietnam, with its two protectorate parts, one in Annam (in the center) and the other in Tonkin (in the North). However, the French refusal to grant full independence to Vietnam angered students not only in Marie Curie but in other elite Saigon schools, like Pétrus Ky and Chasseloup-Laubat, as well as in Hue, Hanoi, and Haiphong. These politically aware students were not dupes. They knew that "association" was the French code word for continued colonial control. It continued to federate Vietnam with its fellow Associated States of Indochina led by royals in Laos and Cambodia. They were all, in turn, members of a wider imperial state run from Paris called the French Union. Their passports left no doubt about where sovereignty resided—in the French Union.

Equally important, Vietnamese students like the women in this book would have all been aware of the wave of decolonization sweeping across Asia in the late 1940s. The radios talked about it; papers could not avoid printing stories about it. The Philippines had secured their independence from the Americans in 1946. The Indonesians, like the Vietnamese, had been fighting for their independence against the Dutch, who finally let go of their colony a few weeks before students took to the streets in Saigon in January 1950. Vietnamese voices on the Right and the Left called on the French to do the same. Since the First World War, Vietnamese of all political colors had never failed to point out to the French that the British had found a way to recognize the full independence of Canada and Australia within a commonwealth. London had now recognized India's full independence in that framework. If the British could do it, so could the French. Paris refused, and for many young Vietnamese coming of age after the Second World War, the French attempt to use the ex-emperor to maintain their colonial rule was the last straw.

It was in this wider context that things took a turn for the worse when the French colonial police, the Sûreté Générale, moved in with force on the protesting students in downtown Saigon in January 1950. Frustration turned into seething anger when the Sûreté shot a student from the Pétrus Ky high school who was trying to help a friend being whisked away by the police. His name was Tran Van On. He was nineteen. Students surrounded him until he could be taken to a nearby hospital free of the Sûreté's meddling. He died a few hours later of a gunshot wound. The news of his death spread like wildfire throughout Saigon and other cities across Vietnam. The French could censor stories, but this one was out of control. Protestors had cameras and were taking their own pictures, printing tracts, and publishing articles whether the security services liked it or not. Nor could colonial authorities prevent students from turning out in huge numbers for the funeral and cortège held for Tran Van On at Pétrus Ky a few days later. That occasion became the site of another demonstration against French colonial rule and those who worked with the French in the form of the Associated State of Vietnam. The Saigon sisters were involved directly or indirectly in these student demonstrations.

Following on this was the arrival on March 19, 1950, of two U.S. naval vessels to the port of Saigon. The French authorities had invited the Americans to make such a call as a sign of support for the French as Mao Zedong's Communist China threw its diplomatic and military weight behind Ho Chi Minh's Vietnam, along with the Soviet Union and the rest of the Communist bloc. In response, in February, the United States recognized Bao Dai's Vietnam and soon began pouring military aid into Vietnam to hold off the Soviet and Chinese Communists at the Indochinese pass. Occurring in the context of this rapidly spreading political activism in Saigon schools, the U.S. naval visit sparked off yet another round of protests, this time hostile to the Americans and their support of the French and their puppet government. Middle and high school students led a march through Saigon, shouting slogans like "Long live Ho Chi Minh's government" and brandishing the red flag of France's enemy, the Democratic Republic of Vietnam. Unable to control the situation, colonial authorities brought in the army. As paratroopers and legionnaires rushed in, one of their military trucks hit a teenager in front of the Grand Marché, killing him instantly and radicalizing the situation even more. The army broke up the protests as the Sûreté opened hundreds of files on those they had arrested in weeks of protests and those they were now following. The French police probably had the Saigon sisters in their sights for the first time from this point.[3] Another incident propelling the girls to action occurred on May 1, 1950,

International Workers' Day. One sister tells of how she slipped out of the house to join demonstrators lining the streets of Saigon.

Again, not all students went on strike or risked expulsion; but for those who did, they suddenly found themselves on the wrong side of the law and often at odds with their parents, many of whom thought that they had lost their Confucian minds. In private, their parents knew better. So did veterans in the colonial security services. This was not the first time Saigon students had mobilized young people in such large numbers. The French arrest of the famous anticolonialist Phan Boi Chau in 1925 and the death of the country's greatest reformer, Phan Chu Trinh, in 1926 had set off similar student strikes and demonstrations in Saigon. Phan Chu Trinh's funeral procession alone had attracted thousands of young Vietnamese critical of French rule. Women had also become politically active in colonial classrooms and through political participation during the interwar period. Confucian tradition had been on trial for decades already.[4] But students in the late 1940s wanted change now more than ever. And unlike in the 1920s, a war was now on inside Vietnam. Underground agents working for Ho Chi Minh were also there to egg the students on and help them cross over to the other side, not into southern China as was the case in the late 1920s but to resistance territories inside Vietnam, oftentimes no more than a bus or boat ride from Saigon and a hike into the jungle, as we discover in this book. (I found the details about linkages between the colonial city and the resistance zones particularly arresting.)

What is sure is that Tran Van On's death converged all sorts of social, economic, and political winds into one crowded hour when hundreds of young students felt they had to act. For the Saigon sisters, that meant joining the resistance, the maquis, and entering Ho Chi Minh's government fighting the French for the country's independence. Some of the sisters made their decision on the spur of the moment. Others discussed their choices carefully with friends and siblings. One refused and stayed put in Saigon but never betrayed her friends. Family considerations crossed everyone's minds when making such decisions: What would happen to one's parents? What would they think? Who would take care of them? There is a human touch to these souvenirs that will leave no reader indifferent.

All of this comes through powerfully in the memoirs of the Saigon sisters, which Patricia Norland has so deftly woven together through countless interviews conducted between 1988 and 2017. One does not have to agree with the sisters politically to appreciate their life stories. Admittedly, I could not help but ask myself while reading their memoirs whether the Saigon sisters were as naïve about the Vietnamese Communists running the resistance and later all of Vietnam as some of their parents had been about the French colonialists manipulating Vietnam's independence. It is hard to believe that these women were not careful in their interviews with Norland to play down the role the Communists played in favor of the patriotic line several of them had toed for the party in their meetings with foreigners for so many years.

But what makes this book so important is that it takes us through the wars through the Sister's eyes, or at least how they recalled it in those conversations between 1988 and 2017 as Vietnam opened to the non-Communist world. We get a better idea of the choices that continued to confront each sister as the First Indochina War ended with an armistice at Geneva in 1954 and the (provisional) division of the country into two halves. Some sisters went north; some remained in the resistance in the South, rechristened the National Liberation Front in 1960. Each sister has a story to tell, and each of them is well worth reading.

Christopher Goscha
Université du Québec
à Montréal

Notes

1. A humanist-minded Frenchman named Marcel Ner ran the Indochinese educational system after the Second World War. He was no reactionary. See http://indochine .uqam.ca/en/historical-dictionary/956-ner-marcel.html (accessed June 21, 2019). Ner was close to another liberal-minded intellectual critical of French colonial policy, Paul Mus. The latter's father was a longtime teacher and educator in colonial Indochina. See my "'So What Did You Learn from War?': Violent Decolonization and Paul Mus's Search for Humanity," *South East Asia Research* 20, no. 4 (2012): 569–93, accessed June 21, 2019, https://cgoscha.uqam.ca/wp-content/uploads/sites/28/2017/01/So-what-did-you -learn-from-war.pdf.

2. Georges Boudarel, *Autobiographie* (Paris: Jacques Bertoin, 1991).

3. For more on these events, see Boudarel, *Autobiographie*, 101–8.

4. Micheline Lessard, "The Colony Writ Small: Vietnamese Women and Political Activism in Colonial Schools during the 1920s," *Journal of the Canadian Historical Association/ Revue de la Société historique du Canada* 18, no. 2 (2007): 3–23; and David Marr, *Vietnamese Tradition on Trial (1920–1945)* (Berkeley: University of California Press, 1981).

Preface

While scores of books on twentieth-century Vietnam have been written by and about soldiers, diplomats, and journalists—nearly all of them men—this book offers the unique perspective of a group of privileged women immersed in a French lycée who rebel and fight for independence from France. This book traces the lives of nine girls who meet at Lycée Marie Curie in 1940s Saigon and remain friends in today's Ho Chi Minh City.

Children of the elite who worked for the French, these young women graduated from the lycée in 1950 and followed divergent paths. One group traded their schoolgirl uniforms for black pajamas and joined the maquis (literally, "brush," meaning underground or resistance). Others were sent abroad by worried parents. A third group remained in Saigon, leading double lives to serve the resistance. In the 1980s, these women, the Saigon sisters, reunited in Ho Chi Minh City.

Voices of women of their age and status are rare and offer insights on the call of nationalism, the impact of Confucian values on women, the toll of war on families, the disillusionment that can follow a life dedicated to a cause, the perseverance of women in professions despite societal upheaval, and the bonds of friendship that endure the trauma of war. Their stories are unique not only because few peers took the same path but because it is unusual for women to speak up in societies shaped by Confucian thinking. The perspective of the Saigon sisters sheds further light on a tumultuous period of history from which lessons continue to be learned. Ken Burns's television series on the Vietnam War (2017) further testifies to the ongoing fascination with studying the war.

The rarity of Vietnamese women telling their stories reveals itself in the dearth of oral histories. One of the few is *No Other Road to Take* (1976), the memoir of Nguyen Thi Dinh, translated by Mai Elliott. Mai Tu Van, in *Vietnam, un peuple, des voix* (*Vietnam: One People, Many Voices*) (1983), provides insights into reasons many women are inhibited from speaking to foreigners. Arlene Eisen's *Women and Revolution in Viet Nam* (1984) contains excerpts of individual accounts of struggle during the war. Lady Borton's work, including *After Sorrow—an American among the Vietnamese* (1995), renders sharp detail to the lives of peasant women during the wars. Karen Gottschang Turner and Phan Thanh Hao turn a rare spotlight on women at war in North Vietnam in *Even the Women Must Fight* (1998). Duong Van Mai Elliott (the translator cited above) wrote *The Sacred Willow* (1999), a saga of four generations in her family. Sandra C. Taylor's *Vietnamese*

Women at War (1999) portrays the "long-haired warriors," peasant women who used weapons in combat against the French and Americans. Expatriate Vietnamese continue to contribute powerful testimonies about life in Vietnam, and some of these accounts are by women, such as Xuan Phuong's *Ao Dai—My War, My Country, My Vietnam* (2004). Going further back, a gripping account of a revolutionary woman in the 1920s is by Hue-Tam Ho Tai: *Passion, Betrayal, and Revolution in Colonial Saigon—the Memoirs of Bao Luong* (2010).

Nevertheless, we have not heard stories of women among the elite in colonial Saigon who remained in their country, forsaking safety and comfort to struggle for independence and enduring great sacrifice. We have not heard privileged women describe in detail how they adapted to life in the jungle, whether facing bombing raids, malaria, deadly snakes, or other trials. How did they juggle double lives working for the resistance in Saigon? How could they endure having to rely on family members to raise their own children? Why, after being sent to study abroad by anxious parents, did several women choose to return to serve their country? How could they bear open-ended separation from husbands? How did they cope with sending their children to villages to escape the bombings of Hanoi? In spite of the maelstrom of war, how did they forge careers? And how, in spite of dislocation and distrust following the end of the war in 1975, did these women find each other and rekindle their friendships?

This oral history answers these questions in rare and vivid detail. In their own words, the women interweave themes of colonialism, questioning of Confucianism, origins of nationalism, women in the resistance, and friendships that survive war and separation.

This book came to life through a chance encounter. Between the end of the Vietnam War in 1975 and normalization of diplomatic relations between the United States and Vietnam in 1995, only a small number of Americans obtained visas to visit Vietnam. In the absence of government-to-government relations, a nonprofit organization called the Indochina Project promoted people-to-people exchanges by organizing conferences and trips to Vietnam. The genesis of this oral history stems from one of those visits.

In April 1988, a group of Americans arrived at Ton Son Nhat Airport in Saigon. Sponsored by U.S. church groups, the visitors wanted a firsthand look at daily life in Vietnam to assess what limited aid to provide given the U.S. trade embargo then in force. As a staff member at the Indochina Project, I went along to learn more about the situation in-country.

To evaluate conditions and priority needs, we talked with officials, aid workers, and academics. One afternoon, we met in a private home with one of the few trained social workers in the Socialist Republic of Vietnam. It seemed to me that the people who had briefed us in earlier meetings obscured or downplayed social problems; on this day, though, we met Nguyen Thi Oanh, a kind-faced, fifty-six-year-old with a halo of gray hair, who described a different reality. A drawn-out war from which many people emerged poor, isolated, and traumatized had produced social problems that Oanh described as devastating. Street children, unemployment, drug use, the disabled, domestic abuse—Oanh provided the most clear-eyed insights we gained on the whole visit.

Afterward, I approached Oanh to thank her for being candid and asked where she had gone to school. Her reply—"I studied down the street at Lycée Marie Curie"—caught me by surprise. We were in a Communist country, a former French colony, and this English-speaking social worker had attended a lycée that still functioned in downtown Ho Chi Minh City, as Saigon had been renamed? Oanh explained she had been a boarding student at Lycée Marie Curie and her experience there had shaped her studies, career goals, and friendships. "I still have friends from Marie Curie," she added, "though we're only a few." She explained that the "indigenous" girls allowed to study at Marie Curie came from wealthy families whose parents worked for the French. By the late 1940s, an anti-French independence movement swept through the countryside into the towns at the same time Oanh and her friends became aware that their people, "les jaunes" (yellow people), were treated as inferiors. While they saluted the French tricolor in the school courtyard each morning, were assigned French names, won prizes awarded by the French education department, wore *jupes* (skirts), and studied Vietnamese only as a second language, Oanh and her friends began to engage in the growing student movement against the French.

Oanh said the year 1950 was pivotal: three fiery confrontations in Saigon stoked student anger. Students no longer wanted to be cloistered in French lycées and participated openly in protests and marches. Saigon was at a boil, Oanh recalled; in 1950, she and her friends were scattered, pulled into different worlds. Several girls were sent abroad to study, others donned black pajamas and joined the maquis, and a few stayed in Saigon to care for their families while quietly supporting the resistance. "We were unsure if, and when, we would meet again," Oanh said softly.

By the time I first met Oanh, in 1988, most of her classmates had moved abroad and returned only for visits. She pointed out that postwar reunions of Lycée Marie Curie students regularly took place in France, the United States, and other countries where large populations of Vietnamese found themselves.

Our conversation set my mind whirling. Why had Oanh and her friends taken different paths from their Marie Curie classmates? Why had they stayed when so many left? How had city girls endured life with the resistance based in the jungle? How had they built a family or shaped a career? A half century on, what influence did Lycée Marie Curie have on them?

FIGURE 1. Courtyard of Lycée Marie Curie, built in 1918 by the French and where the Saigon sisters, daughters of privileged families, met in the 1940s. Oanh, on the right, 1989. Courtesy of the author.

I asked Oanh if I could meet her friends. After a long pause, she agreed.

One by one, she introduced me to eight friends we came to call the Saigon sisters: Tuyen, with whom Oanh boarded at the lycée and whose brother, Luu Huu Phuoc, played an epic role in the girls' political awakening; Le An, who followed her father into the maquis, where she performed in a dance troupe that followed the troops and entertained soldiers before battle; Sen, the "beauty queen," who trained and worked in the maquis but returned to Saigon to help her sick mother; Lien An, who left the lycée to become a teacher in Hanoi before eventually returning to Saigon and becoming principal at the once-prestigious Lycée Chasseloup-Laubat, the boys' school equivalent of Lycée Marie Curie; the serene Xuan, an elegant woman and first to leave Marie Curie for the maquis, where she met her husband, Lau, both of whom studied in London before hearing the call of the country to return.

Finally, Oanh made it possible to meet three other lycée friends who are siblings: Minh, the eldest, stayed in Saigon, cared for her parents, helped the resistance, and juggled jobs in law, education, and music. Trang joined the maquis and learned to cope with life in the jungle before returning to Saigon to lead a double life as a spy for the resistance. She later studied at the Tchaikovsky Institute in Moscow before becoming the first woman to conduct Saigon's symphony orchestra.

By way of serendipity, the third sibling, Thanh, was serving as a diplomat at Vietnam's mission to the United Nations, where I went to visit her. I wanted to meet the girl Oanh said a professor at Lycée Marie Curie had derisively asked, "Who do you think you are, the Joan of Arc of Vietnam?"

Thanh, wearing a silk *ao dai* (traditional full-length tunic) and a stone face, invited me to sit in her office. As if to test my story about knowing Oanh, she asked to see a picture; I produced a photo of Oanh and me in Saigon. Thanh relaxed. This small act, I realized later, contributed to gaining trust and a visa to expressly interview Oanh and the Saigon sisters.

I flew back to Saigon in November 1989, with a tape recorder and thirty Maxell cassettes. Lodging with Tien, a friend of Oanh's whose house stood two blocks from the leafy campus of Lycée Marie Curie (the only school allowed to retain its French name after 1975), I spent six weeks interviewing the Saigon sisters and their friends and relatives. Tien told me years later it had been forbidden to lodge foreigners; filling out the form required by local police to explain who was staying with her, she finessed it by writing "famille lointain" (distant family). We met one on one for interviews and as a group for meals and outings. At restaurants, husbands drank Saigon beer while everyone feasted on *cha gio* (spring rolls), *banh xeo* (savory pancakes, stuffed with shrimp and sprouts), and whole fish covered in tamarind or other tangy sauces.

A favorite place to share a meal was at the home of Mme Tuong, who became a surrogate mother to the sisters after the death of her daughter Suong. It was at Suong's death in 1981 that several sisters reunited for the first time since the end of the war. Death anniversaries are a vital ritual in Vietnam that family and friends are loath to miss. Over the years, Mme Tuong welcomed the sisters to her home near Ton Son Nhat Airport. Her gracious villa overflowed with exquisite pottery, lacquer vases and hangings, and bouquets of fresh flowers. Referring to Mme Tuong's house as a salon for artists, writers, ex-government ministers, and others, Oanh dubbed her the "Mme de Chevigné" of Saigon.

Into the 1990s, the sisters continued to gather at Mme Tuong's on her daughter's death anniversary. The ritual repeated itself. Removing shoes at the door, the women climbed upstairs to Suong's shrine: a large wooden table crowded with photos, bowls of fruit, a bottle of wine, vases of flowers, and a pot of sand in which to place incense sticks. One by one, the sisters lit incense, bowed three times in front of a large photo of Suong, and plunged the incense sticks into the pot. Thin clouds of incense perfumed the air. Afterward, Mme Tuong offered the sisters a gourmet meal over which they shared stories about Suong and other memories.

Apart from the gatherings at Mme Tuong's villa, most of my interviews with the sisters took place in a room I rented at Tien's home on busy Nam Ky Khoi Nghia Street, an old French house with high ceilings and wooden shutters. In 1989, the streets of Saigon were rivers of bicycles and motorcycles. The sisters arrived one by one—by scooter, on bicycle, or on foot. It was the rainy season, and I felt guilty when some of the women arrived soaked and Tien quickly produced a change of clothes. Another challenge was street noise. Especially the more soft-spoken women were hard to hear over the squawk of motorbike horns, jingle of bicycle bells, and rumble of occasional trucks.

I also sought out interviews with relatives and friends, like Mme Tuong, the husbands of Le An and Xuan, and Tran Van Khe, a musical genius who helped spark the sisters' political awakening while still at the lycée. By coincidence, I had met Tran Van Khe in 1988 while at the Indochina Project; he was living in Paris and had obtained a scholarship to the United States. Only later did I realize the role he and Tuyen's brother had played in the 1940s to inspire students across Saigon to fight for independence. I also interviewed Oanh's mentor, a Belgian priest named Father Jacques Houssard, at his retirement home in Belgium. He spoke not just about Oanh but of his onetime friend Ngo Dinh Diem, the assassinated first president of the Saigon-based Republic of Vietnam.

Most interviews were conducted in French and the rest in English or Vietnamese (with a translator). I transcribed the thirty cassettes and pieced interview segments together into a timeline for each person; these interviews form the core of the book. Since 1989, as the sisters shared new information with me in interviews, I filled in and extended each timeline. I edited the transcripts for clarity and context (i.e., through occasional editor's notes or by identifying a historical figure or poet referenced). I translated Vietnamese (*che*, sweet soup) or French terms within the text (a *surveillant*, "monitor") to keep the flow of a story. In a few instances, translations of other materials the women shared are included—lines from poems they carried in the maquis, lyrics from songs that incited students, excerpts from the diary of Trang's deceased husband, and a letter Thanh wrote to Xuan at Tet (Lunar New Year) in 1950.

For all the sisters revealed in interviews over a period of three decades from 1989 until today, they also held back for several reasons. Given the influence of Confucianism and the value put on women who remain in the background, it was hard for the sisters to talk about themselves. They weren't used to it and found it uncomfortable. Some held back because, compared to those who had endured torture or worse, their sacrifices seemed small. Others wrestled with disillusionment as they witnessed the egalitarian society they had fought for distorted into one of greed and corruption. This is also a reason for not identifying all the interviewees by their full names.

As I write this preface in 2018, several of the sisters, whom, I regret, did not live to see their lives in print, have passed on. Through this oral history, however,

I seek to ensure that the stories of each of these young privileged women who rebelled will endure.

When the French established their colony of Cochinchina in 1867, they set up two separate systems to educate French and *indigènes* girls. In Saigon, the city that was considered the "pearl" of France's colonies in the Orient, the Lycée Marie Curie was the premier school for girls of privilege. Founded in 1918, it fills a Saigon city block with thick-walled, two-story tan colonial buildings topped with brick-red roof tiles. Beyond the arched gateway stands a pedestal with a bust of Marie Curie; soaring trees are sprinkled across the ample courtyard.

Vietnamese girls were not allowed to attend Lycée Marie Curie until it was decided that daughters of Vietnamese working for the French who had become naturalized citizens could study alongside the French girls. Opening up schools to all girls who passed an exam reinforced France's *mission civilisatrice* and assimilated local elites to accept French culture and preserve the political status quo even as other colonies negotiated for independence.

In the 1940s, lycées also opened to indigènes from poorer backgrounds if they passed stringent exams. The Vietnamese girls who studied at Marie Curie in the 1940s were given French names, wore French school uniforms, and were immersed in the curriculum imported from the French Department of Education in Paris. They could choose Spanish, English, or Vietnamese—as a second language.

Most of the fortunate Vietnamese girls who attended Marie Curie came from families whose greatest aspiration was for their girls to earn a *diplôme* as a stepping-stone to a stable and safe future in France. Among these privileged girls, a handful sought a different future. Rebelling against the French colonial government, they wanted only to devote themselves to freeing their people. In their own words, these lifelong friends—the Saigon sisters—share their stories.

This book is made possible by the Saigon sisters sharing their stories on Maxell cassette tapes decades ago, as well as across countless meals, cups of *ca phe*, and reunions in Saigon spanning 1989 and 2017. Deep thanks also to their husbands, children, friends, and mentors who shared so many reminiscences.

Many supporters cheered the editor on to record these narratives, starting with two dearly departed friends, Huynh Kim Khanh and George C. Wilson. Other steadfast believers include Helen Chauncey, Arnold "Skip" Isaacs, and Tommy Vallely. Linda and Murray Hiebert, my bosses at the Indochina Project, made it possible to visit Saigon in 1988 and meet Oanh, who introduced me to the other sisters. While recording interviews in Saigon in 1989, I was well cared for by my landlady, Tien—an old friend to the sisters and now to me. Tangible encouragement in the early years came in the form of grants from the Association for Asian Studies, the Samuel Rubin Foundation, and the Vietnam Veterans of America Foundation. Sincere thanks to Kenton Clymer for appreciating the value of sharing these stories.

Throughout this project, I benefited from the love and understanding of my parents, Don and Pat; spouse, Angela; brothers and sisters-in-law, Dick and Mary, and David and Sue; and dear relatives and friends too many to name, though special thanks must go to Daniel and Karen for their keen eyes and edits. No one is an island.

While several of the sisters have passed, I hope their spirits and their families may also draw solace from knowing their stories are not forgotten.

Timeline

39	The Trung sisters, Trung Trac and Trung Nhi, revolt against the Chinese.
939	At the Battle of the Bach Dang River, Ngo Quyen drives out Chinese forces, ending one thousand years of dominance; King Ngo Quyen declares Nam Viet independent.
1288	General Tran Hung Dao routs Mongol naval forces at the Bach Dang River.
1427	Chinese forces surrender to Le Loi, leader of the new Le dynasty.
1867	French military forces consolidate control and establish the colony of Cochinchina.
1884	The Patenôtre Treaty established French rule over Annam-Tonkin.
1887	The French administration absorbs Laos and Cambodia and creates French Indochina.
1930	Ho Chi Minh organizes the Indochina Communist Party (ICP).
1940	Japan implements a strategy to fold colonies in Southeast Asia into the Greater East Asia Co-prosperity Sphere; usurping French control, Japan seizes Cochinchina in 1941.
1941	After Japan's invasion, the Indochina Communist Party organizes a guerrilla force, the Viet Minh.
1945	In March, Japanese forces launch a coup against the French.
1945	On August 15, the surrender of the Imperial Japanese Army ends World War II.
1945	Ho Chi Minh declares independence of Democratic Republic of Vietnam on September 2.
1946	France attacks the Viet Minh in Haiphong, launching the war of resistance, maquis.
1950	Three incidents galvanize students at lycées in Saigon to join the maquis against colonial rule: January 9, French police shoot and kill the student Tran Van On; March 19, two U.S. warships dock in Saigon; May 1, International Workers' Day sparks massive marches.
1950	The United States recognizes the government of South Vietnam under Emperor Bao Dai.
1954	On May 7, the French defeat at Dien Bien Phu ends French involvement in Indochina.
1954	The Geneva Accords, May–July, divide Vietnam at the Seventeenth Parallel and mandate democratic elections within two years; massive migration of Catholics and others south; some southerners go north; Ngo Dinh Diem named prime minister under Bao Dai.
1955	Ngo Dinh Diem deposes Bao Dai in October, becomes president of the Republic of Vietnam.
1960	National Front for the Liberation of South Vietnam and National Liberation Front (NLF) set up as a coalition to galvanize the insurgency against the Diem government.
1963	President Diem is overthrown and killed.

1964	The Gulf of Tonkin Resolution approved by the U.S. Congress authorizes military action in the region.
1968	The Tet Offensive launches a combined assault on U.S. positions by Viet Cong, Communist guerrillas operating in South Vietnam, and the North Vietnamese army.
1969	U.S. troop strength in Vietnam peaks at 554,000 and then begins to decline.
1970–1973	Peace talks are held among the United States, North Vietnam, South Vietnam, and the National Liberation Front, culminating in a cease-fire agreement.
1973	In March, the last U.S. troops leave Vietnam.
1975	North Vietnamese troops invade South Vietnam and take control of the whole country.
1976	The Socialist Republic of Vietnam is proclaimed; Saigon is renamed Ho Chi Minh City.
1986	Doi Moi (Renovation) is ratified by the Sixth National Congress to liberalize economic, and to a smaller extent, political policies.
1995	The United States and the Socialist Republic of Vietnam establish diplomatic relations.

THE SAIGON SISTERS

Part 1
THE CAUSE
Youth at Lycée Marie Curie to the
Geneva Accords, 1954

THANH
"Our Hearts Beating for the Cause"

Minh speaks for all the sisters when she asserts they were the "generation at the crossroads." Their hometown, Saigon—the capital of Cochinchina, one of three parts of the Indochinese Union created by the French in 1887—was ground zero for French colonial political and economic power. The French introduced the French legal code and then, to give legal primacy to French citizens over indigenous subjects, a separate code for the indigenous population. The French determined the exchange rate of the Indochinese currency, the piaster. In 1917, the French formed what came to be the much-feared Sûreté Générale (security police). To strengthen control, the French exploited the loyalty people felt toward the Nguyen dynasty by crowning Bao Dai emperor in 1926 and sending him to France to be groomed for a future role. Saigon boasted a busy port, architectural treasures like Notre Dame Cathedral and the Opera House, and a sophisticated cultural scene. It gained a reputation as the "pearl" of the Orient.

Born in the early 1930s, the Saigon sisters attended Lycée Marie Curie at a tumultuous time. While anticolonial movements were emerging in India and elsewhere, the "superior" French focused on strengthening their rule. Vietnamese who studied abroad found aspects of Westernization appealing, and some rejected Confucianism as a barrier to a modern Vietnam. The use of *quoc ngu*, the romanized script that replaced Chinese characters, spread quickly and helped fuel debate about a post-Confucian society.

The French dangled promises of political change and self-government in front of their subjects, leading some to collaborate. But talk of cooperation was born of necessity: fewer than 35,000 Europeans lived in Indochina during the colonial period, so many locals had to be trained as civil servants. In 1940, about 17,000 French civil servants and military officers lived in Saigon. As the sisters grew up in Saigon, France sought to finesse a balancing act: uphold tenets of its liberal and republican heritage while maintaining a cruel and immoral colonial system. For many Vietnamese, nothing would substitute for being treated equally.

On the global stage, in 1937, Japan's imperial army invaded China to expand its Greater East Asia Co-prosperity Sphere. With Japan on the border with Indochina, the United States and the Soviet Union grasped the geopolitical value of Vietnam. In 1939, Germany attacked Poland; a year later the French surrendered to Germany, and Marshal Pétain replaced Charles DeGaulle to lead Vichy France. Tokyo, coveting Tonkin and the railway from Hanoi to Kunming, pressured the French to allow troops to enter Tonkin in exchange for allowing French sovereignty in Indochina to continue. The Japanese administered the monetary policy in the colony and extracted huge amounts of rice and resources. Japan's occupation caused a famine that, by 1945, killed over a million Vietnamese peasants.

On March 9, 1945, not trusting the French to continue to collaborate, the Japanese launched a coup de force ending eighty years of French rule. Backed by the Japanese, Bao Dai proclaimed Vietnam's independence as the "empire" of Vietnam. His prime minister, Tran Trung Kim, lasted only until the Japanese surrender in August. The revolutionary leader Ho Chi Minh, who had returned to Vietnam in 1941 after years in France, the Soviet Union, and China, embraced the Comintern's policy to build united fronts to establish all-powerful alliances—under Communist control. Also in 1941, a united front emerged in Vietnam: the Viet Nam Doc Lap Dong Minh Hoi (Vietnamese Independence League), known as the Viet Minh, with Ho Chi Minh as its leader.

The August Revolution of 1945 enabled the Viet Minh to fill the vacuum left by the Japanese, both in Hanoi, where Ho Chi Minh announced the independence of the Democratic Republic of Vietnam (DRV) on September 2, and in the South, where Tran Van Giau declared the launch of an insurrection. Emperor Bao Dai formally abdicated any role in support of the French, handing over the dynastic seal to the provisional government of Vietnam.

The Fontainebleau Conference, July–September 1946, was a final attempt for the French government to work with Ho Chi Minh and the Democratic Republic of Vietnam. It was undermined by the high commissioner of Cochinchina, Thierry D'Argenlieu, when he unilaterally proclaimed the provisional government of the Republic of Cochinchina and—after a rightward political shift in France— the French Socialist and Communist Parties did not support Ho Chi Minh. This eleventh-hour conference produced only a draft accord reinforcing France's economic rights in northern Vietnam and left the problem of Cochinchina unsolved.

In December 1946, the French went to war with Vietnam to suppress Vietnamese nationalism and rebuild their colonial state.

In 1950, approximately 22 million people lived in Vietnam, and the Democratic Republic of Vietnam was estimated to control about half that population. As the DRV struggled to build a united front, volunteers dispersed to organize a network of national salvation associations based on gender, age, religion, and profession. The Communists ran the Viet Minh and exercised power through popular committees at four levels: zones, provinces, districts, and villages. The Viet Minh and Lien Viet had parallel offices within the committees: running the state and mobilizing the masses were to work in tandem. (Lien Viet was short for Hoi Lien Hiep Quoc Dan Viet Nam, Association of United Vietnamese People, the overarching political front that included patriots who did not join the Viet Minh within the front.)

President Harry Truman declared his doctrine of containing Communism in 1947; the following year, the high commissioner of Cochinchina, Léon Pignon, framed the battle against the DRV as crucial to the Cold War the West was waging against Communism. After Mao and Stalin recognized the DRV in January 1950, Pignon promised Western leaders to keep Indochina free of Communism in exchange for military aid and acceptance of the French colonial presence. In March 1950, two U.S. warships cruised into the port of Saigon. Students, including the Saigon sisters, took to the streets.

On July 9, 1949, Thanh stood in the courtyard of the prestigious Lycée Marie Curie and received top prizes awarded by the French high commissioner for Indochina. Wearing a skirt, blouse, and long braids, "Julie" (as she was called at school) accepted her prize, a tome of French literature, for having distinguished herself in both studies and conduct. Less than a year later, Thanh left her home carrying a small bundle, crossed the street, and boarded a bus bound for the countryside to join the resistance against the French.

How did Thanh immerse herself in a French lycée—drinking in Victor Hugo and Balzac and La Fontaine and winning prizes ahead of her French and métisse classmates—and then choose to leave behind comforts, further study, family, and friends to don black pajamas and live in the jungle? Her account of that transformation is detailed and vibrant, perhaps because, while she became one of the most politicized sisters, she never lost her passion for French literature, film, and poetry.

Thanh is an unexpected figure in the maquis, not just as a woman and the child of Saigon's elite but for revering the language and culture of the colonialists against which she chose to fight. While growing up "on the hinge" of feudalism, she also was immersed in the culture of liberties of the West. As a child, she reveled in French novels and poems and movies and plays and songs and, even, entertainment magazines. Through a passion for movies, she also learned about American culture. Plunging into life in the jungle, she worked with peasants and villagers while finding small outlets to express herself—writing poetry, copying famous poems, decorating the walls of a thatched hut.

While generous in sharing captivating specifics about her youth—from a childhood brush with death to her skill at designing notebooks she and friends carried in the resistance—Thanh only sparingly reflects on the toll that joining the maquis takes on her family. She admits she was married "too young" to an officer in the resistance but only rarely refers to their two sons' struggles with mental and physical illnesses. Eloquent in her absolute dedication to fighting the French, Thanh appears to don blinders when it comes to expressing the price paid to fight for the cause.

Thanh

I was born in Saigon in 1932, the first of three girls born a year apart—Minh, me, and Trang. Our father, Nguyen Van Duc, worked as an engineer for public utility projects during the regime under the French. His father came from peasant origins in a poor province. Papa was so poor that landowners hired him and his brothers as laborers. He was one of ten children, and his parents could not take care of them all; three older sisters drowned because there was nobody to watch them. People believed that the poorer the family, the bigger it needs to be. Vestiges of old thinking teach people that no matter how many children they have, there will always be enough food.

Father grew up watching buffalo in the rice fields and catching fish to sell to buy rice. He and his brothers walked far from the village to fish in the marshes. After rising tides brought in the fish, the boys built dams to capture them before the water receded. They fished at night or else the fish died quickly in the heat of the day. Papa left at four or five o'clock in the afternoon, two buffalo pulling a crude cart with wooden wheels. Reaching the pond by seven or eight, they pulled the fish out of the water and loaded them in the cart, pouring on water to keep them alive. Papa was only seven or eight years old and got so tired. The buffalo knew the route, so he rested on the back of a buffalo going home. Sometimes, though, he fell off, but luckily his brothers picked him up before the cart rolled over him.

Papa was eager to learn to write and read. He didn't even have a table to write on; he squatted in front of a plank of wood and set his books on it. He studied the characters used before Vietnamese was Latinized. To make paper, he cut squares out of banana leaves and used a wooden stick to carve the characters. When oil in his lamp ran out, he caught fireflies and piled them up to have light to read by.

In the last year of his life, 1987, Papa developed glaucoma and could no longer read. He had gone half blind years earlier, having been arrested and tortured under the French. In his final years, he asked a niece to write down his memoirs. I found his notebooks. His memoir has no periods, no commas, no grammar at all. But he remembers everything about his childhood.

Despite the poverty around him—peasants did not even have running water— he found an uncle who gave him money to study at a school outside the village. When he ran out of money, he had to drop everything and go home. Each time, friends and professors urged him to return: "You study so well—continue." His brothers were completely illiterate and seemed content to catch and sell fish. Papa was the youngest, and his brothers pushed him to continue studying; they agreed to work harder to give money to "the little one." His brothers asked their wives and children to work harder to harvest and sell more rice and asked other relatives to go to the forest and cut wood to sell. The family spirit was strong. As Papa later rose in society, he knew it was due to his brothers. Because he was brilliant, Papa passed exams and went to study in Saigon, where he was one of the few children of peasants to study at Lycée Chasseloup-Laubat. One day, one of his brothers appeared at the lycée to bring him a couple of big fish and chunks of firewood. That's all they had to give; they thought he needed these things.

The French administration held a contest for entrance into the only university, in Hanoi, where Father wanted to study public works. He passed the exam and traveled by boat to Hanoi in 1926. He completed his studies at age twenty-three and became a *fonctionnaire* (functionary, civil servant) as a technical agent in public works. He also decided he needed to marry and raise a family. He met my mother as he was preparing to return south.

A friend told him about a lady with a daughter who was a boarding student at Hanoi's selective École Normale Supérieure (a teacher-training college). He asked if Father wanted to meet the lady. Mother came from a good family of public servants under the French. After this first interview and a "viewing" of his future bride, a matchmaker told Father the family agreed he could pursue the young woman. When my grandmother went to the boarding school to pick mother up on weekends, she rode in the family *pousse-pousse* (rickshaw), and mother sat next to her. Father pedaled his bicycle alongside, as mother was not allowed to sit on the back of his bicycle. That was a touching part of their courtship. Back at the house, he asked "Little Sister Six," as she was called according to birth order: "Since you will be taking exams soon, are you having any difficulties with math? May

I come and help explain it to you?" He was good at math. She accepted, and they spent Sunday afternoons doing her homework. They also talked about the *Kim Van Kieu* (a poem in 3,254 verses by Nguyen Du, 1766–1820, about a young woman who, to support her family, ends up a prostitute; an epic story considered a vehicle to express the tumult of the times and the beauty of romantic love), singing its verses together. He knew French literature, too, having read Victor Hugo and other authors.

My parents had a traditional courtship. Before marrying, they never went out by themselves. The decision to marry lay between him and her father. Since suitors had to bring relatives to joint family gatherings, and he lived far from his village, he found someone to represent his family. My mother's family saw he was serious: he had a diploma; he wore a tie. Once the decision was made, Father telephoned his parents back in their village and shared the news. He observed the custom of the groom's family offering presents to the bride's family. Since his parents were poor, they borrowed money to buy a pair of gold earrings and a ring. Father and the woman he chose to represent the family presented the gifts and asked for Mother's hand in marriage. In his memoirs, Father recalled a gathering soon after: Mother—wearing an ao dai and her hair rolled in a chignon—served cups of tea. She dared not let her eyes meet his. He was deeply moved and so distracted he had no idea what he said to her. Throughout the event he remained standing, not daring to sit down.

After passing end-of-term exams, they left school with diplomas, and Father brought her south, so he could work in Saigon. By custom, a young woman follows her husband. This was the first time Mother had been to the train station; they took the Trans-Indochina train to Saigon. It was an epic odyssey from her house in Hanoi to Saigon and by road to father's village in Long Xuyen Province: the return to the groom's village, where he presents the bride to his family. Mother felt as if she were on a different planet. At the triumphal welcome in the village, she drew attention as a woman from the North. Everyone wanted to see her; it was like a show. Lamps hung everywhere, and people bowed in front of the altar to the ancestors.

With a diploma and a job, Papa was able to get a good position in society. He helped build our house, bringing stone blocks from his village to place as foundation stones. Each brother contributed something. To repay this debt, Papa chose a nephew from each brother's family, brought him to Saigon, and helped him attend school and find a job. That captures his family's spirit.

Soon after my parents married, Mother became pregnant. The firstborn, a boy, died of dysentery at the age of one. My sister Minh was born in March 1931, me in August 1932, and Trang in November 1933. We kidded Mother about having children in such rapid succession.

Both parents spoke French and became functionaries under the French. With her diploma from the École Normale Supérieure, Mother taught at a primary school. She prepared her classes carefully. She had beautiful handwriting; her notebooks modeled exquisite calligraphy. Mother was also as strict as a disciplined teacher. She never cuddled with us, never hugged us.

Growing up, Minh, Trang, and I wore the same clothes, cut from one big piece of cloth. We each had a plate, a bowl, and an enamel cup, which we washed and put back in the cupboard after meals. We each wrote our name on our cup. Our parents never gave us pocket money while we were at Lycée Marie Curie. While other parents gave children money to buy street food, we took three meals at home and did not snack in between. We never asked for money. On Sundays, Mother asked the cook to prepare a big pot of *che*, a sweet soup made with beans and coconut. This was our one dessert. Otherwise, we had no cake, no candy, nothing sweet.

When Trang and I joined the maquis, we reminded each other how we never asked for anything, never cried or asked Mother to buy this or that. We realized we had become highly disciplined. This would help us a lot.

Our parents sent us to French schools. In general, people at this time wanted to have a diploma, a good life, to rise in rank and have a career. For us, things were a little different.

Ever since we were young, Papa taught us about our glorious history driven by patriotism. He taught us we are Vietnamese and we must chase out the occupiers. He taught us to love the homeland. Even when we joined the maquis, he only worried because we were girls; had we been boys, he would have approved right away. That reflected the feudalism in him. He was progressive and modern in sending us to a French school, where we read books by the French, while half of him remained feudal with its traditions about women being good girls with traditional virtues. That tension was the drama in the family.

After the August 1945 revolution, the anti-French movement in Saigon brought together many intellectuals. At home, we talked about national heroes and their struggles against foreign invasion. We have a long tradition of resisting invaders from the North. In the mid-1930s, students at progressive schools joined the movement. Father sponsored a group of progressive students that included Tran Van Khe, Luu Huu Phuoc—the older brother of Tuyen, also at Marie Curie—and Mai Van Bo, who always placed first in his class at Lycée Pétrus Ky.

They made a perfect team: Luu Huu Phuoc composed music, Mai Van Bo wrote lyrics, and Tran Van Khe conducted and performed. Decades later, I would work with Mai Van Bo when he was ambassador to France during the Paris Peace Accords. These three friends, who all spoke beautiful French, were very close. They put their passion and gift for music in the service of the revolution, organizing fantastic choir performances and staging plays about Vietnamese heroes, like the Trung sisters and Le Loi. At the same time, they needed intellectuals as patrons.

My father and his friends started an organization called Société pour l'Amélioration Morale, Intellectuelle et Physique d'Indochine, SAMIPIC (Society for the Moral, Intellectual, and Physical Improvement of Indochina) to support these students. They wrote the anthem that called for students to "wake up and march on the road forward." This was not a revolutionary song that explicitly calls for chasing out invaders. In the 1940s, songs had to be circumspect and simply evoke historic moments, like big battles against the feudal Chinese, the victory at the Bach Dang River, the brilliance of the battle at Ai Chi Lang. Each battle had a song, and its lyrics were distributed and broadcast to students.

"Ai Chi Lang" (Fortress Chi Lang) tells a story of the Chinese being drawn into a mountain pass where they are ambushed from both sides. It opens with drums pounding and cymbals clanging to capture the drama of the attack. Luu Huu Phuoc annotated the musical notes: "Here, beat the drum, here, strike the cymbal." Papa taught us to play the drums and often recalled the battle at Ai Chi Lang and how we achieved victory over the Chinese.

Students supported by SAMIPIC came to our house to perform plays. Every day, we listened to their music, learning the songs by heart. After all, music ran in our family. Papa encouraged us to learn music from the age of six or seven. Minh studied piano with a well-known pianist, and the rest of us learned to play mandolin and banjo. Minh and Trang also played the accordion. Coming from an upper-class family, we could afford an accordion, a piano, a drum, and cymbals. We also fashioned a drum set out of boxes, big and small, and sticks. We assembled enough instruments to make an orchestra, and Father arranged a family concert every Saturday night. At first, it felt like a duty. We were little and didn't really know or like music yet. We were forced to play because Father liked it. But he made it possible for Minh and Trang to learn piano and for all of us to appreciate Beethoven and Mozart. Later, we thanked Papa for helping us learn to love music.

These three close friends—Tran Van Khe, Mai Van Bo, and Luu Huu Phuoc—organized a big performance at the municipal theater built by the French in downtown Saigon. They included a play by The Lu. [Ed. note: The Lu, 1907–1989, was a member of the Literary Self-Strengthening Movement launched in 1932. These writers used the spread of quoc ngu, a writing system based on the Latin alphabet that made the flow of ideas easier than the use of Chinese characters, to access Western literature and ideas and build a community of artists that challenged Confucian traditions and championed the rights of the individual.] Written completely in poetic verse, The Lu's play is about three fairies who fall from the sky and take off their wings to sing and dance. Hearing a woodsman approach, the fairies pick up their wings and fly back up to the sky—except one, who doesn't have time to gather her wings. The woodcutter captures her and hides her wings.

The fairy and woodcutter fall in love and are expecting a child. It is a beautiful love story. Each day, birds sing to the fairy, who, by chance, finds her wings. Clutching them in her arms, she starts to dance, realizing her wings can fly her back to paradise. Suddenly the birds are sad and ask the fairy, "Who will feed us if you go?" Offstage, an orphan describes a dream about the comfort of being home with his mother on a wintry night. The fairy hears this and throws away her wings. Even if life in paradise is easier, she will stay on earth. Even though she needs to work hard and has a husband to care for, it is on earth where she discovers what it means to love.

Since the play was also being performed in the North (the Viet Bac), authorities in Saigon could do nothing. It was hardly patriotic or revolutionary: this is a story about fairies! However, it was performed along with a one-act play about the Trung sisters. [Ed. note: Trung Trac and Trung Nhi are sisters who led the first uprising against Chinese rule in AD 39. Also known as Hai Ba Trung, the Two Ladies Trung, they are considered by many Vietnamese as the most revered heroines in Vietnam's history.] In this play, Trung Trac learns her husband, taken hostage by the Chinese, is dead. She orders an insurrection against the Chinese. Wearing the white shawl of mourning, she prostrates herself in front of her husband's altar, having sacrificed her husband for the homeland. Along with her younger sister, Trung Nhi, she calls her lieutenants—all women with experience commanding troops—and orders who will go where to carry on the battle. In the final scene in front of the altar, Trung Trac faints into Trung Nhi's arms, and the play ends. The whole play lasted only thirty minutes.

Father took us to this play and told us more about our history and our heroines. We began to realize that women had been decision makers under a matriarchal system in feudal times; but, with the spread of Confucianism, our national heroes had all become men. As the French and Vietnamese cultures intersected, freedoms increased and feudalism was questioned. A lot of women stood up for their rights. They did not want to be stuck at home anymore. It was an extreme view—who would take care of the children if everyone left home? But this was part of the romanticism of the time. Open love meant women ignored their parents and could love and be loved as they pleased. Some women became prostitutes and were seen as dirtied and depraved. In this atmosphere, parents feared their daughters would go astray and warned, "If you go freely with boys, you will fall in this trap." That was the mentality. It was considered unusual that our parents let us attend some classes at Lycée Chasseloup-Laubat when it was co-ed. In the confines of home, Mother always said, "Be careful of boys."

Mother raised us as she was raised—the daughter of the elite, who spent her childhood sequestered at home. Her parents came from the South but moved to Hanoi, where her father worked as a customs commissioner for the French. She was a boarding student for ten years, coming home only on Sundays. She never went out alone. Mother was a young feudal woman. At the same time, she was cultured and studying for a career.

Father always told us about our ancestors and about his love for the country. He spoke with emotion about the students he supported, the ones whose patriotic and revolutionary songs we memorized starting when we were ten years old. It was completely natural. We grew up in the revolutionary ambiance.

Even Hollywood inspired us. We ran with excitement to the Majestic Theater on Rue Catinat to see *A Song to Remember* (1945), starring Cornel Wilde as Chopin. [Ed. note: Rue Catinat, named for the French military commander Nicolas Catinat, 1637–1712, was the lifeblood of downtown Saigon: a treelined street bordered by such buildings as the Opera House, completed in 1897, as well as chic stores, restaurants, and theaters. The finest theater was the Majestic Theater, located in its namesake, a glorious hotel facing the Saigon River.] What a revelation to see an American film about Chopin's patriotism as the Prussians occupy his country. Chopin escapes into exile, leaving Poland secretly at night. Crossing the border, he picks up a handful of Polish soil and kisses it. I remember that scene vividly; it resonated in my heart since we, too, were under an occupier. In Paris, Chopin meets Franz Liszt. One scene shows them sitting side by side at a piano, playing a duet, "La Polonaise." Liszt and Chopin each plays piano with one hand. Then they turn to each other, reach out, and shake hands. Their eyes sparkle with inspiration. This scene stays fresh in my heart. Cornel Wilde looked handsome and elegant, an idol playing the role of a patriotic musician and composer. After that, each time we heard "La Polonaise" played over the radio, the song stirred a lot of emotion.

We saw *A Song to Remember* several times. We didn't tell our parents since it was forbidden for girls to see movies that were all just "big love stories."

We loved movies. Our situation was just as Marguerite Duras described in her book, *Un barrage contre le Pacifique* (*The Sea Wall*), about a French family living in the Mekong Delta. [Ed. note: *The Sea Wall* is autobiographical; Marguerite Duras, 1914–1996, was born in the Mekong Delta and described hardships her impoverished family faced in Cochinchina.] The narrator's children, Joseph and Suzanne, are poor; whenever they can escape to town, they run to the movie theater. It was a welcome distraction to see love stories and beautiful actresses. Joseph and Suzanne discover another world. It was the same for us. We knew only our house and school, but then, through film, we saw the outside world.

We didn't even care that concessions were not sold at the Majestic: we came to see a film, a work of cinematography! We must somehow have gotten pocket money from one of our uncles because we were able to buy *Cinémonde*, *Ciné-miroir*, and other magazines with pictures of actors and actresses. We hid them at home.

Another American film we adored, *Marie Curie* (1943), starred Greer Garson as Madame Curie. After her husband, Pierre, dies, she continues to research on her own and comes to be accepted as a professor at the Sorbonne. She is applauded as the first woman scientist at the Sorbonne. She was a model for us—our idol. And here I was, attending the lycée bearing her name!

We also watched American movies, but they were not very memorable. In Indochina, Westerns were called "Far West films"; we did not know the term "Western." Scenes of cowboys riding horses and shooting rifles had a romantic aspect to them, but nothing deep.

I adored movie stars and sketched French and German actors in an album. Trang praised my drawing, saying she could tell right away who was who. She gave my notebook a title: *Thanh's Works*. I drew Michelle Montgans, Daniel Darieux, Cornel Wilde, and Merle Oberon, who played Georges Sand, Chopin's lover when he goes to France. I drew my favorite pastoral scenes. I drew all the time! I arranged to exhibit my drawings at home in a small room upstairs and invited my family to *Thanh's Exhibition*. I loved drawing as much as I loved movies.

Our parents did not understand. They wanted us to read serious books, not watch movies with people embracing and falling in love. Movies could make young girls want to run away and fall madly in love. There were rules for girls raised in "good" families that were intended to instill fear about all that might happen. We were *à la charnière* (on the hinge) of feudalism.

I was in my fourth year at the lycée when my teachers said there was a good film in town that I should see. *Les Visiteurs du soir* (*The Devil's Envoys*, 1942), set in the Middle Ages, is by Marcel Carné, a French director who made the film at the time France was under Nazi occupation. Since we were learning French history, this was cited as an example of how to recreate history. A French teacher recommended *L'Éternel retour* (*Love Eternal*, 1948), a modern adaption of the French love story of Tristan and Isolde in which the king asks Tristan, a knight, to help him find a queen. Tristan falls in love with the would-be queen. Theirs is a pure love. She is to marry the king but loves Tristan, who is mortally wounded in battle. Another woman loves Tristan but sees whom he really loves; she then reads a letter Tristan wrote to Isolde asking to see her before he dies. He asks Isolde to raise a white flag if she can come see him and a black flag if not. Every day, Tristan asks the other woman: "Do you see the flag?" This goes on for days. The woman says she does not see it until, finally, one day she says, "Yes, I see it. It's black." He dies. But it had been the white flag, and Isolde arrives only to find him dead. She lies next to him and dies. They find each other in eternity. This story was retold in a modern setting but with the same ending. It's a return to history. It was a beautiful love story that had nothing sensual or erotic about it.

I also liked poetry and wrote poems at school. I described tropical nights, the moon playing in the trees and the mysteries of the forest—simple poems. Our French literature professor liked me because I came in first in classes on writing and literature. About half of my classmates were French, some of whom were children of colonials. A minority of Vietnamese called indigènes came from the bourgeoisie, who were able to send their daughters to the lycée. Some Vietnamese students were weak and did poorly. It is a little strange, but I was always first in my class. The French admired me and spoke to me with respect.

A professor introduced me to a book, *Poil de carotte* (*Carrot Top*), by Jules Renard, about a boy who does all the chores around the house. People heap their concerns on him, the youngest, and he suffers in silence. One evening, his mother realizes she forgot to close the chicken coop outside. If it's not closed, a wolf will eat the chickens. She orders the red-haired boy to go, even though he is afraid of the dark. Building up his courage, he darts out and back. Our class assignment was to capture the story's action and figure out how to stage it. I arranged the story into three scenes: the order from his mother, his exit, his triumphal return. I kept it simple, but touching. The teacher read my outline in class and used it as a model. It was often like that in school.

My mother loved poetry but was not allowed to read poems about love. In the years from 1935 to 1947, many famous poets spoke about open love. This period marked an opening, an opportunity, as feudal Vietnam encountered French culture. Along with colonialism, the French brought a wave of French literature and the romanticism of Victor Hugo, de la Martine, Chateaubriand—all the poets who sang of love. This fresh wind encountered a Vietnam that was blossoming and shaped a generation that created beautiful love poems that had been forbidden. The most famous of these poets is Nguyen Du.

Nguyen Du's most famous poem, *Kim Van Kieu*, is about a beautiful woman who prostitutes herself to earn money to rescue her father, who has been wrongly accused of many crimes. He is arrested and put in prison. *Kim Van Kieu* portrays how a whole society can be degraded. The social stratus of mandarins is depicted as full of rotten and corrupt people who demand bribes to get someone out of jail or threaten to slander them further. Kieu's father is a mandarin with integrity but also a victim of slander. Kieu devotes herself to saving him. The poem is very progressive. As the daughter from a good family, Kieu meets an educated young man to whom many women are drawn. Kieu falls deeply in love. She discovers he lives behind her house, and she can reach him by passing through a door at the back of the house. When her parents are away, she passes through the door to find her love. For the daughter of an upstanding family to do this was progressive at the time! It became a classic. My mother knew verses by heart. All classes, high and low, liked it. Peasants sang it. It was a phenomenon. My mother did not, of course, read passages about Kieu sneaking off to see her husband; she sang passages about Kieu who, while in the brothel, is thinking about her parents. Sitting alone in the pavilion where she receives clients, Kieu watches the sun set and reflects on her mother, her father, her childhood home. This handful of verses describes Kieu gazing at the horizon, the river flowing, a sampan in the distance, and her wondering, who is on it?

Father liked *Kim Van Kieu* too. But when he wrote poems about the family, he used the feudal approach. His poems were about how Minh is a good student, the qualities of the ideal young woman, and about all girls being good, loving their parents, cleaning the house, cooking well.

At school, I loved to read. I wanted to be a storyteller because I was given a gift for languages, especially French and English. Before I was ten, I read *Alice in Wonderland* with a dictionary at my side. Flipping pages to a new word, I covered the definition with one hand and guessed its meaning. Teachers at Lycée Marie Curie said I read French clearly and encouraged me to read works of theater, too. The lycée had a lending library, and I read a lot of books in French. I read novels in secret since Mother did not approve. Somebody—it might have been Father—gave me a weekly magazine for French girls called *La Semaine de Suzette* (Suzanne's week), featuring stories and cartoons. We loved it. Another weekly gazette, *Fillette* (Little girl), had extraordinary stories and color illustrations. Even when called to the dinner table, I brought a book and read while eating. Father scolded me, saying all excess is harmful.

I read so much I became nearsighted when I was thirteen. I couldn't see the blackboard at school and didn't understand why. I asked to sit in the front row but could still not see the board. One day my uncle, who wore glasses, visited the house; by accident, I picked up his glasses and suddenly saw everything in detail: dust and spider webs in the house, clouds in the sky, leaves on the trees. I hadn't seen any of these before! My parents could not believe I was nearsighted. At night, I often forgot to turn on the light because I was so carried away by stories and history. My parents took me to buy glasses.

Between classes, we found ways to have fun. We bicycled to the zoo and strolled around. Oanh and I sometimes brought bread and snacks to picnic in the zoo gardens. We walked along Rue La Grandière to admire the big French department stores. On one corner stood a store full of luxuries, like perfume and record players, sold by women wearing makeup. Music tinkled in the background. It was a little piece of the West in our midst! The perfumes smelled like civilization itself!

And there was Rue Catinat. It throbbed with activity and oozed luxury with its *grands magasins* (department stores) and theaters in Eden Center and the Majestic Hotel. Classmates and I ran errands on our bicycles; our school bags tucked into the front baskets, we pedaled two by two down Catinat soaking up the beauty of the street and its storefronts, reveling in the shade of the orange-fringed tamarind trees. We called this to go "Catinater," or "la Catinage"—trolling down Catinat. Rue Catinat also channeled a lively rumor mill, which my classmate Oanh called "Radio Catinat." We liked to go to the Portail bookshop on Catinat to read beautiful books about France and the world.

Influenced by the patriotism of my father and his friends, their music and plays, and other activities, we became more and more aware of resistance activities. In 1946 a couple of us transferred from Marie Curie to co-ed classes down the street at Lycée Chasseloup-Laubat because Marie Curie did not have upper-level courses. We met boys who talked about wanting to do something for the country. One of them took the political training course in the Plaine des Joncs (Plain of Reeds). [Ed. note: An inland wetland in the Mekong Delta, this swampy area was used as a base of resistance by the Viet Minh and later the Viet Cong.] Everyone was excited. We were told if we didn't take the course, if we didn't get training, we could not join the revolution. You had to train and study, and here was a specific course for students of Saigon! Xuan had the chance to go. I went later.

When the student who finished the course returned in 1947, he organized a meeting at the house of an intellectual. There, we founded an association of patriotic students of Saigon. We passed around its statutes, articles one, two, three, and so on. Comrades from another organization urged the association to create its own clandestine journal, so we started *Cuu Nuoc* (Save the country). It featured poems and articles to encourage the movement. We made copies using a Roneo copy machine. Passing *Cuu Nuoc* among ourselves, each was responsible for her class—Trang for her classmates, Minh for hers.

I liked to contribute articles to *Cuu Nuoc* and entered a short story contest. This was when we dreamed of going to the maquis. I wrote a simple story, "Dreaming of *Bung Bien*," about a young student imagining going to the anti-French zones of the maquis. That was my mood. He imagines the combatants and nurses carrying backpacks on the march toward liberation. He wakes up and realizes it was only a dream. I won a prize for the story. I don't have a single copy anymore.

We also printed our own *tracts* (leaflets). After school, we bicycled to Sen's house, hoping her father, whom she called "a real dictator," was not home. We closed the door to her room and set about our work. Sen pulled a bowl out of a drawer, a small bag of flour out of another, and a wide and shallow pan from under her bed. On her desk were arranged a gold-trimmed fountain pen and a bottle of purple ink. Sen filled the bowl with water from the kitchen sink. I took a sheaf of onionskin paper from her desk drawer, the sheets crackling between my fingers. We congregated around the desk as Sen poured flour and water into the bowl and stirred it into a thick white paste, telling me when to add drops of water to get just the right consistency. Sen spooned the paste into a shallow pan, smoothing it evenly across the top.

Gripping the fountain pen filled with purple ink, I locked my face in concentration as the pen's tip carved words on our white "pad of paper." It felt like writing on bread dough. I pushed the pen tip and ink across the soft white surface, pausing to let the ink bleed into the furrows of each letter: "Vive l'indépendence." When it was available, we preferred fashioning a pad out of agar jelly extracted from ocean plants because it made a smoother surface, but supplies of this slimy substance were unreliable.

Trang, Le An, and Sen took turns pressing sheets of paper onto the inked message. Thin paper allowed us to draw more than the average of ten copies from an initial inking. Cheaper, thicker paper meant fewer copies per inking. I complemented Sen on her supplies. She laughed: "Don't thank me. Thank Lycée Marie Curie!" Bit by bit, Sen had been tucking away supplies of paper and ink.

Before it was time to go home, each of us had taken a turn with the fountain pen. Among our messages were "À bas le colonialisme" (Down with colonialism) and "Vive Bac Ho" (Up with Uncle Ho). Trang grumbled that the sheets didn't allow longer messages, like "The Vietnamese people will never tolerate colonialism" and "Collaborator and colonialist alike will see the people rise gloriously against them!" I reminded her we just had to do the best we could with what we had, but I also agreed with her. I had also composed quite a few sentences I'd like to have put under the noses of those who thought we Annamites were resigned to our lot.

We left hundreds of sheets to dry in the privacy of Sen's bedroom. All that remained was to distribute them, which could be tricky, as Oanh recalled years later. One day, after the bell rang at the end of our physics class, she jumped up to file out of class. In the line ahead she noticed a student carrying a stack of papers wedged between school books. Accidentally, the papers slipped out and fluttered to the floor. Oanh lunged forward to help pick them up, whispering: "Thanh! I should have known it was you! Someday it won't be friends picking up after you, my little rebel." I dashed out of the classroom before Mme Conan could see what happened.

Distributing tracts called for creative, word-of-mouth tactics. I always carried a supply at the ready. A demonstration around a particular event provided an obvious outlet. But it was important to have copies handy for unexpected opportunities, too, such as a swearing-in ceremony for inductees into the Jeunesse d'Avantgarde, JAG; by the 1940s, JAG included over a million young people. My own induction took place in Le An's bedroom with a longtime member of JAG serving as master of ceremony.

Different political leaflets were tailored to different audiences. Some were for the public; others were more focused, like the one aimed at Vietnamese students at Lycée Marie Curie: *A Flock of Vietnamese Birds,* with its subtitle, "A Call to Participate." Never more than four or six pages, the tract was passed hand to hand, silently. Several styles of handwriting flowed across the pages, depending on who was available to write. I was often asked because my clear penmanship was appreciated. If I was too busy to write, I was asked to review the final version and invent design flourishes to decorate the corners of each page.

As part of the student association, one of our assignments was to distribute secret documents coming from the liberated zone. We passed the papers, hand to hand, to those who needed updates from the maquis—which truck had been sabotaged, which convoy of French soldiers attacked. Zones 7, 8, and 9 were cut off from the North, making it important to share news from there. [Ed. note: The Viet Minh divided Vietnam into nine zones, numbered north to south: 1, 2, and 3 in Tonkin; 4, 5, and 6 in Annam; and 7, 8, and 9 in Cochinchina. Zone 7 was home to military campaigns just north of Saigon. Zone 8 was the Plain of Reeds, and Zone 9, the Ca Mau liberated territory.]

By 1948, we started carrying clandestine pamphlets and journals in our school bags. One of the journals, called *Struggle against Invasion,* was revolutionary. We read them in secret and passed them on. Our parents grew suspicious.

Performances for students continued to be held at the municipal theater. Organizers found clever ways to weave in inspiring themes. Between two historical plays—*Tuc Luy* (Tears of Earth) and *The Debt of Me Linh,* the geographical capital of the Trung sisters—a separate scene took the place during the intermission. Girls and boys, dressed in white, recited a poem by a famous musician who had died young. The first words were: "Tonight, on the deserted river bank, I leave my wandering soul to go beyond this life, to come back to the distant days, to the souls of those who died for the country."

It was an appeal to ancestors from every corner of the country to gather on a deserted riverbank and allow us to think of them and all they did. A meditation spoken through a beautiful poem, this was a prayer call to the memory of ancestors who had died for the homeland.

At home, I organized theater skits on the second floor, which we had to ourselves since our parents rarely came up. In a big room, I hung a curtain to separate a stage area. Before each play, as the curtain rose ceremoniously, Trang and I stood in white ao dais and led the singing of the national anthem that was forbidden at the time and later became the anthem. Our audience usually consisted of uncles, nieces, and others in the extended family. Since Mother worked, we had help to maintain our big house, so I invited the maids to watch, too. Especially when my parents were out, we sang and solemnly saluted the revolutionary flag: I made one by gluing a gold star on red paper. After saluting the flag, we read a poem: "This evening . . . I call the wandering souls of all the martyrs and national heroes."

I imitated what we had seen at the municipal theater, like a child imitating adults. Anything we could understand, we copied.

One time, there was a knock at the door. It was not the police; it was Mother. She yelled, "Unlock this door! What are you doing in there?" Everyone jumped up, and we hid the flag and stage props before opening the door. Mother asked, "Who is the ringleader of this affair?" I confessed and took responsibility. She said, "Lie down," and hit me with a rattan broom. She worried we would draw the attention of the police. I took it stoically and didn't cry. She suspected we had forbidden publications but could not find them.

In public, walking along the street, I carried journals and newspapers about the underground in my school bag. Unafraid, I left my bag open, knowing that, since I was dressed like a French girl, police would never suspect girls like me of circulating clandestine materials.

Friends of our parents had a house in an alley behind our house. That family had daughters, and the youngest joined the maquis. Her older sister immediately suspected us of luring her sister to the maquis and came to our house, demanding, "Where is Thanh? You are all troublemakers! You sow trouble in our house and family!" She insulted me. She was not at all patriotic. I stayed upstairs while she yelled in the salon. Mother suspected we had a role and feared we planned to join the maquis as well. Mother suspected me most. The next day, she put Trang and me in a car and sent us to stay with a cousin in Bien Hoa, north of Saigon. Bien Hoa was miserable. We stared at the Dong Nai River in front of our cousin's house and dreamed about the *bung bien*, the maquis. We imagined others already in the middle of a political course.

Surrounded by French students and teachers at Lycée Marie Curie, we still got news from the liberation zones. We heard about soldiers enduring privations to liberate our country. The poor soldiers—when it rained hard, we worried about how they could survive. They must have been suffering so! As fifteen- or sixteen-year-olds, we let our imaginations run free. When a movement to gather provisions was launched, we contributed by knitting clothes for the soldiers, who must have been shivering in the damp, cold forests. On days designated for collecting money, Trang and I gathered donations. But it was not enough to give money. We had to feel the deprivations. Trang and I decided we would not eat all day because we were empathizing with them. We were so young. We didn't eat all day, and then, feeling so hungry, we decided we had to eat or fall down weak and be unable to attend school. We ate so much; our stomachs couldn't handle it, and we threw up. We hid this from our parents, who would have spanked us.

It's all to say, we were young. We were children.

After a while, it became clear that professors in the lycée's disciplinary committee suspected me of agitating among students. On a prominent wall in the school courtyard, administrators posted lists of students meriting *félicitations* (congratulations) or *blâmes* (discipline). It was funny because I saw my name among those to be congratulated and among those to be disciplined. Appearing in front of the discipline committee, I was berated for "bad behavior" and received a warning and threat of being expelled. I couldn't help but think how this bulletin board was the same where, with nobody around, I had once stuck a drawing of Uncle Ho in honor of his birthday. It was risky. I had done it and dashed away. I didn't know if someone saw me. I was convoked again soon after with a severe warning, but they did not have hard proof of the charges.

Father had made us go and see patriotic performances, so we imitated what we saw and began to put on historic plays at the lycée, as well. Mme Ourgaud, who taught French in Trang's class, held progressive ideas. We took advantage of the lycée approving of students putting on plays. We'd all gather—secretaries, students, and anyone else interested—and I'd choose and direct a play in which everybody played a role. Tall and strong, Trang played the role of young men. Before the end of the school year, before saying good-bye, Mme Ourgaud helped us stage Molière's *Bourgeois Gentilhomme*. Trang wore a white wig and dressed as Monsieur Jourdain. One of the scenes that made a big impression was of Jourdain and his servant who mocks Jourdain's dress and manner while his master mimics a nobleman: a bourgeois pretending to be a noble.

Another powerful influence on us was our teacher of Vietnamese language and literature, Mme Lanh. While we were supposed to learn everything in French, she helped us discover our own language and literature. The primary foreign language offered was English; as a second foreign language, we could choose between Spanish and Vietnamese. As Vietnamese, we learned Vietnamese as a second foreign language! As luck had it, Mme Lanh was very patriotic and made us feel like we had an accomplice. She taught us the epic poem *Kim Van Kieu* and made it possible to study its verses in Vietnamese. She had to be circumspect. When a surveillant walked by the classroom, we spoke in French. As soon as they left, Mme Lanh spoke to us again in Vietnamese. The French did not grasp Mme Lanh's influence on us.

We also learned about the legend of the areca and betel nut and its lessons about loyalty and devotion. Chewing a bit of areca with betel nut is an ancient tradition still observed in marriages. The groom's family brings areca nut in a cloth: the symbol of happiness and conjugal love. In this fable, a virtuous young woman

FIGURE 2. At Lycée Marie Curie in 1948, Mme Lanh taught Vietnamese language and literature, including the epic poem *Kim Van Kieu*. Her classes inspired "indigenous" girls to learn more than French history and culture: they learned to take pride in Vietnamese language and culture. Courtesy of Nguyen Binh Thanh.

falls in love with two brothers. One brother seduces her and marries her. The other is so sad he disappears into the forest and wanders for days. He is weak by the time he reaches the edge of a stream and dies of hunger. Buddha transforms him into a white rock. Meanwhile, his older brother—brokenhearted his brother left without saying a word—ventures into the forest to find him. He too dies of hunger and is transformed into a tall, straight tree with clumps of branches and a plume of leaves that stands next to the white stone. The young bride wanders into the forest to search for the two people she dearly loves. She reaches the edge of the stream, dies, and is transformed into a vine that climbs the height of the tree, unwinding its whole length, creating a beautiful image of a young woman dying and extending the length of the tree.

At this time, there is a good king who cares for his subjects, who in turn love him. One day he goes hunting in the forest. His people have told him about the brothers and bride who disappeared within weeks of each other. Nobody knows where they are. By chance, the king comes to the stream and notices the towering tree. No other tree soars so straight and tall. Then he sees a cluster of nuts. Nobody had heard of such a tall tree or strange fruit or had seen their leaves and nuts. The king is curious and, unafraid of being poisoned, collects a leaf and a nut. He cuts the nut into six or seven pieces and rolls them in the betel leaf, puts this in his mouth, and chews. When he spits the saliva onto the stone, a white piece of limestone, it turns dark red. He wonders what it means.

This fable is poignant in talking about young people searching and caring for each other: the elder brother for the younger, the wife for her husband, conjugal fidelity between husband and wife, the love between brothers. They died because they could not find each other. The king is so moved that he decrees to his subjects that, from then on, at every marriage, to wish the couple happiness, one must eat betel with the areca nut with the *chau* (flowers) from the tree's vines, which are small and white with a delicate perfume that is light and hard to identify. All three must be mixed together. This story is rich with meaning.

I had transferred back to Lycée Marie Curie in 1949 when the school officials decided girls could not, should not, study alongside boys at Chasseloup-Laubat, and added upper-level classes. During this, my last year at Marie Curie, the movement against the French bubbled up across Saigon. The zone of resistance in the North, the Viet Bac, tied the resistance to the socialist camp around the world. From the liberated zone, people traveled to China, the USSR, and other countries. All this resonated in the South. As students, we ached to be part of it.

One of our first clandestine activities was to pass the word that President Ho Chi Minh's birthday was coming on May 19, so we should all wear white. The day before, I'd run around reminding friends, in a casual, friendly way, "Tomorrow is Uncle Ho's birthday; everyone wear white." I didn't have to remind Minh and Trang; they already put their white ao dais out to unwrinkle. Tuyen, Sen, Le An, and Lien An could usually be relied on. Only Oanh, the least political of us, needed to be reminded. During recess, we stood apart in the courtyard trying not to draw attention and risk being disciplined. We stood in groups of three or four. Trying to make it look random, a bunch of us—including Xuan, Le An, Oanh— gathered quickly to take a photo. We don't have any copies.

At one point, I was asked to come before the lycée discipline committee, a group of teachers who met in a big hall. If you were suspected of a serious offense, you were summoned before the committee that dispensed sanctions and punishments. Worse, they filed reports with the local police. The committee also decided which students deserved to be congratulated. They asked me questions— lots of questions. One teacher declared: "That's her, the Vietnamese Joan of Arc." They expelled me. I am not sure how I was able to return to Marie Curie after that. My parents must have intervened and made promises.

In July 1949, before separating at the end of the school year, we put on a performance. I organized it at school and called it an end-of-school event, to say good-bye to each other. We would sing and dance; that would be all. We didn't want the head supervisor to make trouble for us. We performed three skits.

The first, *Pilgrimage to the Perfume Pagoda*, with music by Tran Van Khe, was completely innocent. A fifteen-year-old girl lives with her family in the North during feudal times. She wears an ao dai and visits the pagoda with her parents. They reach the pagoda by boat and climb hundreds of steps to the pagoda, which is inside a big cave. Old ladies go to make offerings to the spirits; the young visit to ask for children. One day each year, everyone visits and a huge crowd forms. Set in the 1920s, the girl asks permission to accompany her parents to the pagoda. She puts on shoes, a beautiful dress, and a hat and rides with her mother on a horse. Midway, they meet a young, well-read man. Intelligent and dapper, accompanied by his young assistant, he is going to the pagoda. To reach the pagoda, they have to stop overnight. That night, she dreams about the handsome young man, who was gallant and considerate toward her and her parents. The next day, after making offerings, each goes their own way. That's all. It's the simple memory of a young woman. She never sees the young man again.

Tran Van Khe came to our house and sang a song he composed about the story. We used his music and song for this first piece. The young woman was played by a beautiful classmate who later joined the maquis but came back early because she could not bear the hard life. She married, had children, and stayed until 1976 or so, when she left for the United States.

Playing the role of the young man, I wore elegant clothes and carried a scroll of paper, showing he could read and write. I borrowed one of Father's black tunics with a double lining—one side black, the other a stunning yellow. I turned it inside out and looked elegant in the bright yellow tunic with a red handkerchief. We invited friends, students, and Mme Ourgaud, who sympathized with the revolution and came to applaud us.

The second play, spoken in verse, told the story of a national hero, Tran Quoc Thoan, who lived during the time of General Tran Hung Dao. We found the play's verses in a journal. Furious at the Chinese invaders, the young man grips an orange in his hand and squeezes it until it bursts. The hero was played by a classmate once active in our group who later had to follow her parents to Paris.

In the play, Tran Quoc Thoan has two guards—armed companions always close by. Xuan played one guard, and I played the other; we used batons as weapons, and the hero wielded a long stick as his sword. I suddenly thought, This is it; everything is in our hands. When we bicycled home after the play, nobody noticed us carrying our batons with radiant pride. It was incredible: we put ourselves in the skin of our characters! It gave us inspiration; it gave us strength; it gave us energy.

We found the third play in a journal. It tells the story of a soldier in the army under the leader, Le Loi. Many young people unite with Le Loi at his headquarters in the mountains at Lang Son. The story is about the young man, his horse, and his sword. Midway on a journey, he stops at the hut of an elderly peasant who asks to whom the horse belongs. The young man, played by Trang, says it belongs to him and dismounts to rest and talk. Trang loved to play the role of boys or men. She had painted a mustache, dressed all in black—clothes, hat, belt—and carried a sword. She looked dashing, and the audience oohed and aahed. The play succeeded fully in telling the same story of a young man going to the maquis. It captured exactly how we felt.

In between plays, a student sang a solo—not a rousing march but a song that expressed our mood. In her beautiful voice, Tuyen sang patriotic songs composed by her brother Luu Huu Phuoc. Tuyen was our nightingale.

The event was a big success.

The year 1950 was a watershed. On January 9, a thousand students gathered in front of the ministry of education of the *fantoches* (puppet regime) to demand the release of students arrested weeks earlier at Lycée Pétrus Ky. A savage repression followed as police tried to disperse students. We stayed into the afternoon to press for the release of our comrades. Police used fire hoses and, by midafternoon, started firing shots. Many students were wounded as they scattered. I saw blood dripping from skulls. A student named Tran Van On was taken to Cho Ray Hospital, where he died of gunshot wounds. Students rallied around his body, so policemen could not take it away and make it disappear. We took the body to his school, Lycée Pétrus Ky. January 9 became the National Day of Students.

On January 12, a river of people—students, cyclo (pedicab) drivers, shopkeepers—streamed into the streets of Saigon for Tran Van On's funeral procession. Delegations arrived from Hanoi, Hue, and the Mekong Delta; having traveled the length of the country, they represented the strength of the movement.

On March 19, another important date in our history, a big anti-American rally was organized to protest the arrival of two U.S. warships, the USS *Stickell* and USS *Anderson*. The people of Saigon—mass movements of workers, intellectuals, and other groups—marched to demand the immediate departure of the U.S. war vessels. Their presence came across as an operation of intimidation. We resented Americans coming to aid the French by putting on a naval parade in the port of Saigon. Revolutionary forces in the city organized demonstrations of more than half a million protesters. American flags were torn and burned; American jeeps, set ablaze. March 19 became the national day of anti-Americanism for the whole country.

After March 19, the next major protest was by city workers on May 1, International Workers' Day. Knowing our parents would not let us participate, Trang and I got up before dawn and slipped out of the house to join the protesters. We were afraid to go back because our parents would punish us, though not because

FIGURE 3. Siblings Thanh, Trang, and Minh, at Tet 1950—a pivotal year for all the sisters. As Minh explained, "We were the generation at a crossroads." Courtesy of Nguyen Binh Thanh.

our parents were unpatriotic. They often admonished us: "You children can't do anything yet. Adults will make the revolution, not students like you, who should study and stay at their benches in school and earn diplomas. After you graduate, they will listen to you then. You will be accomplished women. Now, you are just little schoolgirls. Follow your studies."

We did not agree. We could no longer stand being in the classroom. As students in Saigon who used paintbrushes and inkwells at our desks, we came under the spell of Luu Huu Phuoc's song telling students to "Put away the inkwell and pen; the time has come to go to the front!" Everyone sang it.

After the protest march, we hid at Le An's home for a few days. Mother and Father worried when we didn't return. Minh, being the good child and more conservative in temperament, didn't dare undertake the folly Trang and I did. We were more adventurous. I had asked Trang to come with me. It seemed safer, less alien, to go with her. She accepted right away. We contacted comrades about going into the maquis.

Meanwhile, Minh told our parents she knew where we might be hiding. Finally, they realized they could not stop us, and Father declared, "Come back. We will help you prepare—we will give you what you need to go to the maquis." And they did. Mother sewed a black *baba* (loose top) and pair of pants for each of us.

They bought raincoats, shoes, medicines, and bags to carry our supplies into the jungle.

Confucian thought dictates that we respect older people, parents, and teachers. Children are raised to obey parental wishes. But at some point, struggling to fulfill our parents' wishes and also answer the call of our people and nation, we had to choose one voice over the other.

After saying good-bye to our parents, Trang and I left. On May 10, as we had done on May 1, we got up early, dressed, and grabbed our knapsacks with the clothing Mother had prepared. We wore colorful, flowery babas. We crossed the street to the bus stop at the entrance to the Parc Maurice Long. A woman liaison agent appeared shortly, and we waited for the bus west to Tay Ninh and the Cambodian border. Rue Verdun is a very long street stretching west. The bus rumbled past the outskirts of town, and soon we saw rice fields along both sides of the road. We were en route to the Eastern Zone, while our friends Le An and Sen were going to the Western Zone.

We were leaving for an unknown period. At any cost, we wanted to go to the jungle.

Our liaison signaled the bus driver to stop before the next town controlled by the French. It was still early as we started out on foot to reach the liberated zone. Trang and I imitated our guide's walk. It wasn't the straight line of a city dweller but the roundabout walk of a peasant. She avoided guard towers—built at surprisingly short intervals—manned by French and legionnaire soldiers from other colonies. At noon, we ate at the home of partisans and continued despite the heat and slippery mudbanks along the rice fields. Our muscles began to hurt as if we'd been beaten.

At dusk, we heard human voices and recognized the singing of a song about Bac Ho (Uncle Ho). The singing grew louder. We stumbled out of the dark into a small clearing surrounded by *paillottes*, thatched huts made of tree branches and tall grasses.

For the first time, we breathed the air of the maquis.

Lots of students in the January 9 movement joined the maquis. We didn't hesitate to give up our schooling, *de plein gré* (willingly). We regretted nothing. We did not think about graduating and getting a diploma; that was ordinary and would not serve the country. Even if we were young, the country needed us to join the soldiers in the resistance.

Trang and I were in a group of ten from Saigon. We were the only two from Marie Curie; others came from middle-class high schools. Most of the boys we knew in Saigon did not join because many sons were sent to France, carried away on huge ocean liners. My parents were conservative and, frankly, doubted we girls would make it in a school system abroad. Anyway, we would never board a ship bound for France. We wanted to participate directly. It was our dream. That's how we thought as we departed for a resistance base in the Seventh Zone.

Having us go first to a base where a cousin was in the resistance offered my parents some small consolation. As part of our initiation, we learned how to make things out of natural materials, how to cook, and how to plant manioc.

Mother worried a lot about all the hazards we would face: malaria, torrential rains, cold weather, bombing raids. She worried most about me because she had already once prepared my funeral.

I'd always been thin and prone to illness. I had asthma since childhood and, at thirteen, suffered acute inflammation of the kidneys. My body puffed up so much that when Mother poked me with a finger, it was swallowed up by skin. While my parents started planning my funeral, Mother had a brainstorm. She asked an uncle, a doctor in Can Tho, to take care of me since doctors in Saigon had given up. She hired a special car to take me directly to Can Tho. I lay in the back seat—my feet had ballooned out, and I could not even wear sandals.

My uncle administered shots, antibiotics, and infusions of an herbal tea made of the roots of *tranh*, a plant that grows in the countryside. He said my blood had been poisoned, and I had to drink tranh, take medicines, and avoid salt. I ate a strict diet of bananas, mangoes, and rice. My kidneys began to function. The tranh purified my blood. Of course, it took a lot of discipline to not eat a single grain of salt for two years. I put that discipline to use later.

My uncle saved my life. And while the disease was horrible, I remember fondly living in my grandmother's house next to my uncle's clinic. Out back, a tall screen of bamboo stood next to a little spring. Playmates and I strung up a small tent by the water and pretended to prepare a picnic. We put on plays. For my role as a princess, I laced a red hibiscus around each ear, its yellow pestle swaying elegantly when I moved my head.

Cured, I came back to Saigon in 1943 and started classes again at the Collège des Jeunes Filles Françaises, as Lycée Marie Curie was then known. I found it easy to pass exams and quickly made up for the two years of schooling I had lost.

So it was my mother who worried how I would handle life in the maquis. I still suffered asthma attacks at night. How could I be thrown into life in the jungle and forest? There would be no medicine. How could I endure all the severe conditions? All I could think about was Luu Huu Phuoc's song, "*Len Dang*," exhorting brothers to march bravely down the path!

In the maquis, I walked so much I no longer had asthma. There is nothing better than physical exercise to get rid of asthma. I ate well, my appetite stimulated by the fresh air and atmosphere of the forest. Being in nature did me a lot of good. We had a lot of physical exercise marching along for hours and decamping from place to place to escape bombings by the French. Reaching a new camp, we dug trenches to protect us during bombing raids, and soldiers cut down trees to build houses and tables. One of the hardest tasks was to dig wells; it was a relief when a downpour formed a natural well.

At camp, we fashioned everything out of tree trunks tied together using *lianes*, creepers that festoon the forest. Tree trunks were lashed together to make sturdy beds and chairs. In the kitchen hut, a primitive mud stove had two large holes opening on top and one on the side in which to feed wood. Two pipes ran out of the back of both stove openings, directing the smoke several meters deep into the bush.

Our food staple was manioc. It grows quickly, over the course of about three months, and fills the stomach. Twice a day, morning and evening, we ate a mixture of rice and manioc. For variety, we added groundnuts and salt. But manioc is not very nutritious and destroys red globulin cells. Sick people avoided it, especially women, because it increased mucous flow, draining their energy. If we ran out of manioc, we substituted *mang le* (tender bamboo shoots) and cooked *mam ruoc* (liquid of tiny fermented shrimp). Mam ruoc was even cheaper than *nuoc mam* (fish sauce). And it tasted that way. At first, Trang could not let it pass her lips. A sympathetic friend gave her a small GIBS brand tin of salt and pepper. She rationed out a pinch with her rice but, at the end of a month, ran out and tried the fetid mam ruoc, which made her cry. She got used to it.

Everyone in the camp received equal portions of food. A metal bowl was filled with manioc and rice hash and turned over on a plate. The bowls came from coolies escaping their French masters or were taken on raids on plantations where the bowls served to collect sap from rubber trees.

We also drank from these metal bowls. A favored drink was well water boiled with lianes, which girls also used to wash their hair. Lianes reputedly kept our hair black and youthful looking.

To satisfy a craving for sugar, we concocted our own form of che, the sweet bean pudding Mother used to make on Sunday afternoons. Instead of beans we used manioc and sweetened it with black sugar, a local, unrefined sugar.

Each morning, a metal rod rapped against the door of our huts to announce time to get up and eat. After the 5:00 AM reveille, we mechanically folded our mosquito nets and sheets and stuffed them into our backpacks with our extra set of black pajamas. Backpack on, we reported outside and counted off by number. We learned to move as a unit, following instructions: "Right, forward, left, rest."

We looked forward to bathing in a stream by the camp. Boys walked a few hundred meters away along the stream and jumped in without any clothes. Girls jumped in with clothes on, not just to preserve our modesty but so we could wash our clothes at the same time. When we got out, we hung our clothes to dry and put on our other set of pajamas.

Girls of course had to deal with their menstrual periods and made sanitary napkins out of pieces of mosquito netting folded over several times for absorbency. We soaked it in mud to dye it brown or in crushed leaves to turn it green. Nothing white, which could be seen from the air, could be left out to dry. I used strips of mosquito nets tied together to make sanitary straps to hold the napkin in place. When soiled, the netting folded into the pocket could be replaced.

To decorate their huts, even soldiers planted and watered orchids. It was a small refinement. We braided bamboo to make pots and hang plants with violet, orange, and yellow blooms. The men shared their flowers with us on festival days. At the first independence celebration on September 2, orchids were not yet in bloom, so girls used colored paper—bought by the agents assigned to make purchases in town—to fold yellow, rose, or blue paper into flowers. We picked big, wide leaves and stuck paper flowers in their centers. Boys teased us about our handmade flowers. During other celebrations, we vied to see who had the best decorated hut. Everyone won; we did it for fun.

In 1951, we decorated our huts to celebrate Tet. Our group of a dozen girls, aged seventeen or eighteen, was led by a woman a few years older. The first day of Tet, boys came to wish us a happy new year and admire our artistic flourishes, especially in comparison to how they had tried to decorate their huts.

We also added color to our huts by creating *journaux muraux*, journals that were arranged on a mural. The larger huts had bamboo partitions that doubled as public message boards. Each of us wrote an article, poem, or popular verse about daily life and pinned them to the board. To color the board red, we used *mercurocum*, a bright antiseptic. Trang developed a reputation for witty designs. One was of a girl who, told to be serious during a meeting, curls her lip into a smile at the corner of her mouth. Trang painted the concealed grin on the partition and wrote underneath: "Can this young female combatant be adhering to a military stance while wearing a sly smile?"

At the same time, we remained constantly alert, backpacks at the ready if we had to decamp. Everything had to fit in a backpack. We each had two sets of pajamas—one to wear and one to carry in the pack—along with a canvas raincoat and hat. Many packed a tiny tin of GIBS brand toothpaste. Fitted with a wick and filled with oil, it could also serve well as a lamp. Papers, maps, and all documents were folded into baskets at either end of carrying poles. The poor cook, weighed down by pots and casseroles, looked like a one-man bazaar. Walking single file, we followed each other by the light of the moon. We had to monitor each other because, by early morning, any one of us risked falling down from lack of sleep.

We had to cross streams with rushing water reaching our waists. Girls kept their clothes on, but boys took off their pants and put them back on when they reached the other side.

We put on plays from *cai luong* (traditional theater). Real cai luong celebrities came from town to train us. I saw my first cai luong play in the maquis. It told the story of General Tran Hung Dao. We made a stage by laying planks across a clearing and improvised a mandarin's costume using cardboard and colored paper. In our zone we did not have trained actresses, so one man in particular—with a pretty face—played the roles of women. He wore makeup that agents had bought in town. We introduced a lot of plays that were new to the local people. We worked with artists of *ha boi*, also a kind of traditional theater, who went to the maquis.

We learned songs and dances from the Western Zone as well as the Viet Bac. Most foreign songs and dances came from China and the Soviet Union. One popular Soviet play is about a soldier whose face is horribly burned by a bomb explosion. The nurse who attends him is his great love. Despite his disfigurement, she still loves him. Our leader translated the play. I played the nurse, though my enthusiasm for the stage was low because of my handicap: taking my glasses off on stage, I was myopic. The deep love between the nurse and soldier is unforgettable.

We performed for a stream of delegations moving north and south for conferences. As the showdown at Dien Bien Phu neared, more songs from the North paid tribute to minority groups helping the army close in on the French, including as porters inching supplies and armaments up the mountains. One of the songs was "Pinong Oi" (Little brother). A popular march, "Van Cao," urged audiences to "go forward to liberate Hanoi."

We also faced challenges. *Ram cham quap* was the name for the deadliest snake in the bush. Huge ants burrowed into our skin, making it hard to rip one off without taking off a piece of skin. We risked slicing our fingers on sickles used to harvest vegetables and herbs. I had to go to the hospital for a week because of malaria. Poor Trang had a tooth pulled without anesthesia; I held her and heard the pincers grind at her tooth. To ease pain and brace for an operation or amputation, soldiers sang marches and other patriotic songs.

Crossing a stream could also be treacherous. Walking to the manioc field meant crossing a rushing stream with a bridge made of a tree trunk with a rope as a handle. Once, returning alone at dusk, I found the torrent of water covered the bridge. My bare feet groped the tree trunk, and I inched along the submerged bridge. I was alone and could not swim. I thought, "If I slip, nobody will know what happened to me." I felt safer moving as a group.

I had to admit envy of the entertainment troupe from the Fifth Zone; they wore trim pale gray uniforms made of a tissue called *sita*. We dreamed of those uniforms; they were the only thing we coveted. We were embarrassed by our black pajamas.

But overall, we were happy. Everyone was young, our hearts beating for the cause. We laughed a lot, especially in the evenings, when we gathered to dance and sing and perform short plays. In the forest, we sat on tree trunks around a big fire. We would dance around the fire, read poems, and sing about the revolution and how we were going to liberate the nation. Trang immediately joined the artistic ensemble of the Seventh Zone army. They were impressed she could play an accordion seized during an attack on a French convoy. Otherwise, there would not have been any hope of finding an accordion in the jungle! She became quite a celebrity with her accordion. Given the name Chi Ba (older sister number three), Trang provided the soundtrack during theater performances and screenings of silent films.

Films were projected on a white sheet strung between two trees in a small clearing. We hiked three or four hours just to see a film. The first film I saw in the maquis was set in Soviet Armenia and showed peaceful scenes of children in school and fields of flowers. This captured the dream for which we now suffered; it made real our hope for a free, independent Vietnam with food and schooling for all. As we watched, Chi Ba played upbeat Soviet songs. During sad movies, she played melancholy pieces. She was imaginative and changed soundtracks so they wouldn't be repetitive. Her strength and stamina enabled her to play for hours. Soldiers appreciated what she did and liked her a lot. Chi Ba was more well-known than I was.

Wherever we relocated, my core work remained in propaganda. Girls and women formed a union of liberated women of the Seventh Zone that included a congress and president.

Assemblies were called to honor the achievements of soldiers; they were honored and decorated as a way to encourage them. To make flags for these ceremonies, we crushed quinine that came in dark yellow pills and used it to paint the golden star on a field of red. Girls also sewed badges for these heroes.

When I worked in the Seventh Zone with a group of women for the patriotic front, one of my fellow workers was Le Thi Rieng. She helped me with my propaganda assignments. I liked and admired her. We taught together, educating peasant women and winning them over to the cause of the revolution. We knew how to talk with youth and women. Rieng came from a simple, peasant background and could work the fields.

Wherever we set up camp, we cultivated small pieces of land. We burned the forest before planting grains of rice in paddies; because tubers grow better than rice, we also planted manioc and sweet potatoes.

Rieng liked poetry and composed poems. In the maquis, people carried a *carnet*, a small notebook, or a diary with verses and poems, usually by poets from other countries. Rieng and I carried poetry notebooks, and she often asked, "Can you please copy this poem into my notebook? I like your handwriting." She liked how I arranged the page, ornamenting it with small designs and pencil sketches. Le Thi Rieng was assassinated during the Tet Offensive in 1968.

We dedicated passages to people we knew who had been martyred on a certain day. The first martyr in my family was a handsome man not even twenty years old. The French captured and tortured him, stretching him out in the sun to die. I wrote a dedication based on an article his father wrote about his son's death: "In the struggle of the universe, each person is a combatant; life is an endless struggle. To stop struggling is to fail, and failure means death. To stop struggling is to await slavery. The combatant is most fully alive, living next to death but also living above death."

I filled my carnet with poems by the poet of the revolution, To Huu (1920–2002), imagining a bond with him because he published his first poems in clandestine journals while studying at a French lycée. He combined the revolutionary fervor of the time with the traditions of our people. He lived with the peasants for many years, and his poems touched many different kinds of people. One of his poems I copied was titled "Mother," which starts:

> Who will return to the village to tell mother,
> That this evening, far away, her child thinks of her,
> Aren't you cold, mother, in this bitter wind,
> Blowing from the mountain, mingling with the rain,
> Mother is cold, planting rice,
> Feet in the mud, hands pushing the seeds deep down,
> With each seed she plants,
> She thinks of her child.

The poem ends:

> I am going to the distant Front.
> I love you, Mother.
> I love our country like another mother.
> When the enemy is chased away, I will return forever.
> The mother with gray hair in the evening,
> Heard inside her the voice of her child.

To Huu also translated poems by foreign poets, including a popular poem by the Russian poet Konstantin Simonov, who fought in World War II as the Soviets tried to hold off the Nazi armies. In his poem "Wait for Me," a soldier at the German front writes to his fiancée back home. It opens:

> Wait for me, I will return;
> but wait for me forever,
> even when the rain's coppery tones darken your sadness.

And the poem closes:

> Wait for me,
> I will return defying death,
> "How well he did to come through that" they will then explain.
> Those who awaited me so little
> for lack of knowing that I could make my way through fire safe, by your
>   hope.
> Only we will know, we two,
> if I survived more than any other, it was you—
> You waited for me.

Many of us copied this poem into our notebooks.

I also composed poems and showed one to a poet in the maquis. He said it wasn't bad. Words came easily, and I wrote them down in short verses. I didn't use a classical style. I continued for many years to write poems when I was alone.

When they weren't teaching or writing, artists and writers were well known for drinking a lot of tea. Coffee was a luxury, and sugar extremely rare. Trang and I heard artists joke, "The stronger the tea, the better we write." Squatting at the foot of a tree or stretched out in hammocks, they swapped stories. In the jargon, it was called UTQ: *uong* (drink), *tra* (tea), *quau* (strong).

My sister Trang and her fiancé, the writer and soldier Nguyen Thi, walked into the forest together to clear a patch of jungle and plant manioc. If they had a baby, they wanted to have food for the infant. Whenever he had a day or two off, Thi ·vent to cultivate their small parcel of land. With no way of mailing a message, how could the lovers communicate when to meet and work the land together to have food for their baby? When he waited at the plot, she didn't come. She might be assigned to play accordion for the soldiers or receive his message too late. So he cultivated the land by himself. We learned this from his diary, which he kept right up to Tet 1968—almost twenty years later. His friends brought it to their daughter in 1975, along with a handkerchief and his vest.

It breaks my heart to read the poems he wrote about their honeymoon. I think their daughter has the page on which he wrote their initials, TT, initials Trang and Thi's child would have regardless of whether they had a boy or girl. He illustrated and painted his poems and journals with lovely designs.

For me, my personal life was much simpler. I did not have so many romantic stories. There were a few evenings when my future husband and I met in the forest—moonlight is beautiful in the forest. We sat on logs, chatting together. We did not make many plans for the future; each of us had our work to do. But he was already older, and they rushed us to marry in the maquis—too early. It was at the end of 1950. He was an army officer and already considered a big leader. When sports and races were organized at camp, my husband was never among the first to cross the line. At thirty, he was already older than most.

At our marriage at the end of my first year in the maquis, army officers attended our simple ceremony; we offered tea, cookies, and peanuts. Since none of our relatives were at the wedding, my husband and I used a short vacation to visit them. We traveled by sampan. During a downpour, Minh, Mother, Trang, my husband, and I ended up huddled together under the sampan's rounded tin roof. Mother was shocked men and women could be so close to each other: her thinking remained feudal.

I returned to Saigon to have our first son. While at home, I marveled at the luxury of taking a shower: water came out of a tap and disappeared into a drain! I reveled in the feel of water pouring onto my skin and lathering it with soap. Pure joy. It was hard to leave my son in the care of my parents and Minh and return to the maquis.

We had a son and put him in the care of my mother in Saigon. One year, on his birthday, I woke up before the others and made a small wood fire to warm up. It was foggy and cold. I wrote a poem, "Nhu Con" (I miss my son).

After liberation in 1975, when I traveled often on diplomatic missions, my husband could no longer stand being alone, so he found someone else. I did not reproach him. You have to sacrifice something for the revolution. It might be a career. It might be family. In my case, starting in 1950, I was able to pursue a career that was part of the revolution.

In 1954, with the French defeat at Dien Bien Phu in May and the Geneva Accords in July, members of the resistance transferred north of the Seventeenth Parallel. My husband and I prepared to go, but Trang returned to Saigon. Seven or eight months pregnant, she could not risk the travel. She thought she could give birth right away and join her husband in the North, all within the three hundred days the Geneva Accords allotted for movements north or south. She expected to take one of the last boats north. Each time the arrival of a boat was announced, Thi expected her to be on it. But her comrades needed her to stay in Saigon to maintain communication lines with the resistance. She could not leave everything. She had ties in the resistance that had to be nurtured and sustained in Saigon.

Peace seemed to be at hand, and people celebrated. I worried about what would happen to Trang, who stayed behind in Saigon. I went to the southern coast to take a Soviet ship north.

2

TRANG

"Living a Contradiction"

Trang inherited her family's gifts for languages and music. "Lucie" excelled at the lycée. Trang credits learning French with raising her political awareness: it allowed her to read about French and Soviet resistance against the Nazis. She also delighted in French books, plays, and movies though they reinforced the feeling that girls came second to boys. No matter how many prizes she and her sisters won at the lycée, her parents expected them to stay on the sidelines as Saigon roiled. The tomboy in the family, Trang tried to show her physical strength by gardening alongside her father and repairing bicycles; still, all she heard was girls are to "walk, don't run," and "smile, don't laugh." Trang chafed at the thought of mirroring the cloistered life in which her mother grew up; she wanted, quite simply, to live more. To be free.

Like Thanh, Trang craved the chance to join the movement to rid her country of its colonial master. Confucian norms expected of women were unfair: If boys could join the maquis, why not girls?

Supported by her older sister Thanh, Trang also donned black pajamas and took a bus out of town into the jungle. In the resistance, she got up at dawn to go to the fields and plant crops. She kept working as the sun beat down. She learned to fish and forge across streams. She wanted to prove herself a female cadre equally dedicated as the men.

One small incident in the jungle changed the course of her life. She mastered an accordion left behind by French troops, which she played for soldiers as part of a musical troupe; she was determined to earn the respect of soldiers and show them what a woman could accomplish. Her strength and endurance made an impression. Eventually, her musical talents and dedication led her to be the first Vietnamese woman to train at the Tchaikovsky Institute to be an orchestra conductor—and then the first woman to take that stage in Saigon.

Unlike Thanh, Trang is reserved and spare in her narrative. One friend surmised Trang had borne such sorrows she became an emotional "turtle." A romantic love story that bloomed in the jungle was disrupted by the Geneva Accords; the father of her child took a ship to the North, while Trang stayed in Saigon to have their baby. When the resistance needed her to remain in Saigon as an agent, Trang asked her sister Minh to raise her daughter. Trang and Minh arranged periodic visits, so Trang could glimpse her child, setting a time to leave her in a baby carriage as Trang casually strolled by and cooed at her. Trang called it being a visiting mom.

[Ed. note: Trang's story is one that was not recorded on tape. What follows is based on interview notes, her husband's diary, and articles in Vietnamese newspapers she shared.]

Trang

I was born in 1933, a year after Thanh. Father was one of the first civil engineers to graduate from the University of Hanoi in the early 1920s. When he was offered a high-level position in the Ministry of Public Works, he refused it. Colleagues assumed he had hoarded enormous wealth, as many collaborators did; they assumed he could do that if not from a salary, then by owning buildings. Driving around Saigon, people working in the ministry often pointed out buildings they owned. Father owned none. The French administration urged him to continue studying in France and apply for citizenship and adopt Catholicism along the way. Again, he refused.

Father joined a group of intellectuals to form a legal organization, Société pour l'Amélioration Morale, Intellectuelle et Physique d'Indochine, known by its French acronym, SAMIPIC, with the goal of making life better for people in Indochina. SAMIPIC supported students, introduced jobseekers to colleagues, and gave young patriots a cultural and literary foundation to draw on in the struggle for independence. Men like my father, Nguyen Van Duc, masked their patronage of politics by supporting culture and the arts. Students gathered at our house to rehearse plays about heroic figures. We came home from school to find these men and students in our house; we listened to their talk of patriotism and memorized their revolutionary songs. We girls were in the atmosphere. It was *tout naturel* (completely natural) we would hear a voice urging us to join the struggle.

Student choirs sprang up all over town. Thanh, Minh, and I rehearsed songs and verses on a stage we fashioned in a room upstairs.

I studied at Lycée Marie Curie from 1943 until 1950 and left at the age of seventeen. The lycée provided a base of education and was especially important in teaching us French, so we could read about the French and Soviet resistance against the Nazis. I read journals and books by French people who questioned colonialism.

At the same time, we thought about leaving home to get away from Father's feudal thinking. He donated so much and risked so much to play a role in the country's liberation, but he did not think women had a role to play in that cause, at least not at our age.

We were living a contradiction. Father sent us to a Western school, while remaining feudal to his core, believing girls should not be with boys, and they can't do everything boys can. Despite our grades and prizes and being able to play all kinds of instruments, nothing changed his thinking about what women should or should not do. I liked to tinker with bicycles and was good enough that people paid me to fix their bicycles. I played the male roles in dramas at school. My sports scores were twice as high as anyone in my class. I was like a boy! But not in my father's eyes. Thanh agreed with me that even if we had wanted to go, Father would never have sent us to school in France. Yet our friend Xuan's father, also very traditional, believed a woman could succeed in a classroom abroad.

Growing up, I enjoyed working in the garden with Father, planting yum-yum fruit trees, lemon trees, gladiolas, and spectacular orchids. We were awed by one particular orchid: it was purple with alabaster-smooth, tongue-shaped blooms that encircled a round pendant. While digging in the peaceful setting of our garden, I felt grateful but also angry because we were living a contradiction. It was not only Confucian restrictions, all the *obéissances* and rules, but how they were interpreted. Up and down the length of Vietnam, girls learned to walk, don't run, and smile, don't laugh.

The contradiction wore me down. Respect and admiration for Father coexisted with deep frustration and a sense of submission to him. I could never forget how he helped his brothers rise from poverty. Every year, on the first day of the Tet Lunar New Year festival, cousins crowded into our house to pay respect to the man who had offered them money, a job, or simply advice. But I remained torn.

Similarly, we admired Mother for her schooling, and yet she accepted the feudalism and the idea that women were not equal to men. I agreed conservatism had a good side in how it encouraged the rules of virtue. She shielded us from Europeanization, from becoming libertines. Mother was convinced that even a glimpse of liberties outside the home led to excesses. Having led the life of a sheltered girl at a strict boarding school, she considered co-ed classes dangerous. I hope she knew we did not want to be like our lycée classmates who shrugged their shoulders in contempt, put on airs, and paraded around mimicking the French. I didn't like those girls.

Le An never shrugged her shoulders like others from rich families who became naturalized French. She remained humble. Le An and I helped distribute clandestine student journals and enjoyed each other's company bicycling to and from school.

We continued to feel *soumise* (subjected). I wanted to dwell less on the past. I wanted to live more. I wanted to be free. Thanh understood and had a plan. We left for the maquis after the May Day demonstration in 1950. When we left, I never expected to meet my classmates again, except Le An since I knew she and her father had gone north. I saw Sen once when I came to Saigon to give birth. We met in passing, never really expecting to see each other again.

In the maquis, I was part of a team responsible for planting and harvesting crops. We got up as early as four in the morning to hike and find land to cultivate. When we reached a flat area or gently sloping hillside, the team cut down trees, burned branches, and turned the soil with crude hoes before planting manioc, corn, and soybeans. Imitating Khmer farmers working along the nearby border, I jabbed a wooden stick into the soil and dropped a grain of corn into each hole. The sun beat down on my head, and the muscles in my arms and legs burned. But I did not suffer back pains the way Thanh did. Gardening with Father had prepared me to stoop and dig in the soil. Thanh and I had pledged to each other, "If we get sick, we remain at camp; if it's just our city girl muscles aching, we keep working." We heard others comment on how hard Saigon students worked. Our pride kept us going.

At home, I never cried in front of my sisters. But in the maquis, one thing made me cry: the first time I tasted mam ruoc. When supplies of nuoc mam, fish sauce, ran out, the cook resorted to mam ruoc, a cheaper, smelly fermented shrimp sauce. I figured out a way to postpone using the offensive liquid: a friend from Saigon brought a tin of GIBS toothpaste filled with salt. Adding a pinch to each bowl of rice, I made it last over a month.

To get to one plot of land we cultivated, we crossed the Tha La stream; it was wide and fast flowing compared to the trickle of water in most creeks. I could walk across the Tha La in the dry season, but the water lapped at my knees. The rest of the year, I learned to tiptoe across a tree trunk. Neither Thanh nor I knew how to swim, despite Father having taken us to the Piscine Neptune, the pool open to Vietnamese while the French swam at the Olympic-sized pool at the Cercle Sportif club.

Once, after days of steady rain, we struck out for the fields and found the log bridge over the Tha La submerged. The team and I braided a thick belt of vines and branches and stretched it across the water. Once we reached our fields, we saw only the tips of corn stalks poking up from the water line. All we could do was be patient, wait for the water to recede, and hope to salvage a small yield of corn or manioc.

Trudging back from the fields one day, I first noticed Tan. He was not only a soldier but a writer and poet. He was in charge of entertaining troops and pumping up their spirits before battle. He had tawny brown skin from working in the sun. He had many admirers. It was said a writer and poet has a "special soul." His handsome face seemed haunted by a serious expression, and his eyes bore into their targets. He was consumed by the cause.

As one of the eager city recruits, I was obsessed with proving worthy of the maquis. We accepted and adapted to the daily basics. I wore black pajamas. I wanted to show I could be a female cadre equally dedicated as the men. I tried not to think too much about Tan. When I did, warm feelings flowed through me. I could not control those feelings. Our family's Confucian morality seemed distant to me; harder to ignore was the revolutionary morality—the personal code of conduct tightly tied in with the political struggle. We were to fight *against* personal needs and fight *for* the cause.

One small event in 1951 changed my life. While working in the fields one day, soldiers from our camp intercepted and captured a French patrol. They seized a

FIGURE 4. Trang, left, and Thanh overcame their parents' opposition and joined the maquis, the anti-French resistance, in 1950. They traded a comfortable life in Saigon for the daily trials of life in the jungle. Courtesy of Nguyen Binh Thanh.

black musical instrument that had a panel of white "fingers" along one side. It was an accordion. One of the camp leaders knew my family had a musical background and said, "She's one of the musical Binh daughters, and she's strong as a tiger; let's see what she can do with such a physically demanding instrument." I knew what to do with an instrument I had played at home and at the lycée. The leaders were impressed and asked me to join the theater and dance ensemble of the Armée du Septiéme Zone, the army of the Seventh Zone.

Our troupe was made up of ten singers, dancers, and musicians. We were dispatched to help the people in a *xa* (village) whenever torrential rains flooded their rice fields. At the xa, I rolled up my pajama legs, stood in a row of peasants knee-deep in muddy water, and gratefully accepted a straw conical hat against the sun as we tried to salvage the harvest. In the evenings, we performed popular songs to buoy the spirits of the peasants. Our troupe operated on its own separate schedule, leaving camp by boat at dawn and reaching a xa by midday.

Another of our duties was to entertain assemblies of political and military personnel. Music and poetry circulated north and south through congresses bringing together combatants from up and down the length of the country. It was like the circulation of blood in a body.

I stood out not only as one of few women but because I carried this bulky and bizarre instrument, which few peasants had ever seen. I attended hundreds of reunions grouping cadres from the provinces and leaders of the *armée populaire* in the Eastern Zone. At night, we traveled by small waterways, sometimes hiking beyond where boats could go.

One evening, the team left camp on foot at sunset. As I walked along a path with deep ruts made by a buffalo cart, my foot slipped into a crevice, and I twisted my ankle. My comrades waited for a cart to come and load me and the accordion onto it. That night, I assured my camp leaders I could still play music. Balancing on a tree stump, I cradled the accordion in my lap and opened the meeting with a patriotic song. At intermission, a cadre came up to me; he saw the peasants staring at this woman playing such a bizarre instrument. When the cadres were summoned to reconvene, peasants asked him, "What is that instrument she plays?" Thinking of a similar instrument he had seen, he said, "It's a ken," a wind instrument. He knew that wasn't quite right, so he added, "It is a ken . . . banjo."

After the close of the congress, cadres returned to their provinces and spread the story of the woman with the ken-banjo. Accounts of the ken-banjo played by a woman appeared in the *journaux muraux*, murals drawn to decorate the walls of huts. It became a favorite story passed on from one entertainment ensemble to another, the kind of tale shared when sitting around and relaxing. Later, when I was arrested in Saigon in 1958 and isolated in a prison cell, I learned from one of my interrogators that the man who coined *ken-banjo* turned out to be a traitor.

Four decades after that congress held in the forest, old cadres who were there still recognize me and come up and ask, "Do you still play the ken-banjo?"

I am still associated with another nickname from the maquis: "Chi Ba," elder sister number three, a term of respect. Leaders and combatants appreciated my energy and endurance. The square collar on my short-sleeved shirt made me look like a boy, which was fine with me. Since I dressed like a man, people at camp thought our unit of artists was all male. As the only girl among the artists, I grabbed every chance to prove myself. Everyone in the camp would march for three or four hours to see a film in a clearing in the forest. As the audience faced a white sheet strung between trees, I sat behind them and played a "human soundtrack." I adapted music to the mood of each movie or play. During gloomy parts, like when Russian soldiers marched against the Nazis, I played one kind of music. When news reels flickered and flashed across the sheet, I improvised musical riffs to keep up with the mood. During films about the fight against the Nazis, I liked to perform beautiful Soviet folk songs. One film ran so long my fingers began to go numb. I didn't want to disappoint the troops, so I mentally blocked out the spasms in my fingers; despite the throbbing pain, I disciplined myself to ignore it. Troops thanked me for keeping the music going.

A film about Soviet Armenia celebrated peaceful scenes of children studying in schools surrounded by fields of yellow flowers blowing in a breeze. This captured the dream for which we struggled and people suffered: the dream of achieving a free, independent Vietnam with food and schooling for all.

Our unit had a chicken, a rarity in the forest, and I decided it should be introduced to a rooster. A friend from Saigon gave me a bit of news I took as a challenge: a rooster was being kept at another encampment. I volunteered to bring the rooster to our camp, and the task was confided to me. On a moonless night, I struck out across fields and swaths of bulrushes, their sharp shoots pricking my sandals. I stumbled into the muck of a forest swamp and groped my way forward, dreading the bloodsuckers glued to my legs. I scrambled up a steep incline covered with tall, sharp grasses. Reaching the encampment with the rooster, I asked one of the leaders if I could borrow it. He couldn't believe I had even attempted the trip just to get a rooster! He caught it, and I tucked it firmly under my arm and returned to camp that night. Many in the unit laughed at how I dedicated myself to such a small cause. But after this and a few other adventures, people praised me for my good spirit and elected me for emulation as a *combatant de production*.

It was hard to keep up a good spirit during the year of famine, 1952–1953. A ration of rice, measured in a tin of condensed milk, had to last two to four days. We mixed the rice with manioc or sweet potato. Some people added the rind of manioc even though it did not provide any nutritional value. People scoured the forest, sifting for edible leaves and tubers, wild bananas and roots.

Artistic troupes continued to travel and work with villagers in the fields or simply lift the spirits of the peasants. Once, weak from hunger, our troupe stopped to burrow into one spot and tend a fire to cook tubers we had dug in the forest. We boiled the tubers for three days, but they were hard and inedible. They seemed to defy nature.

No matter what happened to us, I yearned to be a model combatant.

Even the elderly and others who had retired gave up their quiet lives to participate in the cause. Grandmothers, their gray hair pinned up in a chignon, their sun-dried skin wrapped in loose black pajamas, grouped into what were called *chignon brigades* to demonstrate for the release of husbands and sons held in jail. Grandmothers carried supplies in secret: a bent-over, betel-chewing grandmother drew scant attention. Women hid antibiotics in yellow and green squash or in jars of nuoc mam. Military and medicinal supplies were concealed in all kinds of containers: Miner Brand cans of sweetened condensed milk, handbags woven like baskets, rambutans and other fruits. Explosives were wedged into tins of Craven "A" Virginia cigarettes, and documents stashed in cavities hollowed in tree trunks.

Once, Thanh nearly gave herself away while carrying medicines and messages from our house on Rue Verdun to contacts who would take them to the jungle. She hailed a pedicab from home and lugged a large ceramic jar, supposedly of nuoc mam, onto the seat next to her. When the bicycle driver swerved sharply to avoid hitting a Peugeot, the jar rolled out of her reach and shattered on the sidewalk. Luckily, its secret contents spilled out of sight of the police officers who arrived on the scene.

Another source of inspiration to do as much as we could were the martyrs. I knew the names of early women revolutionaries, such as Nguyen Thi Dinh, who left her one-year-old son with his grandmother while her husband was imprisoned on Poulo Condore, the prison island known for men being tortured in front of women. Nguyen Thi Minh Khai attended the 1935 Socialiste Internationale and devoted herself to fighting the French. I knew prisoners at the dreaded Catinat Sûreté (security police) headquarters on Rue Catinat who were classified as Communist or not yet Communist but in favor of the party.

Closer to home, Lycée Marie Curie students were detained for marching in the Tran Van On funeral. Some were released when their parents intervened, but one—twenty-three-year-old Duy Lien—was imprisoned at Catinat for months. Duy Lien withstood torture and revealed nothing. She was sent to Chi Hoa, a gray, circular building on Saigon's outskirts, where she recuperated and organized classes in geography, literature, and other subjects that prisoners could teach each other. Duy Lien circulated a handwritten newspaper called *Brisons les chaînes* (Break the Chains); if male prisoners could circulate a newspaper, so could the women.

We also knew about the first woman taken to Poulo Condore, sixteen-year-old Vo Thi Sau (1933–1952), who had followed her sister's advice: "You can't stay in school; we must act." Both sisters joined the maquis; Sau was recruited for an attack and killed a provincial chief. She was caught and taken to Chi Hoa prison, where her mother brought her clothes. Years later, I learned Sau had secretly been moved to Poulo Condore, where a January 1952 entry in the prison file recorded her death.

I composed music to accompany poems by a favorite poet, Tran Huu Thung (1923–1999). One of his poems, "Tham Lua" (Going to visit the rice), is set at harvest time and condemns the French patrols that hunt down anyone who plants or harvests rice. I arranged music to accompany the story of peasants slipping into the fields in the black of night to bury a rice paddy where the French wouldn't find it. But the French did uncover the cache of paddy and burned it.

All this time, I wondered where I stood in a long line of admirers of Tan. From the time we met in 1950 until 1953, I nurtured only the faint hope he had even noticed me. Then I received a letter from him:

> On July 18, 1953, the company has a celebration on the eve of departure to a new battle. One has to be a soldier, a combatant of the national army, to understand what it means to leave for the front. Later in the night, at the end of an entertainment program, drunk with inspiration, together with comrades, with Trang, we launch into songs, "Artists, leave for the front!" Into the evening, Trang plays her accordion and verses are sung without interlude. Each one feels the blood boiling in his veins. Then we draw it all to an end, very late in the night. Before going to sleep, the idea suddenly strikes me, "I love Trang. I will make my life with her." A furtive thought that never leaves me again. Hand across my brow, I can no longer fall asleep, and stare with wide open eyes at the silent forest. . . .
>
> The hardest part is to make my love known to Trang. Tomorrow we will already be separated. After the battle, will I be able to return alive to tell her, "Trang, I love you"?

I was very moved. But it also made me think about Thanh's marriage to a soldier leader: the family only learned after the fact that they had gotten married in the jungle. Her marriage shocked the family and showed me the conflicts that could arise from mixing marriage and the cause. Thanh joked privately about how her much older husband, already in his thirties, always came in last in sporting events organized at the camp. She told me he had written fantastical love letters, by which she meant absurd and crazy. She wrote back, trying to assure him she could be nothing but a burden to him. While he was *couronné* (crowned) with rich experience, she was irreparably *ignorante*, a novice in all things. Thanh described herself as a young recruit who "knows and understands little." At first, he desisted. But he and other older colleagues grew impatient and agitated; girls from Saigon, it was said, could calm them. Years later, other women from the maquis said they were told only the girls could satisfy the leaders. At the same time, it was considered an honor for a leader to select and sweet-talk a young recruit. Other girls acted jealous about the attention given to Thanh. All this aroused my suspicions about becoming deeply involved with anyone in the maquis.

Thanh married without our parents' knowledge, slipped back to Saigon to give birth, and returned to the maquis. Once, Mother brought Thanh's little son to the jungle for a brief visit. He lived in the family compound in Saigon under the care of his grandparents and Aunt Minh; he was hardly the only niece or nephew Aunt Minh parented! For the Saigon census, my parents omitted both my name and Thanh's. As for Thanh's son, they listed his mother as Minh and, for safety, his father as "unknown." This tarnished our family's upstanding reputation, for which my mother suffered deeply.

During this time, Tan was in charge of entertainment for the troops and sought out every chance to talk with me. He confessed he was amazed a young woman could master an instrument as complex as the accordion. Tan had to leave for battle, on the eve of which he wrote in his diary:

> Nothing is less sure than my return to tell Trang about my love for her. But how will I have the courage to tell her now?
>
> The best way is to write a letter. In the still of the night, I think of all the words I will write to her. . . . My precious love letter! At the first glimmer of dawn, as soon as there is enough light to see, I jump up with a start and begin writing, all in one flowing motion. My comrades are not yet awake. The words dance, rising and falling in half darkness. . . . The love letter of the soldier before his departure to the front will perhaps lead to a yes, if only because of that? My hand trembles with emotion as if at the hour of first gunfire in battle.
>
> For my whole life, I will remember that day, July 21, 1953.

He did return. At Tet in 1954, we organized a simple wedding followed by a three-day honeymoon. We knew we'd be lucky to find snatches of time together. We never shared a home but resorted to random rendezvous at a clearing across from the Tha La stream that we thought of as our little patch of land. When I became pregnant, we planted manioc to have something to feed the baby. When he had a day or two of leave, Tan hiked across the countryside to cultivate our piece of land. He signaled me when he would be going and waited for me each time.

But I had to perform all over the region and often received the note or a verbal message through a friend only after he had come and gone.

A day or two at a time, we were able to spend about a month together at our clearing by the Tha La stream. The leadership "awarded" us the plot by Tha La as a special dispensation in exchange for contributing to the revolution. At dawn, we woke up to the cries of forest monkeys. I liked listening to nature's music all around us. Getting up early, we heard deer pawing at plant roots and chewing leaves. In the late afternoon, the shriek of a rooster often pierced the forest. We joked about having a manioc plantation. We worked it all day and felt refreshed by the soft damp leaves that brushed against our faces and necks, bringing relief against a merciless sun. Over time, I noticed the green manioc leaves we had planted during our honeymoon reached over our heads.

The loveliest time of day was early evening when a luminous golden moon hoisted itself into the dark blue sky, where it kept us company. If we had a baby girl, Tan wanted to name her Moon, but I preferred the name Autumn, since we had courted then, and I had read Tan's love letter in autumn.

Our lives and those of hundreds of thousands of compatriots changed in July 1954 with the signing of the Geneva Accords. Pregnant and weak from malaria, I stayed south to give birth. Tan, a talented and valuable member of the army, would go north. He wrote:

> The memory of the white coned hat you waved tirelessly to bid me a last good-bye at Cao Lanh remains indelible in my memory. My wife, my love, there you go back to the occupied zone carrying in you a drop of my blood.
>
> God, each day, each hour, no matter what I do, I don't stop thinking about you and this little being who is like both of us. Don't you feel a sweet pride, as I do?
>
> Whether it's a boy or girl, this child will carry the name we decided on together. And you, just like me, understand it will be our "little Tha La":

My little moon, Papa asks you:
Who brought you into the world? "Papa and Mama."
What are Papa and Mama's names? "Tan and Trang."
Whose eyes do you have? "Papa's."
And your nose, it comes from who, my sweet one? "Papa."
And the mouth? "It's Mama's."
Where is your place of birth? "Tha La. The North. Saigon. The South.
    All of Vietnam."
What will you do when you grow up? "I will learn music, piano, like
    Mama. And I will become a soldier like Papa."

Do you love Papa and Mama? "Very much."
Papa and Mama love you very much, too.
My love, I think so much of you and our child who will be born.

[Ed. note: Tan's friends, finding the diary after his death, gave it to Trang in 1975.]

The 1954 Geneva Accords specified three hundred days for people to move north or south and that elections would be held within two years. [Ed. note: Negotiations to end the war in Indochina began at the Geneva Conference on May 8, the day after the resounding defeat of French forces at Dien Bien Phu. The United States and the State of Vietnam proposed disarming the Viet Minh and allowing the State of Vietnam control over the Democratic Republic of Vietnam, but this idea was ignored by other delegations. China and the Soviet Union pressured the DRV to a settlement in which they gave up territory and population for a promise of later reunification. The accords split Vietnam at the Seventeenth Parallel, with the North governed by the DRV and the South by the French Union until internationally supervised elections were to be held in 1956.] So we thought the longest period of separation would be two years. Knowing we had to part, Tan planned to meet my mother before going north. Combatants going north grouped at the tip of land at Cao Lanh. Thanh escorted me, pregnant and suffering from malaria, to our home in Saigon. On November 1, I delivered a healthy girl named Autumn.

I began my work to monitor resistance activities in the city by listening to clandestine radio broadcasts and reading leaflets. A few days after Autumn's birth, I received a letter from Tan. The night of our daughter's birth, he had left the southern zone. He expected to be back in two years, at the latest.

I continued to work for the resistance. To do that, I had to rely on my sister Minh; she made it possible.

3

MINH

"Generation at a Crossroads"

Minh venerates her father as a model of hard work and endurance and defends her overprotective mother, who, after all, never left the house or school until she was twenty. Minh felt the impulse her younger siblings did to join the cause but also the tug of the dutiful daughter. "Cécile" resented saluting the French tricolor flag every morning in the courtyard of the lycée and having to resort to a *Encyclopédie Larousse* to picture the flag of Vietnam.

Cécile learned to apply her talents in French, teaching, law, and the piano, to deftly straddle both the calling of family and country. She started out reading about the French youth under German occupation, singing songs from the maquis, and learning folk dances. She gave piano lessons and donated earnings into a fund for the cause. Eventually, Minh performed a risky role as liaison for her sisters and others in the resistance when they needed to pass on information or acquire medicines and other basics that could not be bought in the countryside.

Not only did she take care of her parents and her family at the Binh compound on Cach Manh Thang Tam (August Revolution) Boulevard, Minh was a surrogate mother to nieces and nephews. She admired and envied her sisters for committing wholeheartedly to the cause. Bringing her mother to see Thanh in the jungle, Minh romanticized the "intoxicating" atmosphere of the jungle, while detailing the sight of Thanh trying to light firewood to cook after a hard rain. "Maman looked stunned," she recalled, "as Thanh cooked by the damp wood that produced dense smoke and a foul odor." These visits must also have reminded Minh of the compensations for staying in Saigon.

Minh claimed fewer gifts than Thanh, whose decisions in the family carried more weight. Minh places herself in the shadow of clever and strong-willed sisters even as she excelled at the lycée, studying relentlessly to defeat French classmates on the academic playing field.

Minh was heroic in nurturing family members, from babies to elders, throughout the war—a pillar in the chaos. What would her sisters have done if Minh had not taken care of their parents and their children?

Beyond the crucial role as family anchor, Minh stayed in town and led two lives.

Minh

Thanh, Trang, and I—each a year apart in age—ran around together as one, whether at school, playing games, or doing household chores. When Maman made dresses for us, she cut out one, two, three pieces from the same material. When our parents bid us good night, they rattled off our names all at once: "Good night, Minh, Thanh, Trang!" They were strict, and we greeted them formally, bending slightly forward. We were reprimanded if a door slammed.

My father came from a peasant background. He is a self-made man. Compared to his past, we are privileged. He is the only one who broke out of his traditional peasant family. Every time he came home from school, he worked in the countryside with his brothers. They caught country rats, fattened on the rice paddy, to eat or sell for a little money to help father study. He was a model of hard work, endurance, and tenacity.

Mother came from the leisure, *semi-aristo* class. Up until she turned twenty, she never the left the house or school; no wonder she always worried about us. Even if I came home late from studying, she worried. Her parents were functionaries who transferred to Hanoi, where she met Papa. As part of our education, he made us take lessons in piano, violin, mandolin, and guitar; each learned an instrument, so we could form an orchestra as a family. He had us study piano with Mme Thi, who was naturalized French and came back from Paris with her husband; her sister, Mme Lien, was the mother of Dang Thi Son—the winner of a major prize at the Chopin competition. In my last year of high school, 1950, I studied with Mme Lien and won first prize in a piano competition organized in her home. Aside from classical music, we played a lighter repertoire: French singers in vogue, like Tino Rossi, whom Papa adored.

My patriotic spirit awakened while I studied at a French lycée; from the time we were little, every morning we had to salute the French flag, the *tricolore*. We did not even know what the Vietnamese flag looked like. I had to look in a *Encyclopédie Larousse* to find a flag of Vietnam displaying a dragon on a yellow field, which

I figured stemmed from past dynasties. Each time we saluted the tricolore, I began, instead, to see the yellow flag in my mind.

By 1943, many of us participated in youth sports competitions, school songs, and the daily salute to the tricolore, all of which awakened in us a love of country. [Ed. note: Mobilizing youth and stirring independent thinking later became known as part of the Ducourau movement, named for a Frenchman who became a sailor at age sixteen and worked for the Free French fighting the Nazis.] After the August Revolution in 1945, it was all about the movement. We launched ourselves into the common cause of independence. Some left for the maquis; others continued the struggle in town. We learned the folk dances of the popular movement. I joined a troupe of six students, three pairs of dancers, and performed in front of French professors and intellectuals and at student reunions. We performed the dance of the paddy harvest. After dancing, we acted out the life of peasants, disguising ourselves as babas wearing black pajamas. French authorities, however, considered the dances rebellious and dangerous.

We sang songs from the maquis, several of which were officially prohibited because they targeted students. We read pamphlets about the exploits of French youth under the German occupation. We read books from Editions d'Hier et Aujourd'hui (Yesterday and Today Publishers) and La Jeune Garde (Young Guard) that were filled with progressive ideas about Soviet youth. I was enthralled to learn about these clandestine activities, the camouflaged side to life in the city, the ardor of young militant patriots, the sabotage undertaken for the cause, and the horrible arrests under the Hitlerian regime.

In 1945, we read books about the youth in the French resistance. We nourished ourselves on this literature, on the feeling of people in France resisting the Nazis. Part of our awakening was due to the same patriotic awakening as in the French. As early as 1943, students of my father's generation had begun to organize musical performances at the Opera House. We went as little kids and chased each other up and down the aisles. Tran Van Khe led the singing of our student march in French! It was striking that here was a march like any other, but he got everyone—even the French—to stand and salute! There was no flag. Just seeing the French stand up and sing along was extraordinary. That march later became the national anthem.

Given the name Cécile at Marie Curie, I wore the school uniform. I dressed simply because I did not like coquetry: I wanted to rise above the mundane to pursue a noble cause. It was not an issue of conceit but internal pride that pushed us to ignore what was superficial and therefore useless. I was strict with myself in following a line of moral conduct. In a time of combat—of hostilities and dangers threatening the life of our people—I felt we could not allow ourselves to be carefree and enjoy life. People were dying; blood flowed everywhere. This pushed me to study hard and encourage classmates to listen and follow my example. I also gave piano lessons to girls and contributed all that I earned into a common fund for the cause.

I studied the sciences, such as geography, and social sciences, such as law. In 1950, graduating with licenses in both, I began teaching at a school for girls, Collège Gia Long. I taught geography during the day and took evening classes at the faculty of law. I wore an ao dai but no makeup. I braided my hair and coiled the braids around my head instead of having a permanent at a hair salon like everybody else. Girls wore their hair one of two ways: short and free to the wind or curled. I always rejected coquetry—until there was an incident that made me realize I would be better off conforming to everybody else.

It happened on January 9, 1951, a year after the burial of Tran Van On. Students observed the anniversary by wearing the color of mourning, white, and planting incense sticks at the foot of trees in the school courtyard. It marked a silent political demonstration by the youth movement I had participated in the year before. When I saw police agents converge from all sides to crush the demonstration and arrest the youth, strong feelings churned inside. I felt overwhelmed; the emotion made me literally pale with anger. A policeman remarked: "Who is this professor who feels so much for these students?" I realized then I needed to put makeup on, so my feelings would not be so obvious. I felt what the students felt, but I had to cover it up.

As the eldest, I felt responsible for our parents and didn't dare leave home to join the maquis with Thanh and Trang. I had to take care of my parents and my children. In our home, everyone was treated equally; that said, I always thought Thanh was more decisive, and her decisions carried more weight. By comparison, I have fewer gifts. Trang is the quiet one. I was the one to represent our family in matters related to the extended family, and, as the eldest, my sisters could lean on me. They could rely on me.

From the time my sisters joined the maquis, I followed the war from a distance, dreaming about its atmosphere of freedom—freedom to be part of the resistance. I stayed in town where I led two lives. I continued my official activities, where, in the eyes of students and teachers, I was a law student and teacher of geography. In secret, I engaged in the movement and worked under orders of the Committee of the Resistance of Saigon-Cholon. In small groups, we met at prearranged places and took political training classes that set a program of action and orders to be carried out.

I had only three opportunities to breathe the intoxicating atmosphere of the bush. I accompanied Maman to see her daughters when they had short breaks. The first time, we traveled to a muddy, swampy area in the Eighth Zone in the heart of the Mekong Delta. A liaison agent fixed a rendezvous at the house of a friend living in the center of the small town of Sa Dec. We spent a night and changed into black shirts and pants before taking a boat into the liberated zone to see Thanh. The black outfits had never been used: they smelled new, and the material felt stiff, making it awkward to walk. But everything unfolded as planned, and we reached a group of huts built on stilts in the shade of coconut trees. The peacefulness of the scene, the morning freshness, and the smell of the soil invigorated me. Moments later, Thanh and her husband welcomed us, and we all stood in the middle of a group of cadres. It was the first time Maman saw her daughter in a political setting so different from her own.

The life of peasants shocked Maman. Thanh and her husband lived in one of the straw huts divided by a partition. A hard rain had fallen and soaked the firewood in the kitchen. To start a cooking fire, Thanh blew with all her might; when a little flame came to life, she struggled to protect it from the wind. Maman looked stunned as Thanh cooked by the damp wood that produced dense smoke and a foul odor. She shook her head and sighed seeing her daughter work so hard. She had *le cœur gros* (a heavy heart) thinking about home, where we didn't face such coarse conditions, and somebody was always there to help. We stayed in peasant homes that had no doors; they were more or less open-air. Maman felt disoriented.

For me, I was thrilled to breathe the freedom we didn't have in town and to see people working together like one big family motivated by the spirit of fraternal solidarity. All that without any worry about the police in Saigon.

On the second visit, Maman, Thanh's one-year-old son, and I headed northwest to Tay Ninh to see Trang in the Seventh Zone in the jungle closest to Saigon. Trang had just married and wanted us to meet her husband, a writer in the army. Wearing black clothes, we got off a bus to follow a woman liaison agent who walked a little ahead of us. We were disguised as villagers returning from the market with baskets full of purchases and provisions. This time, we were questioned en route by guards at the blockhouse near a bridge. Thanks to phrases agreed on in advance and learned by heart, we were able to pass. But it gave me the jitters. I remained ill at ease.

The path to the meeting place was rough and rutted, and we weren't used to walking for so long. Toward dusk, we were trudging along an embankment on a narrow, muddy path, and with each step our feet kept sinking into the muck. As night fell, we found ourselves in near darkness; our black clothes didn't make visibility any easier. I carried Thanh's child on my hip and kept my eyes peeled for any obstacles in Maman's path, all while barely able to spot the tracks left by the agile liaison just ahead. I was exhausted. I opened my eyes wide to stay awake and on track. Suddenly I heard sounds far up ahead, familiar voices full of joy—the voices of my sisters trembling with impatience and excitement to greet us. Finally,

I reached the edge of a rice field and this time put a foot on firm soil. I was at the end of my strength but happy to see my sisters and new brother-in-law.

Our third visit to the maquis took us not to the bush or jungle but along the road to Chau Doc, where my father first met Thanh's husband. We chose a place that did not compromise Papa, who still worked as a functionary for the French. We met at a house close to the national route where the bus could stop and let us off. Thanh's son would be meeting his father for the first time. Everything went according to plan. I counted the kilometer milestones along the road and signaled the driver to stop at the door of a communal inn, where we got off the bus. We overnighted in the house of a Catholic family. It was there that Papa met his revolutionary son-in-law and that my brother-in-law had the joy of embracing his first child. We talked about many things throughout our one night together—politics, the movement's social goals, and family affairs. The next morning, Papa took the bus back on his own, and we stayed another day, so my brother-in-law could learn to bottle-feed his son and enjoy the delight of being with his first child.

When the Geneva Accords were signed in 1954, Thanh went north and Trang stayed south. I continued to live a double life in Saigon. It was the start of a difficult time for us all.

4

LE AN

"The University of Life"

Born into wealth, Le An scorned her mother for coming from a family that adored everything French and for being a lady of leisure who stayed home. Le An worshipped her father, an engineer who worked for the French in public works before siding with the resistance in 1945. In 1950, Le An participated in the protest over the death of a student killed by authorities: a black-and-white photo shows her clutching one end of the Lycée Marie Curie banner as students flood the streets. Following her father and friends into the resistance, Le An adapted to life in the jungle.

Le An embodies resilience. In one small black-and-white photo, she smiles wearing a white silk outfit in front of her family's villa; another shows her barefoot in black pajamas leaning against a palm tree in the jungle. She grew up detesting the taste of fish but learned to catch and eat fish out of a dried coconut shell. Used to eating French food seasoned with Maggi sauce, she adjusted to food without seasoning and to appreciating a few grains of salt as a treat. She learned to protect herself from huge mosquitoes and to detach leeches from her body. Used to sleeping on a soft mattress, she became accustomed to sleeping on straw. Anything hung outside to dry in the jungle had to be black, so she learned to make black dye from battery powder to darken pieces of cloth used as sanitary napkins.

On the spectrum of political zeal among the sisters, Le An may be a close second to Thanh. Despite all the dangers, she does not express regrets—not about bypassing study in France, not about leaving her mother, and not about trading a life of comfort for that of a peasant who "could do all the hard work of daily life."

Le An

I was born in Saigon in October 1931. My home village was in Go Cong, about five kilometers from the sea and about sixty kilometers from Saigon. I went to school in Saigon and visited Go Cong once in a while, like when we visited my paternal family for Tet. I attended a private French grade school before starting my first year of secondary school at Lycée Marie Curie. The atmosphere and influence of Marie Curie were completely Western. My maternal side adored everything French. The whole maternal side of my family lives in France; it was on my paternal side that family members rallied to the resistance.

My father joined the resistance in 1945. Mother stayed home. I was drawn to the resistance because of what relatives on my paternal side did and because of the influence my father had on me personally. My grandfather joined a patriotic association, and my grandmother participated in the patriotic women's association. Two uncles went to the resistance with my father, and all three moved to the North. My mother and one sister stayed in Saigon while another joined the guerrillas and became a martyr in the early seventies when she died in a bombing in our home village of Kien Phuoc hamlet.

In 1945, at age fourteen, I began to participate in the movement. At first, I joined out of a sense of fun. Intellectuals in the city had united to take up the resistance in what was a predecessor of the Fatherland Front. My family and the youth movement influenced me, but it was my classmates Thanh and Trang who brought me along into political activities. I first met them at a celebration of the committee of the student movement. Earlier, we had been in the same class but were not close. I knew Thanh's father was an engineer and her uncle the minister of commerce in the puppet government.

I also knew Thanh and I shared a passion for movies. We read *Ciné-vogue* and *Cinémonde* and worshipped stars like Ingrid Bergman. Trang borrowed magazines, sometimes returning them with clandestine journals from the movement rolled up inside. Later in 1949, Thanh and Trang planned a ceremony to recognize me as a member of the association of students. We met at my house and conducted a simple, touching ceremony. Thanh, already known as a student leader, read out the association rules, regulations, and duties, and I took the pledge.

In groups of ten to fifteen students, we organized artistic meetings, poetry readings, and musical concerts. We always posted one person as a guard outside. One way to organize in secret was to rehearse school plays, by Molière and others, and in the middle of rehearsal, stop to discuss politics. We had more dynamism than students in the North.

Beginning in 1947, I spent three years at Lycée Marie Curie. I studied *Kim Van Kieu* with Mme Lanh, who was a good influence: she opened our eyes to our own language and culture! At the same time, Tran Van Khe and Luu Huu Phuoc were organizing plays to educate the people, in an artistic way, to be aware of what was happening in the country. I heard about Tran Van Khe's aunt, Mme Tran Ngoc Vien, and her dedication to fighting the French.

Beginning with the time my father went to the maquis in 1948, he sent people to our house in Saigon with letters asking for supplies. Some people stayed at our villa, which police did not suspect since our neighborhood catered mostly to foreigners. After 1950, though, the flow of visitors increased, and police began to suspect.

I first set foot in the liberated area in 1948 when Mother and I visited Father. He had worked as an engineer with the public works. Father, who knew Thanh and Minh's father, had trained as an architect and built houses. To visit him, we walked barefoot all night across the countryside. In some places, the water in the rice fields came up to my waist. Mother remained in the city and sent news once in a while. Father worked with the foreign service.

The whole time I came to spend in the maquis, I walked barefoot because I stayed in the Western Zone, where we didn't worry about giant ants. In the Eastern Zone, where Thanh worked, everyone had to wear sandals.

We walked all night, getting our clothes soaked and not stopping to eat, so we would arrive before daybreak. At four in the morning, we took a sampan on a

FIGURE 5.   Le An in front of her family's villa in an elite part of Saigon at Tet, circa 1948. From a well-to-do family, Le An left her mother to follow her father into the resistance. Courtesy of Le An.

narrow river to the first stopover, where we could have something to eat and take a bath. We navigated the winding swamps because we had to avoid major routes. We spent three weeks with Father. Mother had agreed to visit him since she knew how much I absolutely wanted to go. When I saw Father, he said, "If you want to join, go to Saigon and get your things." After three weeks, I returned, and this time I brought Sen to train with me.

I carried black pajamas, a toothbrush, toothpaste, a mosquito net, and a sanitary napkin made out of a piece of black mosquito netting. I made a "pocket" in which to put folded pieces of netting. It was all very primitive. Anything hung outside to dry had to be black. We made black dye from battery powder boiled in water. Boiling the pieces of napkin first made them gray, then darker each time. Girls had two or three pieces each; we never threw them out. We also used old clothes that were going to be thrown away as extra napkins. We had to be innovative. For the toilet, we had yellowish toilet paper that we of course did throw away.

In 1949, I was always dashing around in the streets because I belonged to one of the most active youth movements in Saigon. This movement of southern resistance sprang up when the French returned to power. The resistance hiding in the jungle directed the Saigon Cholon branch of the southern region student association. Networks operated all over, but people didn't know about them; it was all done undercover.

Several historical events punctuated the year 1950. On January 9, police shot a student during a protest, and we took the body to display it at his school, Lycée Pétrus Ky. Delegations of students came to see the coffin and light incense. A group from Marie Curie came to pay homage. Police arrived and started hitting students; luckily, I have a strong skull. They herded us into trucks and took us to Catinat to take our fingerprints and photos for the police archives. Seven or eight of us from Marie Curie were arrested, including Trang and Sen. Police lined us up in rows of girls and boys, including Tran Van On's classmates from Pétrus Ky and delivered a lesson in morals: "You are from well-to-do families yet were clearly raised poorly!" The agent in charge showed us instruments of torture—whips, chains, and ropes. We waited in the courtyard all afternoon, the sun beating down, until our families came to pick us up. We had been arrested before ten that morning. It was dusk.

On January 12, I was one of two students holding up the Lycée Marie Curie *banderole* (banner) during the burial procession for Tran Van On. At the funeral, organizers took up a collection, and everyone gave money. A committee headed by the former minister and lawyer Nguyen Huu Tho, who lived in Saigon and led the movement, counted the money and allocated it for different needs; whenever he spoke at a demonstration, we surrounded him en masse for security. A few hours after the funeral ceremony started, police agents came, and students crowded around to protect him. When the police turned violent, everyone fled like a flock of doves. The battlefield was strewn with hats, shoes, scraps of clothing, and the stones we had hurled at the policemen, aiming for their heads.

Lycée Marie Curie expelled us after the police high commission informed them about our activities. The director, Madame Brissaud, wanted us to be expelled. Our friend Suong had also been arrested, and her mother, Mme Tuong, protested to the police and the school. From a well-educated family and the wife of a prominent physician, she had influence. All our families were well placed, and everyone supported the cause. In my Marie Curie class, Trang and Sen were the most active.

On March 19, Americans arrived to talk with the French about handing over power: they came to discuss our fate, the fate of Vietnam! The resistance knew about it and planned marches. A French jeep was burned, and several of us were arrested near the central market. Thanh gave me leaflets to hand out around town: "À bas les Américains" (Down with the Americans) and "À bas les Français" (Down with the French). We helped make them and found that, by using thick Chinese ink, we could draw about ten copies from each inking. Sen composed her own slogan, "Vive le Vietnam, à bas la Mesquinerie" (Up with Vietnam, down with Meanness).

In May 1950, I went into the maquis for the second time. I hadn't planned to, but the French found out about the student movement, and security agents were chasing us down. Thanh and others like us, more visible than most, were advised to leave Saigon for a while. Mother wanted to send me to France to give her daughter *un bel avenir* (a beautiful future); an uncle offered to pay for me to go. To her, the maquis was far off, and the outcome unknown. But I enjoyed being in the resistance movement so much I didn't go to France. Mother cried when I left and often asked me to come back. She sent money and clothes.

Thanh went to Zone 7 around Tay Ninh. My father worked as a technical expert in Zone 9, way in the South. I joined him after he agreed it would be dangerous for me to stay in Saigon. Sen came with me. Four of us left together: a cousin, a friend, Sen, and me. None of us knew when we would be back. I took the bus to Can Tho and spent a night at Tuyen's house, where I saw her brother Luu Huu Phuoc. The next day, a woman liaison agent took us by sampan into the delta.

The U Minh forest served as the headquarters of the occupied zone. In the South, the head of the health service was Nguyen Van Huong, and he wanted Sen and me to be medically trained. But father wanted me to work with women, so I joined the Women's Union, based about a day's journey south by boat. [Ed. note: The Women's Union was founded the same year as the Indochinese Communist Party, 1930, to mobilize women to the cause of independence. The Communists promised women they would be unshackled from Confucian society if they joined forces against the French. The union organized women to carry out duties across many areas, such as health, propaganda, and education.] Sen and I were sent to the southern regional Women's Union, where Nguyen Thi Thap served as president. Along with youth and peasant unions, the Women's Union formed the Hoi Lien Hiep Quoc Dan Viet Nam (All National Front), or Lien Viet for short. As we moved around the region, we were separated from men—except when we asked them to carry heavy things, go fishing, or help gather wood. There were no markets, so we had to find our own food. Girls threw the fishing nets while boys rowed. We cultivated rice, though not as well as the peasants. Out of thirty women, about half of us were between seventeen and twenty years old. Later, the provincial association in Can Tho asked Sen to go work with them; it was hard for us to separate.

I felt unafraid. We were so immersed in the cause we didn't even think about our security. We didn't think about how, for one, our pictures had been taken by the secret police during demonstrations. . . .

One of the most unforgettable experiences in the bush was to attend performances and sing. Rivers and streams crisscross the southern provinces, so we took sampans to reach the places where plays were staged. If the current flowed in the right direction, a journey took two hours; if the current ran against us, it took three hours. We ate supper at five, climbed on the sampan, and reached the meeting place around eight or nine. We watched performances until three or four in the morning and took the boat back just in time to start the day's work.

The biggest gatherings were organized on special days like Labor Day, May 1; National Day, September 2; Women's Day, March 8; and Army Day. Cadres from different agencies joined amateurs to stage performances. Shows occasionally started late because groups came from many different regions, and we had to wait for everyone to arrive. Some came as late as eleven or midnight. While waiting, guerrillas kept watch for French fighter planes; if they had any inkling a plane was approaching, they extinguished the kerosene lamps and torches.

I found daily life in the jungle engaging and exciting. The group dynamic was so different; I felt a lot more solidarity than I had in the city. We lived in huts made with straw walls and traveled by sampan. In the Western Zone, where few trees survived in the marshlands, we did not sleep in hammocks: we slept on the dirt floor with mats underneath. We had mosquito nets to attach to the straw walls. A cord ran down the middle of a hut with a partition made of leaves from water palm trees. We made lamps by putting a wick soaked in oil on a plate or in an empty tin of Rickles brand mint, used for colic stomach. We built bathrooms out of straw along the banks of the rivers.

Many utensils were fashioned out of metal or baked clay. If we did not even have clay for plates or bowls, we found dried coconut shells and buffed them with lime until they shined. I put two holes in my bowl and hung it in the "cafeteria"; each person's bowl differed a little, so we didn't have to put our names on them. I scrubbed mine well, keeping it clean and shiny. Especially after eating fish, I rubbed it hard with soap that we received at camp in blocks. We used chopsticks carved from bamboo. We ate in groups of five or six, sometimes squatting around the foot of a coconut tree to leave the table to older people.

In the Western Zone, we ate a lot, so our faces were round, while in the Eastern Zone people didn't have enough food, and their faces became thin and their bodies weak. People were sent from the Eastern Zone to the Eighth Zone to eat fish and other foods to regain strength. Nature favored us; for example, the mosquitoes did not carry malaria. The things Thanh had to get used to I never worried about. We stocked rice in big clay jars that reached above my waist. Still, we did not drink water from the river in which we often saw dead dogs floating. On festival days, we ate sweet soup made with chunks of sugar and sweet potatoes or manioc. We made our own nuoc mam. In July 1950, I sent a picture to mother; on the back I wrote, "See how round-cheeked I am!"

When we traveled from one camp to another by sampan, the youngest rowed, cadres sat in the middle, and the heaviest sat at the back because otherwise the sampan couldn't float forward. We took sampans to fish in the afternoons, planting our rods in the stream bed. We came back at midnight to see if any fish had bitten. Three girls took a sampan at a time, with one chosen to row. We had a way of rowing while standing that made a very poetic motion. Others rowed in a squatting position or with their feet. I usually sat up front and checked each pole to see if we had caught anything. I put the fish, some weighing up to half a kilo, in a woven bamboo basket with a narrow neck. We dared not light lamps. Our eyes adjusted to the dark, and sometimes we could see clearly by the light of the moon.

Each day, a team of three was designated to take care of the larger group. The team picked vegetables in the forest, husked rice, and employed its chosen method to catch fish. We went to the forest to collect wood; with shallow streams everywhere, we pulled a small boat along and piled the wood in it. The water came to our knees, sometimes up to our waist.

Sunday was a day of rest. We learned revolutionary songs about women in the resistance, put on skits, and visited peasants, including the elderly mothers of combatants.

We did need a few things from town. Agents who made runs to town brought back toothpaste and letters from family, who in turn sent clothes, medicines, and money. Those going to the occupied zone had to be careful because anyone looking at their thick, hard nails knew they lived in the maquis. We used a small pen knife to cut our nails short. Some agents lived in town and came back now and

FIGURE 6.   Le An in black pajamas in the resistance. She inscribed the photo to a friend on July 7, 1950, stating she was *o que* (in the homeland) and asking if she looked *map* (fat, as if she had gained weight). Courtesy of Le An.

then. They learned to dress like townspeople and took on their manners; some even used limestone to whiten and soften their skin. Some families—like mine and Sen's—sent food, clothing, material, and money for the group.

We did not have to deal with ants in our area, but we had a problem with strangely large mosquitoes. Instead of relying on mosquito nets, we each carried a *nop*, a big basket made out of woven grass. To avoid mosquitoes, we crawled into the nop. But I had a problem; once in, I could barely breathe. I made a hole for my head and put a cloth mosquito net over my face. I still could not get comfortable. I tried this for seven nights but could do no more and started using a regular mosquito net.

To deal with leeches, I carried a piece of lime that repels them, so they drop off. Women who chew betel nut keep a piece of white lime close by for its strength and heat.

We ate some snakes while others were precious because their venom was made into a medicine against rheumatism and other conditions. One kind of snake had a triangular head and a deadly bite; a victim would foam at the mouth and have blood run from their nose before dying. Using the nop as a sleeping bag helped ward off snakes, as well as the mosquitoes.

Every week, we learned self-criticism. On Saturday nights, we criticized what we had done that was good, like helping people cook, and what we had done that was bad. At the end of the month, we picked the best model—the person who didn't quarrel, who sought perfection, who exhibited a spirit of collectivism. Our training and lessons in endurance while in the Women's Union made us good cadres. Although the only child from a rich family, I knew how to do all these things, including planting and harvesting rice.

Each of us carried a small notebook in which to make notes and copy poems.

Sen and I were appointed to the printing team, where we imitated stencil techniques we had learned in Saigon. Because we were educated, we worked in the propaganda team. We read and collected news about women in the world, writing stories down on little file cards. Later on, since we were pretty, the leaders promoted us to be secretaries at meetings.

I was sent to hamlets to teach illiterate women in open-air classes. When I joined the maquis, I wore my hair short and curly, but—to be accepted by women in the countryside—I let my hair grow long to make a chignon. We often used someone else's natural hair and attached it to our own to look natural. We called it borrowing hair. It helps women make a beautiful bun. I looked older in order to be respected by the women. I taught them how to read and a little bit of writing. I wrote on a board using chalk or used sticks or stones to scrawl characters on the dirt floor.

We held meetings with women to educate them about family life, hygiene, and so on. Sen did the same work. We did this in a way that people understood, not rambling on as was done later. Before, it was about the truth; that is how the revolution could win over the peasants. Everything was kept simple, more convincing, not dogmatic. Things were kept real.

The resistance, along with experiences I had while in the north, is for me the greatest university: the university of life. No other university could do what this experience did for me. All this experience taught me to love nature, to love the nation, to love people. No matter who the person is—regardless of religion, country, nationalism. To do good for the human person, that is the thing.

My maternal family side was astonished to see how, as an upper-class girl, I became like a peasant and could do all the hard work of daily life. Growing up at home, I was a finicky eater. I never ate fish sauce; I ate only Maggi, a French-style soy sauce. I especially didn't like salted fish and never ate preserved fish. But after the resistance, I could eat anything. When I lived at home, I could only sleep on a soft mattress; anything else felt painful. Now, I can sleep on the floor, on straw, in one of those flat basket-like woven bags. My whole personality changed. It is something nobody could imagine: this life could transform a person. If I hadn't gone to the resistance, I would probably be in France. I would have studied there and stayed. We struggled against colonialism, but we didn't struggle against French people or the French language. Similarly, we were against American imperialism, not American people.

In the resistance, there were different associations, including one for the Chinese resistance. On the first of October 1952, China's National Day, the government carried out a policy of taking land from rich owners to give to poor peasants. The Chinese resistance in Vietnam wanted to perform an opera about the "white-haired girl," and they met with a lot of associations to find a woman to play the part of the white-haired girl. They picked me. For the first time in my life, I acted on a stage. I played the main role; all the other roles were played by Chinese. The story is about landlords who take land away from peasants. Since I was able to cry easily, my performance was convincing; all I had to do was imagine that this happened to my father. I performed the scenes at night, from midnight to four o'clock in the morning. When the girl goes to the mountain, she is so consumed with everything weighing on her that her hair suddenly turns white. I had to wear white face powder, which unfortunately triggered my asthma. But I could keep going because they gave me two shots before I performed. Cosmetics were so rare we made lipstick by mixing water and incense and applying it to our lips. This play later showed in Paris. Basically, it is the story of a Chinese girl who, facing all the suffering of her nation and people, worries so much her hair turns white.

This was my first acting role. Afterward, the Chinese organization asked me to join them for a year. I traveled around, teaching, making propaganda through artistic activities, and collecting rural taxes on the Chinese patriots. In 1952–1953, I stayed in the Hong Dan District of Bac Lieu Province, a Chinese district with no rice fields—just crops that can be grown on dry land, like manioc and pineapple. A lot of people were Vietnamese of Chinese origin. Between China and Vietnam, there were still many good relationships, so these people were really more like Vietnamese with Chinese culture. People worked with the same resistance organization, but they also focused on Chinese mobilization.

Before 1952, I had never performed. We studied a lot. Because of all the upheaval, we could not organize festivals and big gatherings, not even while on breaks. It was only during 1951–1952, at the end of our studies and the beginning of a rare vacation, we recalled how to throw a party before being separated.

I attended a school for the training of women cadres for about a year, after which the women leaders planned to send me back to Saigon to work in the student movement.

In 1954, I had a choice: go back to Saigon to continue the struggle among students or go north with a troupe of artists set up by the army. I had never been to the North, and this would be a chance to get to know it. If I went north, Father wanted me to study architecture, so I could become an architect like him. This was the period after the Geneva Conference during which the army would go to the North, and everybody thought it would be for two years. My mother went to the bush to see my father and understand what was happening. Nobody saw any problem with me going north for two years. From then on, I have been involved with artistic troupes and related work.

I traveled north at the end of 1954, wondering where my friend Sen would go.

5

SEN

"A Question of Habit"

Sen grew up with a brave and patient mother and a father who was equal parts dictator and saint. Her father was a self-made man who became a naturalized Frenchman as a stepping-stone to a stable future for his children. He ensured his children received a French education. Sen never liked politics but empathized deeply with the suffering of her people under the French. She decided to go into the resistance, where she received training to teach women peasants to read, when not decamping because of French bombing raids. While finding aspects of life in the maquis appealing, especially outdoor life and working with peasants, she condemns several practices, including the party marrying young city girls to older, uneducated soldiers.

While Le An was her closest friend at the lycée, Sen never shared her friend's Far Left tilt on the political spectrum. The two friends worked closely together in the maquis making stencils used to print books on raising children and feeding newborns. They became so close that party cadres separated them since the collective called for the "I" to be wiped out. Sen never joined the Communist Party. She sympathized with peasants but harbored doubts about the motivations of cadres. She observed leaders chasing girls of a different class and concluded that most marriages (in the maquis) were for the worse because couples did not share similar culture, education, and customs.

Sen's independence allows her to examine questions others leave unasked. Why did Le An not return to spend time with her mother, alone and miserable in Saigon? Wasn't it a mistake for Thanh to marry a "complete peasant, to the point that he loved to eat snakes"?

Unbound by political doctrine, Sen found other aspects of participating in the resistance rewarding; it "helped form [her] youth and forge [her] character." Compelled to fight against French colonial power, Sen still believed there were lessons to learn from France and the West.

Sen

My grandfather was a teacher from a very poor family before the turn of the twentieth century. His wife made cakes for him to sell to his students, but he still did not have enough money to send my father to school. So Father sat under the window of the school and learned by listening to teachers give their lessons. When the teacher asked a student a question, he would even answer from outside! Father was intelligent. He had a hard life but became successful and won a scholarship to the University of Hanoi.

My father was a patriot and very hardworking. He did not care at all for colonialists; he became a French citizen only because he worried about the future for his children—my two brothers, four sisters, and me. He shared his view of the French with us, often admonishing us to work hard and gain a good position in society in order to do something for the country. After 1947, he no longer wanted to cooperate with the French and quit his job as a veterinary inspector and became a driver. He bought a Mercury and rented it at three hundred piastres an hour; the income made it possible to send my older brother and two older sisters to study in France.

My mother was shy but also very brave. She sacrificed everything for her children and my father. She once stepped in front of a French soldier's rifle to save her husband! This happened in 1947 when Father sold foodstuffs to people who had ration cards. Each month, the wife of the French commissioner of the Go Vap District, near downtown Saigon, came to buy the products. One day, she told my father, "I can't buy all that's rationed; I will buy just what I need." Father replied, "I am sorry, madame, but if clients don't take all the products on offer, to whom will I sell them afterward?" She became indignant at his unexpected and insolent reproach—which I found dignified and heroic. She told her husband everything that had happened. My mother predicted things would not turn out well.

The next day, the commissioner returned with a rifle in hand and escorted by two French gendarmes. Reaching our house, the commissioner told my mother, "I want to talk with your husband." Father appeared and asked him nicely, "What do you want, sir?" The Frenchman said, "Are you going to sell just the products that my wife chooses?" "No," father replied, "I am sorry. In principle, clients have to buy all the products allotted on the ration card." The angry husband put his index finger on the trigger of his rifle, ready to pull. At that moment, my mother ran in front of the gun and put her hand against the barrel. She prayed in Vietnamese and implored, "Please don't shoot—I beg you." The commissioner dropped his rifle and left without saying a word. Flanked by his two armed gendarmes, he felt humiliated by Mother's courage. He was ashamed. I was there; I saw it.

Mother taught me patience. She endured everything without saying a word. Theirs was not a marriage of love. My father was unbearable. He was a dictator, and Mother suffered a lot. Vietnamese women sacrifice everything for their children. They endure everything to keep the family together. In the past, people did not divorce. You were obligated to live with whoever you chose, or more accurately, whoever the relatives chose for you. You had to stay together until death. My mother advised me to work hard and have a career. She counseled against marriage and even pointed out how adopting a child could be a good way to deflect disapproval. Seeing my mother suffer hurt me. I loved her. We could not counsel Father; he was such a dictator. He did anything he wanted.

Growing up, my siblings and I were so afraid of Father that when he came home from work, we would all try to disappear. One day, he opened the front door and found there was no light on in the room; he said, "You are all like mosquitoes, aren't you! Yes, you like darkness. Well, since you like darkness, get under the sofa!" Without saying a word, we scrambled under it.

But even though he was severe with us, I love my father. I respect his courage, honesty, intelligence, and altruism. Father earned his veterinary diploma at the University of Hanoi. He became a vegetarian because he couldn't stand the suffering of animals in slaughterhouses. He told me about seeing a cow cry when taken to slaughter, and after that, he no longer had an appetite when offered a piece of steak or pork cutlet. That's why I was vegetarian since birth and only became an omnivore at eighteen when I had to eat everything offered in the maquis. I still prefer vegetables and fruits to meat and fish.

Father wanted my brothers, sisters, and me to study in French lycées because he was a naturalized French citizen, and since we were colonized, we could not hope to have a good place in society unless we earned a French diploma.

Under colonization, we had no rights. French people held all the important jobs. Uprisings in the provinces increased, as did the pace of meetings in Saigon. At school, we were considered French. Schoolbooks were printed in France and followed the curriculum of the education ministry in France.

Many students at the lycées and universities supported the goals of the maquis. Marie Curie and Chasseloup-Laubat students had close relations; we organized meetings and produced pamphlets together. After the death of Tran Van On in

FIGURE 7.   Sen (front center), Trang (to the left), and Le An (in glasses) gather with classmates by the lycée infirmary, December 22, 1948. Even Sen, who—unlike Trang and Le An—did not like "politics at all," was drawn into joining the maquis. Courtesy of Nguyen Thi Sen.

January 1950, students felt emboldened and became more aggressive. During the huge funeral procession for Tran Van On, students showed extraordinary discipline—no violence.

I also participated in the May 1 demonstration. In early July, over the course of a week, I thought about whether to go into the maquis. I knew my parents would not be happy. I would have to abandon my studies, while my future depended on them. I wanted to be a doctor, but joining the maquis would mean quitting school at the age of eighteen, having only completed the first part of my baccalaureate. My father was not at all happy about the idea and told me I was too young.

On July 10, 1950, I decided to join the maquis with Le An, who also went by Thu Ha, which means "river in autumn." I could no longer tolerate the savage repression of the French colonialists and Vietnamese traitors and how they treated us after Tran Van On, a student like us, was shot just for demonstrating. Before leaving, I wrote my parents a long letter explaining my decision.

Several of us left without the approval of our parents. Le An is an only child; when she followed her father to the maquis, she left her mother all alone. Her mother felt so alone; she drank heavily. For Le An, the homeland came before everything else. Family came after. Together, we went to the jungle about two hundred kilometers from Saigon. We carried black clothes, a toothbrush, and a little money: everything we needed fit in a small sack. Nothing more.

Living in the jungle was a question of habit. The first few months, I thought a lot about my parents and family. I especially missed my mother, whom I adore. I cried. But afterward, we got used to it. Saigon did not suit me very much, and I easily adapted to the communal life. In the countryside, the clean, fresh air and vast and beautiful greenery of the rice fields and forests did me a lot of good. I also appreciated the innocence and simplicity of the peasants.

In the morning, we woke up around six and shared household duties. Some went to collect river weed; others fished or ground rice by hand. After that, the bran of the rice had to be removed using wooden hammers. That's one reason I still have very broad shoulders. Another daily task was to cut wood. After two hours of manual work, we threw ourselves into the river with our clothes on since we didn't have swimsuits. We didn't want to appear indiscrete in the eyes of the peasants, who weren't in the habit of seeing girls with their legs, arms, and backs exposed. We swam the length of the river.

At nine o'clock, we turned to office work. Political meetings were often called, but since I was not Communist, I could not participate. These were particular meetings for the Communists. About a tenth of our group was Communist. [Ed. note: This is a surprising estimate given that Democratic Republic of Vietnam campaigns to spread Communism had been underway in a concerted way by the Viet Minh since 1941. It also underscores the scope of grassroots desire for independence.]

Not having eaten breakfast, we ate an early lunch. While there was not a lot of rice, our basic diet consisted of produce in abundance: sugarcane, which we sliced in pieces, white beets, pineapples, coconuts, and bananas. As a vegetarian, in the first year, I ate a lot of river weed boiled with granular salt. But we had no small-grain salt, only big crystals we had to crush ourselves. Friends kidded me that I ate "tiger meat" because pounding the salt made a homophony, *cop cop*, which means "tiger" in Vietnamese. Occasionally, Le An's father—who thought of me as his adopted daughter—brought me a bottle of soy sauce: a gift that was at the same time affectionate, precious, and simple. I ate vegetables, fruits, the cream of soy, milk, butter, and cheese but nothing with a fetus in it, like eggs. Nevertheless, I gained weight eating river weed with bowls of rice and because of the fresh air in the countryside. The fresh air and healthy living were like vitamins to me.

The first year, I could not get used to eating meat or fish. To me, they smelled bad, especially fish. Bit by bit, I got used to it. Each week, we were given a few small strips of pork boiled in fish broth cooked with slices of pineapple.

At noon, we rested for an hour and started working again until five in the afternoon. Because we had nice handwriting, Le An and I were put in charge of writing the stencils used to print books on raising children and nourishing newborns. The books were distributed to the people.

After dinner, as we sat in the courtyard at dusk, mosquitoes came at us in black waves. I couldn't stop itching and scratching, and the squashed mosquitoes stuck to my hands—the blood and mosquitoes mixed like glue. It was a relief when we stayed in the homes of local people and slept on the earthen floor or on planks of wood with a mosquito net over us.

Each evening, we gathered for self-criticism sessions. Often, critiques were sensible, friendly, and sincere, but some people used the sessions with bad intentions and the sole aim of revenge against someone they didn't like. We also had entertainment in the evening, starting around eight o'clock. We sang chorus or solo, told funny stories, or practiced folk dances or short plays to be performed at a celebration or festivity.

But night also brought the fear of French bombing raids. Bombing alerts sounded every few days, once a week, or sometimes once a month. We were afraid, but soldiers dug trenches for each person to protect us from the explosions: they were cut deep and straight to absorb the shock.

Avoiding discovery by enemies also meant moving fairly often. We moved at night, sometimes soaked to the bone under torrential showers. Once, in a small village in Bac Lieu named Binh Phu, hearing the first whirring of a plane, I jumped out of my sampan and plunged into the water to hide myself under the *palmiers d'eau* (water palm trees). I tilted my nose above water to breathe. Ten minutes later, after the plane left, I found the prow of my frail sampan shattered into pieces by a hail of gunfire.

I managed to endure almost every trial but couldn't overcome my fear of the leeches that swam in the stagnant water of rice fields and ponds. I preferred pounding rice to picking river weed or shoots of water lily and lotus. I liked to go into the forest to collect wood rather than harvest or pound paddy. We have a saying that captures the profusion of these "water worms": "Mosquitoes whir like flutes; leeches expand like noodles."

Le An and I were together for six months. Party cadres assigned us aliases. Our names were truly predestined; combined, they formed Binh An, an adjective meaning "peaceful, safe." We liked that our names combined into such a positive message. We shared a bed and felt very close, which is why our leaders decided to split us, transferring me to the Women's Union in Bac Lieu and Le An to a theater school.

I realize the leaders had reasons as we each had to have an independent life and not be too sentimental. The war was very demanding, and we had to be courageous and strict with ourselves. In the life of the collective, friendship must be shared and the "I" forgotten, wiped out.

In Bac Lieu, three hundred kilometers south of Saigon, I worked with the peasants—the people. With food less abundant than in the Mekong Delta, we ate only twice a day: at nine in the morning and five in the evening. With a shortage of rice in this region, we mixed grains with manioc or potatoes. The local people knew we were combatants and helped us a lot. Sometimes they brought rice or shared their homes. In return, we did household chores for them and helped harvest.

As part of the Women's Union, I taught reading and writing to the illiterate and taught young women, future mothers, about the basics of hygiene during pregnancy, how to feed infants, and new ways of teaching children. We talked about the duties of women toward the husband and society. We had to explain all that to the people. Young and inexperienced myself, I first took classes by my leaders, the ones we called "elders." To have an impact, I had to gain the sympathy of peasant women by helping them cook, clean, cut wood, and play with their children or younger brothers and sisters while telling fairy tales or teaching them to sing.

We had taken classes not just on helping peasants but on politics. I do not like politics. I don't like it at all. If I did do politics, it was to liberate the people. To this day, I don't like politics.

During my three years in the maquis, I had no contact with my family. I had many relationships with men in the maquis but was totally indifferent to each. I had no conception of love; I thought of myself as a child and thought that love was for older people. I resisted the pressure leaders put on us to marry early. I wondered if young bright schoolgirls were brought to the bush to be married off. While vaunting the poor peasant class, I noticed leaders chased after girls of a different class.

Most marriages were for the worse. Those who married were not from the same class. Most of the husbands were peasants, and most of us were bourgeois, so it was hard to get along. Thanh married a leader who was basically a laborer. It was hard for them to understand each other. The resistance treated people according to class: the poorer you were, the more you were valued. Most people in the maquis were peasants and laborers, not intellectuals. Everyone loved the schoolgirls who were young and beautiful, like Thanh. I thought this was ridiculous. I knew a lot of couples who did not get along at all because of their different class backgrounds. [Ed. note: Sen's view that people with different backgrounds found it hard to understand each other and get along or that the poorest class was most valued refutes the Communist propaganda about a classless society.] If a girl married, it was for the party: by bringing happiness to her husband, she contributed to the interests of the country. But a schoolgirl would have had no experience! She did whatever the party told her. Since I am not Communist, nobody made me do anything. They did try. But while I was young, I felt I knew one could not live with a man of another class. I don't scorn them, I don't dislike them, but I knew that one could not live without sharing similar culture, education, and customs. Thanh's husband was a complete peasant, to the point that he loved to eat snakes.

At the end of November 1953, I received a letter from an aunt saying my mother had been hospitalized. Hearing the news, the president of the Women's Union gave me permission right away to return to Saigon using a false identity card and a borrowed ao dai. My friends were stupefied she had decided with such understanding and confidence. I was lucky she was such a generous and humane leader. She often said to those of us coming from Saigon: "I respect you a great deal. We proletarians and orphans lose nothing by joining the revolution, but for you, young students of the bourgeoisie, it means abandoning your studies, your dear parents, your beautiful homes, and *nem am chan em* [soft mattresses and warm covers] to unite with us in the struggle for our just cause, despite the difficulties— poverty, lack of food, hard work, the risks of bombing and police raids." This woman, the president of the Women's Union branch in Bac Lieu, was wise and strong and a real revolutionary, worthy of the name.

Back in Saigon, it saddened me most to see my mother weak, emaciated, and looking so aged because of my absence of three years. She had contracted pulmonary tuberculosis and lost ten kilos. At the sight of her little sweetheart, she cried with joy. But she was also shocked to find me "made ugly" by skin browned by the sun and a square peasant build. Pounding rice and rowing had made my shoulders strong and my arms muscled; after all, the only way to move around the Mekong Delta was by boat.

According to my father, I could have better served my country by staying in Saigon and studying further. Because I had been a good student, always among the top five in my class, he rued my unfinished studies and, after I joined the maquis, heaped his frustration on my poor mother. Almost once a week, he threw all the dishes with food she had prepared for him to the floor and yanked down and ripped the curtains.

But for me, participating in the resistance, at the expense of my studies, helped shape my youth and forge my character because she [*sic*] taught me endurance, courage, teamwork, the love of work and the future, all of which I could not have learned at school.

At first, I could not stand life back in Saigon. I could not adapt to the traffic, the loud honking of the cars, the dust. I was always sick and wanted to go back.

But my mother wept and threatened, "If you abandon me again, I will commit suicide." At home with my mother, I joined members of my family who taught French in the Michelet and Duc Tri schools. At the same time, I helped friends in the maquis who came to town from time to time to fetch money, clothes, and other necessities.

6

TUYEN
"A Chance to Succeed"

One sister to have come from a family of modest means, Tuyen grew up in the Mekong Delta before passing the exam to enter Lycée Marie Curie. Her family gained prominence through her brother, Luu Huu Phoc, who—along with the music genius Tran Van Khe—composed and performed songs and plays that impelled students to leave the classroom and rise up against colonialism. His song "Len Dang" (Forward we go) became known as the march of the students and spurred them to take to the streets, to the maquis, to any sacrifice needed to expel the French. Tuyen provides intimate glimpses into her brother as well as the political whirlwind he triggered.

Quiet and reserved at the lycée, Tuyen admired Thanh, who was brilliant and "wrote French like an author." Tuyen joined a student group, led by Thanh, and signed petitions and sang patriotic songs. Tuyen helped print leaflets and—at preset dates and times—distribute them around town; it was like a game with the authorities. She reflected, "We amused ourselves—while trembling."

Tuyen is as observant as she is shy. It struck her that Vietnamese students studied better than the French girls, who seemed to think more about having fun. She saw Le An eagerly follow her father into the maquis because she worried the revolution might end before she could be part of it. Tuyen, with her brother Phuoc living in the North, understood how, in every family, there were people who left and those who cooperated with the French. One family would be split in two camps. Tuyen rhapsodized about a philosophy class taught by French professors who introduced her to Communism, "a beautiful, idealistic ideology" and the first ideal she had ever heard of.

Steering her own course between obligations to family and the revolution, Tuyen remains in Saigon. She would have liked to study to be a doctor but accepted that her brother's studies came first.

Tuyen

In 1931, I was born in the town of Can Tho that straddles the heart of the Mekong Delta. My parents were middle class and worked as functionaries. Father did not earn much as a teacher. Mother was a seamstress and, on the side, took care of others' children by providing lodging and meals. She had a beautiful voice and sang just for us.

I am the next to youngest of six brothers and sisters. After they had two daughters, my parents were elated when my brother Luu Huu Phuoc was born in 1921. When I was born, my parents were expecting a second son and were disappointed. After me, they did have another son. My parents spoiled my brothers, and they deserved it because they were very intelligent. All the family's income went to educating my brothers. My sisters stopped studying after high school.

When I was ten, Phuoc was in high school and started composing songs. After writing each one, he asked what I thought about it. In his mind, there had to be a song for every situation: a hymn for his high school, a song for students at university. During the revolution, he composed songs to sing at street demonstrations. He wrote a handful of lyrics to help galvanize students—concise words they could easily remember and sing together. When I was twelve, he made up theater scenes along with songs, enlisting us kids as actors. We invited friends to attend the musical events. The point of these songs was to create a movement—a national movement that his songs would propel forward.

I asked my brother why he didn't compose love songs. He wrote a few short ones, but I didn't think they were memorable. He loved children, starting with his siblings: he loved us first and foremost. When he moved to Saigon and then Hanoi to study, he often used the money our parents sent him to buy books for us. Before he mailed them, he read them and marked the pages to explain words used in the North that we would not understand in the South. He loved to teach children. During the resistance years, he surrounded himself with children and taught them to sing and make music.

Attending school in the village, we learned Vietnamese history and, in parallel, French history. At an early age, we all knew about heroes like the Trung sisters.

My parents were cautious and did not want to let their first son go to France. He won scholarships to study in France and at the University of Hanoi. Mother did not want Phuoc to take the scholarship in France, but by sending him to university in Hanoi in the early 1940s, she did not realize her choice would lead him toward Communism and thirty years of war that took him far from his mother.

In the early years of colonial rule, the French needed a way to quickly train a large number of cadres in every field. They made it easier for anyone to take the administrative exam: students no longer needed a *bachot* (slang for a baccalaureate degree, attained after thirteen years of study) to take the exam—it was enough to have a *diplôme d'études* after just ten years of study. Those who passed and were selected could become lawyers and engineers after just two years at university. Those who studied medicine for four years became *médicins indochinois* (Indochinese doctors). At the time, the people lacked medical care so much that everyone aspired to become a doctor. These graduates were not allowed to have a private practice. All these cadres—judges, lawyers, engineers—were functionaries of the state who could be transferred from one province to another, depending on the needs of the state.

The parents of several Marie Curie friends were part of this first wave of intellectuals trained by the French at the start of the twentieth century. After this wave, the French reverted to requiring the bachot to go to university, and it took seven years to become a doctor and four years to be an engineer and so on.

In 1945, during the Japanese occupation, all offices were abruptly closed. [Ed. note: Japan's imperial army had invaded China in 1937 as part of its plan for the Greater East Asia Co-prosperity Sphere. Tokyo coveted Tonkin's geopolitical perch and pressured the French to let troops enter Tonkin in exchange for allowing French sovereignty over Indochina to continue. The Japanese extracted huge amounts of rice and resources; their occupation caused a famine that, by 1945, killed over a million peasants and turned many Vietnamese vehemently against them. On March 9, 1945, not trusting the French to continue to collaborate, the Japanese launched a coup de force ending eighty years of French rule.] Teachers and cadres were not paid and stayed home. Only small businesses kept going. The resistance organized demonstrations to demand independence and urge people to take up arms against the Japanese. We protested against the Japanese. I stopped going to school. When the French returned to our village armed with cannons, we fled by sampan and lived in another village for a few months. When the French administration was reimposed, we returned to our village. Those who worked for the French did so again; anyone who did not turn themselves in the French went after. Order appeared to be restored.

But there was too much injustice. French cadres, even at the lowest levels, made ten times more than a Vietnamese at the same level. There were too many prisons. People were illiterate and had so little, even in the villages, where only a tiny dispensary took care of many sick people. We desperately needed independence and liberty. There were good French people, but their way of doing things was outdated. They had projects to develop the country, but their methods were bad. It could not last.

While the French administration was in place, life was not so hard in the maquis. *Maquisards* (freedom fighters) came and went. Everyone loved them. We felt close to the combatants. Many were neutral. Others sided with the revolutionaries, quietly, without saying anything. We felt sure the revolutionary forces would win. For young people, it was the fashion to go to the maquis. It was very common, and those left behind were considered cowards.

Even my mother looked for ways to help people when they got sick. She could not earn enough to feed her children, so she bought a stall at the market. Using her business sense, she prepared small packages of everyday medicines she bought in quantity at a pharmacy in Rach Gia, a village to the west of Can Tho. There were so few medicines; anything was appreciated. A pharmacist from Can Tho came to our village looking for someone to sell his products retail—someone he could trust and who had the confidence of the people. Our local administrator recommended my father, a teacher with a good reputation. But it was my mother who did the work. She was intelligent and highly observant. While my father was a good and charitable person, he was not attentive, a quality needed in a good doctor. Mother had that gift. At a time when parents expected to lose half their babies, she raised seven children without one dying. It was unheard of to raise a family without losing a child! Mother ended up doing well with the pharmacy.

My brother Phuoc abandoned his study of medicine to become a musician. When he went to university in Hanoi, he met Tran Van Khe. They formed part of a group of young people filled with revolutionary ideas. With my brother as composer and a *chef d'orchestre* as brilliant as Tran Van Khe, together they made something that caused a furor.

Through music, the revolution had more of a chance to succeed. In 1942, Phuoc composed a song that inspired a lot of people to join the cause; "Len Dang" urges students to march forward, and it became known as the march of the students. Almost everyone knew the song and its simple, easy-to-remember lyrics.

Another song that inspired students was "Ai Chi Lang," which tells the story of the Chi Lang fortress near Hanoi, once the scene of fighting between troops led by Le Loi and Chinese invaders. Le Loi symbolizes what it means to endure a long guerrilla struggle. The music by Mai Van Bo and Nguyen Thanh Nguyen uses the human voice and traditional instruments, like the gong, to stir chords in the listener. The song begins with far-off sounds, drawing slowly near with the *cloc cloc cloc* beating of horses' hoofs:

> Chi Lang, Chi Lang! the echoing sounds of an army approaching
> Fighters battle bravely for their lives, for ten thousand lives

. . . Whose voice is that? To which god, to whose soul does it belong?
   Or does it belong to past heroes?
Urging soldiers on to victory for their country.
To prove that you are from Tien Rong
. . . Try to save people from the misery.
   Sing together the hero's song.
. . . Conquer the South and bring peace to the North
   As in the hero's way.

Following the swelling sounds at the opening, the gong echoes ever more faintly as the song comes to a close. Tien Rong refers to the birth legend of the nation, in which Tien (Fairy) and Rong (Dragon) marry and have one hundred children that make up the Vietnamese people.

Students got in the habit of organizing evenings of song and music. Before, we put on plays—but not musical soirées like those organized by patriotic students who popularized evenings filled with choral music, sketches, and operettas. Adding to the momentum were students on vacation from Hanoi joined by girls from the lycées in Hanoi and Hue, who all descended on Saigon to join students of the Collège des Jeunes Filles Indigènes (School for Young Indigenous Girls), also known as Collège Gia Long, after the first king of the Nguyen dynasty. Groups from Hanoi, Hue, and Saigon would assemble and go up on stage and demonstrate the unity of the country as they sang patriotic songs and performed short anti-French skits—using the cover of the enemy cast as Chinese. I was only twelve but attended all the rehearsals and knew all the performers. Over their two-month vacation, students organized dozens of soirées. Venues were always full; people fought over tickets. Performances were staged in the downtown opera, a theater built by the French, who—while remaining alert—allowed a few gatherings to display how liberal the government was. These students inspired countless supporters. It was the beginning of the movement.

Intellectuals in Saigon also participated in the movement, like Thanh's father, who was an upstanding person. He participated in the struggle early on, before 1945, and supported the student movement that took hold in Hanoi.

In the French education system, students did not have to pass multiple exams. Their way of schooling was more liberal and more modern than ours. In schools for indigènes children, students had to take an exam at several intervals, whereas in French schools, you went straight through twelve years without so many hurdles. At that point, you studied for the *baccalauréat 1ère partie*, followed by the *bac 2ème partie* a year later. For the indigènes, something always held them back or selected them out. I wanted to study with professors who knew French really well. I wanted to understand the French I heard spoken and noticed that Vietnamese who taught French did not have the same accent as native speakers. To study something, it is best to study it in depth and from an original source. I always thought the French schools were better than the Vietnamese schools. As soon as it became possible to enroll, I took the entrance exam in 1947 and started studying at the lycée.

The profession of teaching in our country brings a lot of respect to those who practice it. In the old times, teachers were considered in a class second only to the king and ahead of the father. It was said the order was king, teacher, parent. Everyone had a duty to learn at school. In the past, we learned especially about morality; we did not yet know a lot about science. Young boys—we did not yet talk about girls at school—first learned about loyalty to the king, respect for the teacher, and love of the parents. We still talk about teachers with respect, and the children of teachers are much loved by students—that is to say, by classmates.

During the revolution and coup d'état in 1945, all the educated people took part, especially the teachers. Some had participated before—people who were imprisoned and released several times, chased from school, and forbidden to teach. So other teachers secretly gave them money. When the French forces came back, several teachers went into the maquis. To stem these losses, French colonial forces increased their salaries many times and even gave them raises retroactively. Functionaries who stayed and cooperated closely with France were called *viet gian* (Vietnamese traitors).

In my village, almost all the young teachers left. I always think of them because they were the ones who organized the drives and outings to the countryside. That is how even in a tiny school, in a very small village, young people were organized into recreational activities to help the peasants. Every Sunday, we gathered to go to the fields. In the dry season, we joined the hunt for rats. These outings gave us the chance to see many things, like peasants hunting birds in the fields and coming back to sell them in the market.

But a commune school was never worth a school in the capital, and my eldest sister who became a teacher in Saigon took me with her to live in Saigon. Rich families sent their children to France to have the best circumstances in which to study. My parents lived far from the capital, earned a modest living, and sent money to pay our living expenses. Even if they didn't have the means to send me abroad, at least I should go to the best school in the country. I passed an entrance exam to a French school, where study conditions were better, starting with a class size of thirty students instead of fifty or sixty in a Vietnamese school! Professors of French literature came from France and had updated qualifications.

I passed another exam and received a grant to attend the Collège des Jeunes Filles Indigènes for a year. Before 1945, indigènes were not allowed at Collège Marie Curie, which was reserved for French citizens. Thanh and Lien An had French citizenship. Once the lycée doors were opened to indigènes, I passed the entrance exam and started to study there in 1947. I quickly saw that all three Binh sisters were excellent students. They had not learned Vietnamese at primary school, as I had in my village; they had a Vietnamese teacher from whom they learned the language a long time after I had.

While at Lycée Marie Curie, it struck me that Vietnamese students in French schools studied better than the French. The French in those schools were not really French; many were métisses whose fathers were *colons* (settlers) and cadres and whose mothers were maids who married their masters. As long as parents were married at the time a child was born, children of mixed couples inherited their father's French citizenship at birth. The young white girls seemed to think more about having fun. That's one reason Thanh and her friends studied better than the French. I was in Thanh's class. She was so talented. As hard as I studied, I could not equal her. Thanh was the most brilliant. She wrote French like an author. There were not many like her.

I wanted to study medicine, but Mother persuaded me to pursue pharmacy, which took five, not seven, years to complete. We weren't rich enough to continue beyond that. It was different for Oanh, Thanh, and Minh, whose fathers came from high-class families that were well-off financially. They faced fewer worries. Nevertheless, the Binh sisters were excellent students because they were intelligent and understood the need to work hard to be respected in society. Coming from a modest social class, my family and I had to consolidate all our efforts to get anywhere. When I went to Saigon to study, I had to find a place to stay.

Some friends at the lycée came from rich, spoiled families. For a while, I lived in Le An's house. She was an only child, and her parents had a villa. After her father joined the maquis in 1947, her mother invited me to come and live with her in 1948. Le An had relatives who were in the resistance; they periodically came to the house. I was there; I knew them. There was tension everywhere. It was like that in all the homes—friends came, just for a few days. After Le An's father joined the maquis, she thought only of following him and simply left her mother. In her place, I would never leave my mother. Her mother suffered a lot, but Le An disparaged her for not being a revolutionary. She was a woman of leisure who did not want to leave her house. Le An did not respect her and loved only her father. Le An felt she had to follow her father and join the maquis quickly because the revolution would end before she had done anything for it. That's how she reasoned. After that, her mother was all alone in the world. She had a son who died young.

The time came to look for somewhere else to live. There were no boarding houses for young women in Saigon; it was years later that Oanh, after studying sociology in the United States, established the first *pensionnat* (hostel) for women. I asked to stay at Lycée Marie Curie, where Oanh and I ended up becoming close friends as *pensionnaires* (boarding students). Oanh was already a boarder and had a nice sister who was a monitor. We entertained ourselves and did not worry too much about the class monitors, who shouted at us but did not scare us. We were considered French and dressed as French. Before exams, we carried our notebooks into the bathroom, where there was good light by which to study late. Oanh and I found food at the lycée pretty good. I am easy when it comes to food; I'm not sure Oanh was the same. We ate French food in the cafeteria.

Not long after boarding together at Marie Curie, I met Oanh again, and she told me she had heard about a Catholic scholarship from a Belgian priest named Father Jacques. She won the chance to study sociology in Wisconsin. I asked Father Jacques if there was a grant to study technical science or chemistry; I didn't know what sociology was! If I had known, I'd have gladly chosen it because I wanted to be like Oanh. She and I are similar in terms of talents and academics. Father Jacques explained the only subject to study on scholarship was sociology because that was what the Church wanted. So I stayed and studied pharmacy. My sister, who had started the course four years earlier, shared her books.

In the late 1940s, students needed a pretext to foment the struggle. Young people declared they didn't want to attend school anymore and stayed home. The authorities announced they would close the schools. A big protest broke out at which speakers demanded that schools reopen. There were five or six demonstrations like this; it almost seemed official that students would go into the streets carrying banners and protesting this and that. Everyone was against the authorities for closing the schools. On the eve of each event, the French authorities launched an appeal on the radio: "Parents, keep your children at home tomorrow. There will be a demonstration." Students joined their friends in secret. It was like a game. Once the police came, we left. Each cycle repeated itself. At one point, the lawyer Nguyen Huu Tho got up on a stage to talk, and the police came to stop him, but students protected him. Chaos broke out, and everyone ran, leaving a trail of hats, shoes, and clothes—a mass of people fleeing as one.

Students continued to rally and provide charity around Saigon. One day, a series of fires broke out in a neighborhood where huts were made of straw. Students brought medicines to help the injured and sick. Doctors, like Mme Tuong's husband, treated patients on the spot. Afterward, everyone joined together to sing songs and plan a rendezvous for another day. Fires broke out all over because Saigon was full of straw huts. As soon as there was a flame, it burst into fire. We thought the authorities did it on purpose, but I am not sure because during the dry season, everything was parched because of the sun. Huts were built too close to each other. After several gatherings like that, we organized a street demonstration. Everyone gathered, ready to walk together. By 1948–1949, following several demonstrations, it turned into a general movement with thousands of students.

FIGURE 8. Tuyen, fourth from left, marches in a demonstration with Mme Ourgaud, the lycée professor of French, who defends students protesting the French administration. Trang stands at right, Le An next to her in glasses. On January 12, 1950, a huge march took place against the French killing of the student Tran Van On. The sisters cite the march as a key event spurring them to act against the French. Courtesy of Le An.

In 1950, the last protest took place at the sprawling Ben Thanh central market. To arm themselves against the police, students grabbed pieces of wood off a train that ran on tracks close to the market. A big battle broke out, with merchants siding with the students. Students fled to the Ministry of Education to demand that schools reopen; they waited there a long time. To disperse them, authorities gave police orders to shoot. Police hit students, and many wounded were taken to Cho Ray hospital. When a student named Tran Van On was shot and students carried him to hospital, merchants from the main market soon arrived and donated money and fruit. Girl students nursed the wounded. It was like a fair had sprung up at the hospital! I took up a collection for the wounded and, after asking our friends to donate, brought the money to the wounded. Le An joined the committee set up to manage the money. The hospital was full. The number of demonstrations multiplied.

Thanh and Trang's friends became my friends; we formed a group of students with Thanh as our leader. She was a good writer and drafted petitions we all signed. We began to participate regularly in resistance activities. The ideas came mostly from Thanh.

We were at war against French colonialism. Thanh's sister Minh played music and invited us to their home to sing together and make leaflets marking revolutionary occasions. We mixed chemicals and gelatin—agar made out of water plants—to make a flour pad to print slogans with purple ink. We sang about the youth. All students did this, at every school. At a preset date and time, students coordinated to distribute leaflets around town. We'd arrange a rendezvous at a certain spot and empty our schoolbags at the chosen time. Then, we ran. We amused ourselves, while trembling. We were not against the French but against French colonialism. That's what we said in the leaflets.

At this time, my brother Luu Huu Phuoc was in the mountainous region in the North while the rest of us stayed in the South. Our family was considered to be one of national patriots; the police, of course, did not see it the same way. But they did leave me alone. In every family, there were people who left and those who cooperated with the French. One family would be split in two.

For classes needed to earn a baccalaureate, students at Marie Curie studied with boys at Lycée Chasseloup-Laubat, where—after two years—we were ready to take the exams for the bac 1ère partie and after one more year, the bac 2ème partie. During this first year at Chasseloup-Laubat, we took a class in philosophy. I learned about Communism in the philosophy class taught by French professors. They encouraged us to read Karl Marx and Lenin, but I didn't because I was overwhelmed with classes and did not have a lot of time to read. But in listening to the philosophy professors, I understood Communism. Before, I knew about patriotism, not Communism. In philosophy class, I began to understand. Communism is a fascinating idea, a beautiful, idealistic ideology. I think everyone has difficulties in life, so when we see something that is beautiful, we want to take part in an ideal. It was the first ideal that I knew about it; I found it beautiful.

After all, we were young, with a lot of enthusiasm.

The Music Professor, Tran Van Khe, Luu Huu Phuoc's Lifelong Friend

Tran Van Khe, who came from a renowned revolutionary family, befriended Luu Huu Phuoc in Hanoi in 1940. Their musical talents complemented each other in formidable ways, influencing a generation of students, including the Saigon sisters, who—a half century on—recall inspiring lyrics and performances in fresh detail.

While bonded by their love of Vietnamese music, these two prodigies drifted far apart politically, their lives leading them in opposite directions. "Everything I have done has been neither for one political party or one government but for the whole people. Where the people are, I am there."

Tran Van Khe

Luu Huu Phuoc was in Hanoi from 1940 to 1944, and I was there from 1941 until the start of 1944. We did not have a revolutionary spirit at that time but rather a profound feeling of nationalism and of thirst for independence for our country that was then a French colony. We wanted social justice for the Vietnamese people. Phuoc's father was a teacher who had strong nationalist feelings and secretly helped revolutionaries by giving money. He passed on to Phuoc his admiration for those who fought for independence.

My mother, while the daughter of a rich landowner, belonged to the Thanh Nien Cach Mang Dong Chi Hoi (the Association of Revolutionary Youth [1925–1929]), which became, in the end, the Communist Party of Vietnam. She hosted revolutionaries at our house. That contact with people fighting for independence—they did not talk at this point about socialism or Communism, or at least not in front of a kid like me—made me want to read the pages of our glorious history and the struggles against Chinese domination and against the colonial French.

In 1942, I was at the University of Hanoi, where Phuoc and I collaborated in the context of the Tong Hoi Sinh Vien (Association Générale des Etudiants); he composed and I conducted the orchestra to spread his songs about youth and victories in our history, like the naval battle on the Bach Dang River, the victory over the Mongols of the Yuan dynasty in China, the fifteenth-century victory over Ming soldiers at the Chi Lang Pass, and others. Later, we joined the youth called Jeunesse d'Avant-Garde (Thanh Nien Tien Phong), in the South. I do not know who in the resistance introduced Phuoc to the Communist Party of Vietnam. I have never been a member of the Vietnamese or French Communist Parties.

After going back home in 1944, Phuoc left for the North in 1945 in great danger. They went by sailboat and had to stay away from the coasts, which meant sailing in salt water. As a good swimmer, it was he who swam holding a jar to find drinking water for Ton Duc Thang, a future president, and others. While a musician, he did this kind of work. I admire him; he did not hesitate to sacrifice himself for others. In the North, he occasionally sent publications on which he had worked. But by this time we had fairly different ideas. He was very much for the resistance and the Communist Party, while I remained a nationalist. My feelings differed from his, especially in politics, but we were very close in terms of music.

In the North, Phuoc was influenced by politicians and started writing many marches about politics. He became highly politicized. In his memoir, he said he could have continued to write personal love songs; that would have been much easier because people are easily drawn to love songs. But he deliberately chose to express, as profoundly as possible, all our thoughts. He expressed the feelings of the people, the currents running through the people. That is why the music became seen as a weapon of struggle. That is what he called the music, *vu khi dau tranh*, "weapons in the struggle."

The music Phuoc composed evolved over several phases. Between 1938 and 1941, he imitated the Western style, like that of the French composer Vincent Scotto. These were *chansons du jour*—pleasant, if banal, songs about love. From 1941 to 1945, he composed songs that retraced history and his two great loves, one a woman from Hue and one a northerner. He was sensitive to the beauty and kindness of young women. Above all, he wrote for a young woman from Hue that he hardly knew. The two were unable to meet but shared a deep affection right up to the day she died and he was unable to come to see her. I was their intermediary. The year 1944–1945, in particular, marked the high point of his famous songs about history and about love.

Music is essential to the Vietnamese, as expressed in one of our songs:

> The heart of the country is filled with songs. . . .
> Listening to your music, who would not have tears in
> their eyes. My song shows serenity that life in Vietnam
> flourishes and, like a flower, opens and blooms.

Popular traditions that had glittered in our songs for four thousand years were suddenly rejuvenated. As the resistance developed, music radiated in ten thousand directions.

7

LIEN AN

"Deep Down, We Remained Vietnamese"

Lien An grew up in a francophone family, a "very rich" family, before shaping her own voice and direction. Coddled at home and chauffeured around town, she was one of the students awakened by Luu Huu Phuoc's music to seek independence. The idea of a society where everyone was equal drew her and her friends like Thanh, Trang, and Minh. Bemoaning that women of her time "did not have ideas," Lien An resented the expectation that girls stay home and have nothing to do with politics. She was grateful her mother urged her to get a profession, so she would not have to rely on a husband.

"Simone" used to walk to Lycée Marie Curie with Minh, who greatly influenced her by courageously rallying support for those fighting for independence. "We felt united in being drawn to a society of equality and justice," Lien An asserted. "We believed in that ideal."

Other friends and family members did not share that vision. At a time when students with the means left for France or the United States, Lien An decided to take part in the struggle from Hanoi. An older sister lived in France, and the younger ones did not want to leave their parents. She confided in Minh but was careful whom else she told, knowing "some friends thought like me, encouraged me, while others did not like that I chose this path." She took a boat north, expecting to return within two to five years, after elections were held. It would be twenty years.

Lien An

My father returned from France as an engineer who had adopted French culture. At the time, there were two kinds of people. Some Vietnamese adopted French nationality and wanted their children to think they are French. These families only spoke French among themselves; they did not even speak Vietnamese in the home! Others upheld a sense of the homeland, like my father, who always preserved a sense of *la patrie*. At home with our parents, we spoke Vietnamese. We spoke French only with teachers and friends at school.

Frankly speaking, my mother was a person of few ideas. Women of that time did not have ideas! Women took care of the home. They had nothing to do with politics. My mother did provide some guidance when she told me, "Whatever you want in life, get a profession, so you have an independent life and are not attached or obliged to be attached to a man who works." As a young woman, she wanted to learn to read and be a teacher. My grandparents were very rich, and at that time, young girls were not meant to go to school. Knowing how to read and write was enough, not more than that. My grandparents focused on saving money to educate the last born, a son. My mother did receive a *certificat d'études*. She could have taught elementary school, but her parents refused to send her for further schooling. I knew I wanted to have a husband, a home, children; I also wanted more.

My father worked with the popular front. Everybody got into politics. In 1944, he went to Hanoi with a group of Lycée Pétrus Ky students who had decided to study medicine in Hanoi. He studied medicine for a year and participated in the youth movement with Tuyen's brother, Luu Huu Phuoc, Mai Van Bo, and the others. In 1945, he returned to the revolution and continued to participate in the resistance, but without using a gun. He was involved in radio broadcasting. At the time, there was the Communist Party as well as other parties.

When I was young, we only learned French songs. We never heard songs that incited a sense of patriotism. Then we heard songs by Luu Huu Phuoc that began to awaken us, and we started talking about independence. *Doc lap* (independence) was new to us. The songs and movements of the year 1944–1945 stirred us deeply, as did communiqués and leaflets calling for action. After 1945, many of us felt our consciousness had been raised. Feelings we didn't know had been buried in us were awakened, bit by bit. One friend asked, "But when did this sense of patriotism awaken and you decided to leave?" It is hard to explain. It happened gradually, over time and with the support of people we knew. We can know the facts of what happened, but it would take a psychologist to dissect how it came about.

I attended Lycée Chasseloup-Laubat for a year and then went to Lycée Marie Curie in the late 1940s. We had Vietnamese friends at the lycée. We found it natural to pal around, learn French, have a French name—I was "Simone"—and dress in jupes and blouses, just like little French girls. We did not have a lot of misunderstanding among us. Typically, Vietnamese girls played with other Vietnamese, but from time to time we also had little French friends. My older sister had a very close French friend.

Growing up, I never learned the history of Vietnam; I only learned the history of France. From 1945 on, all our professors were French except for our Vietnamese-language teacher. We learned French as our maternal language and English as our first foreign language. It was hard to find a teacher for other second languages like German, so our second language options were Spanish or Vietnamese. For all the little French girls, Vietnamese was a second language. Vietnamese girls did not want to learn Spanish. We still go and visit Mme Lanh, our teacher of Vietnamese.

It was at the lycée that we discovered a France that was new to us. In our teachers we saw French people who were not colonialists. We learned about a France in which there is liberty, equality, fraternity!

While living in Cochinchina and immersed in a French lycée, we knew we were not French. We were a French colony, but deep inside, deep down, we remained Vietnamese. To start with, we all have black hair! Vietnamese were allowed to attend French schools and absorb the culture, but when the movement for independence emerged, we were ready to contribute to it. We found ways to express this sense of a nation. If some were no longer young enough to go in the bush, people found roles to play in town: raising money for the resistance, distributing leaflets, resisting in different ways.

My oldest friends are Trang, Thanh, and Minh. Trang and Minh were both brilliant in their studies. They always scored in the top ranks of their classes. At Marie Curie, Minh and I were close as we lived across the street from each other. On our way to the lycée, my sister and I walked by Minh's house and called out for her to join us. She was in my class over several years. I was also in class at times with Thanh. These friends and I shared a deep empathy for the events taking place. Minh had an especially big influence on me; she showed a lot of courage in promoting compassion for people in the independence movement. She was in the avant-garde, passing out little brochures that talked about the resistance. I joined Minh and her sisters for events like anniversaries, national holidays, and the president's birthday. We printed little flyers and deposited them around campus or pasted them on the walls. School monitors kept a close eye on us. At one point, the police detained Minh at the Catinat police station.

We felt united in being drawn to a society of equality and justice, not one with a lot of poor people and a lot of rich people. We wanted a society where everyone is equal. We believed in that ideal. We tried as much as we could to create such a society. Over time, what has happened, that is something else. But at this time, we believed that after peace we would live in a new society with real independence and equality. Everyone would have a profession, and there would be no class differences.

Growing up and going to a good school, my friends and I led the privileged life of intellectuals. We were chauffeured to school in cars. We had servants. When I decided to go to Hanoi, I did not tell these friends. Even within my family, we did not share the same ideas. My older sister had also studied in a French school and liked living in France. She is francophone. My younger sisters did not want to leave our parents; they wanted to take care of them until their last days. I had my own thoughts. I said, "Fine, you take care of Maman and Papa, and I will leave. I am going."

At the time, students with the means left for France or the United States. Few went to Hanoi. Shaped by our education, the background of our families, and the influence of friends and classmates, we were already independent in our thoughts and in our judgments. Minh, Thanh, and Trang all took approximately the same path. Still, I only told Minh about going to Hanoi. Tuyen did not have the same idea about heeding the call to go to Hanoi, so I did not tell her. Some friends wondered why I didn't tell them and later asked, "Were you afraid I would hold you back? Why did you go without giving a signal?" I had to be careful. I knew some friends thought like me—encouraged me—while others did not like that I chose this path.

Shortly after leaving Lycée Marie Curie in 1950, I took a boat north. Sailing past the port city of Tourane, now Da Nang, the ship made a brief stop. A fellow passenger, a Frenchman, asked where I was going and what I planned to do. I explained that, being from the South, whatever lay ahead I, of course, would not be staying up north.

I was traveling with a friend who had the address for the house we were to go to in Hanoi, but when we arrived, we were told that our contact had moved. We were in the middle of Hanoi on a cold night. Here I was, unused to being out on my own after being coddled at home as the daughter of protective parents. We each had a big bag and didn't know what to do. We were afraid. But we calmed down and remembered the name of another contact.

In Hanoi, we met Tran Van Giau, a teacher of Vietnamese history in Saigon before participating in the maquis and going to the North. He was the first president of the resistance committee in Saigon in 1945. He wrote books about Vietnamese history. [Ed. note: Tran Van Giau, 1911–2011, had been sent by his family to study in France, where he joined the French Communist Party. He went on to organize several fronts in the South and oversee their merger with the Viet Minh in 1945. After committing violent excesses during the August Revolution, he lost political power and worked in the Ministry of Education in Hanoi.] I had liked history at Marie Curie and learned it fairly easily. That is why, choosing among history, science, and geography, I studied history. History and geography had been cotaught, but in 1954, in Hanoi, the two subjects were split off. We studied one or the other, as with physics or chemistry. At school in Hanoi, we also had hours set aside for learning politics. We had classes in Marxist philosophy and the history of human evolution.

The first years, things went well. We endured hardships in terms of clothing, cold weather, and not having all we wanted or were used to. We ate simply, using rations. In the first years, even the dedicated cadres received funds—though not salaries yet. We accepted life cheerfully. Cadres who returned from the resistance became our models. Later on, we thought they were a bit Maoist but then saw how they lived simply and thought we could do the same. We thought Vietnam could be a country based on that. After the events, bombings and all that, we could not count on that.

When we left Saigon, we told ourselves, "In two years, after the election, we will return." My father said we might not have an election in two years, but at the latest, in five years we would have one. We expected a separation of two to five years, which we could accept.

It lasted twenty years.

Mlle Lanh, Teacher of Vietnamese at Lycée Marie Curie

One of a handful of Vietnamese teachers at the lycée, Mlle Lanh stood out in her ao dais made of local silk and her hair coiled in a chignon. She worked alongside French teachers, some of whom became friends and she would go visit in France. She also committed herself to waking her students up to the glories of the Vietnamese language and literature, especially the *Kim Van Kieu*, a "diamond" that can be read from many angles.

The revolution took root, and two Vietnamese professors Mlle Lanh knew at the lycée left to join. One returned. As the student movement churned, Mlle Lanh stayed on the political sidelines but was unsurprised to learn her classes had helped spur her students on to join the resistance. "I did worry about the girls, but we could not stop them."

Mlle Lanh

The South was a colony, and the French governed directly. In 1917, they built two schools for young women. Completed in 1918, one was for French girls, Ecole Primaire Supérieure des Jeunes Filles Françaises, and one for local girls, Ecole Jeunes Filles Indigènes. The Japanese first arrived in 1940. Right after they were overthrown in 1945, the French decided to transform the college into the Lycée Calmette. On January 1, 1948, it was decreed to be Lycée Marie Curie and opened with twenty-five hundred students, eighty professors, and five primary school teachers. I arrived a year later. My house was so close I could hear the school bell go off.

French served as the language *véhiculaire* (lingua franca) while Vietnamese was taught as a foreign language. As the number of students learning Vietnamese increased, they needed another teacher. In my time, women became nurses or teachers. After a dozen years in administration, I saw the call Lycée Marie Curie issued for a Vietnamese language and literature teacher. Every teacher in my office refused to apply to work in a French school. I was seconded in my role as *enseignante du Vietnamien auprès de la mission culturelle française* (Vietnamese teacher to the French cultural mission in Saigon). I accepted the position because I relished being able to read and teach Vietnamese literature. At Marie Curie, I did a bit of everything. But teaching the language and literature interested me the most. It was not until 1965 that Marie Curie recruited me directly as a language teacher.

Since children learned French from the beginning, most chose to study Spanish and English as a second language. Parents thought it would benefit their children to learn another European language. When I started teaching Vietnamese, I had two students—at different levels!

Vietnamese students all knew the language pretty well because they spoke it with their families. But living among the French since nursery school, they spoke a mélange of the languages. Some could read a little Vietnamese while others could not read a single word. They couldn't write at all. So I had students, ten or eleven years old, at very different levels. I tried to separate them—putting the illiterate to one side. I organized several sections within one class, giving a writing assignment to one while teaching the alphabet to another. It was challenging.

My arrival on campus was a revelation for the Vietnamese students because they had only ever had French teachers. I wore clothes made of the silks from the country; it wasn't for love of country I chose that material but for the price of the silk! Local silk cost a lot less than imported silk. I dressed modestly. As a primary school teacher, I had not been earning much. I also took care of several brothers and sisters, so I had nothing with which to buy expensive clothes. For a long time, I did not realize that wearing local silk awakened something in the spirit of the students.

As I think about it, I realize my appearance—in local silk, long black hair in a chignon—gave some students their first impression of their own country. There was another Vietnamese woman who also wore Vietnamese clothes, but seeing the way she behaved, she could not be said to represent her country. She came from a privileged position and had married well. We contrasted completely, perhaps even comically. I was tiny and thin and wore an ao dai in white silk, *o be* (pants ensemble), and a chignon. She was plump, frizzed her hair, made up her face, and wore jewelry, including diamond rings. She looked more French than Vietnamese.

I did not consciously mean to be representing our country; it really was just a question of money. Before marrying and moving into our house near Marie Curie, I lived five kilometers away; from 1948 until 1950, I walked to and from school. During the noontime heat or going to a midafternoon class, I would make the trip in a cyclo. But going to school early in the morning or returning in the evening, it was a pleasure to walk the five kilometers. On both sides of the road, it was just rice fields—no buildings, no construction, no crowds. It was not at all tiring as long as I avoided the worst of the heat.

I did feel proud about teaching. The biggest delight was becoming attached to the students. After moving into our house nearby, teachers also wanted to have friendly contact.

I keep up ties with some teachers who returned to France. But with some, I experienced a sense of, if not hostility, a certain coldness, which is understandable as they were new to Vietnam. There was also the question of the motivation of those who came to teach—mainly because life was a lot less expensive in the colony. The school headmistress and others were very nice. During the twenty-eight years I taught, several headmistresses were in charge. First, Mme Brissaud, followed by Mme Fortunaire and Mme Caubot. I saw Mme Caubot again in Paris years later. I never complained about the administrators, but among colleagues, we did have tensions.

On break between classes, one French teacher often complained about living in Saigon. She ranted about how the local help bring their whole families to the house and the constant noise of people chattering and children crying. Europeans aren't used to noise like we are. But one day a teacher blurted out, "I just can't stand the yellow vermin." Immediately, I jumped up and marched out the door, with a French colleague following close behind.

We went to the bookshops to buy books for the students. Because my husband made a good salary, I had the means to buy books and documents.

At the beginning, my level of Vietnamese language and literature was higher than that of my colleagues because I had attended a good secondary school with dedicated professors. I was comfortable teaching at the primary level, but at secondary, I felt a little unprepared. Because the tests fell on different days, students had the chance to pass two baccalaureates—one in French and one in Vietnamese. If they failed one, they could try the other. That's why, more and more, students became interested in learning the language of the country. I needed to be able to offer something more substantial than what I taught at the beginning. I had to raise the level of instruction.

After a few years, my husband bought me a house close to the lycée. When he got a good job on the coast, I took all my vacations in Nha Trang or Da Lat. We could even afford a car and chauffeur. By 1950, I was freed up from family obligations: one brother became an engineer in France; a younger sister taught physical education in a local lycée; and another brother became a doctor and married in France.

I was a little to the side of politics. I didn't like politics. My husband, too, only focused on his work. I was aware of political demonstrations in 1950. The girls knew where my sympathies lay. I just did not get involved directly. They knew I approved of what they did. The three Binh sisters were very active and joined the maquis. Lien An also left. Of my Vietnamese colleagues, two joined the maquis. One, a very young teacher of physics, was killed. The other taught Vietnamese language and history and geography; he did return from the maquis.

To my students, I did not appear partisan to either side. I spoke about the country, our culture, and especially our civilization.

Vietnam has had, in effect, two languages: nom and quoc ngu. Before the end of the thirteenth century, we did not have a separate culture. We used a language rich in terms of oral literature—legends, counts, popular songs. The literate studied Chinese characters and Chinese literature. In the thirteenth century, we did not know the names of authors. Some Vietnamese sounds don't exist in Chinese, and vice versa. They took Chinese characters and added marks, so people could read in Vietnamese. Classic poetry, like *Kim van Kieu*, was written in nom. To read and write nom meant knowing Chinese characters—one had to pass by the "bridge" of Chinese. It was difficult! French missionaries realized this impeded the spread of religion. So, in turn, they imagined another written language: quoc ngu. [Ed. note: Based on the roman alphabet, quoc ngu was devised by the Catholic missionary Alexandre de Rhodes, 1591–1660. Just as it made the spread of Catholicism easier, ngoc ngu later facilitated the spread of Western knowledge and ideas, which had huge effects on Vietnam's history, including the rise of Communism.]

I like the works of Vietnamese poetesses. One was a cultivated young woman who had many suitors and refused those she did not find were cultivated enough. Another, Ching Phu Ngam, passed exams and wrote works like "La Chanson de la femme" (Song of the Woman), in which a young wife complains about war while her husband faces the dangers of war. In the poetry in Chinese characters, she shares her travails and her hopes. Doan Thi Diem translated these works to pay homage, and they are even better than the original. I gave extracts to my students in all three languages: Chinese, nom, and quoc ngu.

Kim Van Kieu is like a precious diamond: depending on the angle, it sparkles in a new way, makes a different impression. Years on, I still discover new angles! It is complete with over two thousand verses. In terms of painting, nature, language, and psychology, it is perfection itself.

After I told my students that I would be getting married, they planned a gift they said I would never be able to give away. We all know that couples sometimes receive the same gift and then regift it. The girls would not allow that to happen. They told me, "We ask that you set aside one afternoon, and for that time, you will belong to us, not him. Please give us one afternoon." When I asked where we were going, they said, "It's a secret; we will blindfold you." They came to get me in a car, and we drove to a villa somewhere in the suburbs. I entered the house; there was nobody there. I stood in a large room with a white curtain. They sat me down, and a bell rang out. The girls staged a beautiful play using costumes they had made themselves, cutting cardboard into masks and headdresses and carving canes out of wood. To take on their roles as king and queen and others, they put costumes on over their European clothes. They acted so well! The play was long; I don't know how long it took them to learn it. It was a play I liked very much, having often read passages from it in class.

The students pulled this play off all in secret! They also staged a scene about a young woman on a pilgrimage with her parents to a pagoda in the North. Thanh—our Thanh—played the young man the girl meets along the way. After this final scene, we ate cake, and the girls brought me back. It was a magnificent gift—one that I could never give away.

Le Tay The Thi is an ancient story of China and a young woman who sacrifices herself to save her country. All told in verse, the story includes a spy who is offered up to an emperor to sabotage him and save her country. She succeeds, but the palace burns down. In the history, we don't know the real ending; in the play, the palace and emperor are destroyed. The three authors were part of the revolution: Luu Huu Phuoc and two poets. I will never forget it.

I did worry about the girls, but we could not stop them. Some parents tried to stop their children from getting involved in the revolution, but they couldn't. We had good relations with the parents of the Binh girls. Their father had studied in a private school. He asked for contributions to make a liberal school, Duc Tri. I gave two months' salary.

8

XUAN

"Liberty, Fraternity, and Equality Were Not for Our People"

The family of Xuan's mother owned a lot of land along the Cambodian border. Xuan's father farmed the land and earned a degree from the Hanoi School of Law after which the French promoted him to provincial administrator. Her parents accepted and respected the French way of life, and it was seen as the only way to "move our country and people forward."

According to Xuan, when the Japanese invaded in 1940, "one invader had colonized our country; now a different one occupied our village." For her, seeing the Japanese occupy her father's village provoked a period of awakening: if the Japanese, yellow like us, could dominate the French at least for a time, why not us?

Xuan was sent to Saigon for safety and to be near her paternal grandparents. Her father resigned from his position of privilege and decided he could no longer work for the French. Seeing her father reject a life of prestige and wealth to join the August Revolution, Xuan began to learn more about the Viet Minh; after meeting several, she did not agree they were "pirates."

Her patriotism was also nurtured through the liberal education and friendships forged at Lycée Marie Curie. While Oanh and Tuyen boarded, Xuan and Thanh bicycled between home and school. Xuan read Tolstoy and Chekhov, learned about the American Declaration of Independence, and came to believe that liberty, equality, and fraternity should be for her people, too.

Rejecting a life of wealth and privilege, in 1949 Xuan left Lycée Marie Curie for a three-month course on Marxism-Leninism organized for girls and boys from Saigon. She carried a small bag packed with black pajamas, a black-and-white checkered scarf, a pen, and a watch. She also took a diamond ring to give to the cause.

Xuan

I was born in Rach Gia, on the border with Cambodia, on April 10, 1930. My parents were wealthy: Mother's family owned land bordering the fertile Mekong Delta, and Father's family held land along the Cambodian border. He loved to farm and checked his crops daily, riding his horse in jodhpurs and knee-high leather boots. My mother died when I was ten days old, and my father and an aunt raised me. His success as a farmer and a degree from the prestigious Hanoi School of Law caught the attention of the French, who promoted him to provincial administrator.

As my mother had done, Father accepted the presence of the French—if not with enthusiasm, at least with admiration. My parents walked among the powerful, and they accepted and respected the French culture and way of life. They enjoyed a high status in society and took the presence of the French for granted as something good for our people. It was the only way to move our country and people forward. That was the thinking then.

Father also remained deeply traditional. After hearing the teachings of Confucianism repeated within our home, we subconsciously followed them regarding respecting elderly people, parents, and teachers. At Tet, Father sat at home as if on a throne and waited for visitors to prostrate themselves in front of him.

When I turned seven, Father sent me to the best French school available. St. Paul's, in Saigon, was a boarding school run by French and Vietnamese nuns. My classmates came from wealthy French and Vietnamese families managing farms and rubber plantations scattered across the beautiful green expanse of the Mekong Delta. One girl's family lived on a rubber plantation so far from school that she flew back and forth in a small plane. My aunt made a two-hundred-kilometer trip each way to pick me up for vacation.

Each school day followed a rigid regimen. We woke up at five, lined up in church pews for prayers, sat in the refectory to quickly eat baguettes and jam, and rushed to classes in dictation, reading, math, drawing, science, music, and catechism. My father did not care whether I became Catholic; he cared that I learn discipline and gain a breadth of knowledge. He also found comfort in knowing that the only men I came into contact with were priests.

One day in 1940, my aunt suddenly appeared at school, packed my bags, and hurried me home. The Japanese were invading, and my aunt said there would be bombing. Straddling the Cambodian border, father's village of Kinh Vinh Te lay in the path of Japanese forces. Around four o'clock one morning, they marched into our village, tracked down the administrator—my father—and jailed him. My aunt and I didn't see him for weeks. One invader had colonized our country, now a different one occupied our village.

Our village organized a school where we learned to speak Vietnamese and write Chinese characters. Every morning, I looked out my bedroom window at the rows of Japanese soldiers raising their flag. A small French tricolor fluttered alongside the red-circle-on-white flag of imperial Japan. To obstruct their movements, I hid the sturdy little rowboat they used to ferry across the border; then I told a Japanese soldier the boat had disappeared. The night before, I had buried it downstream under layers of broad palm tree branches.

Father was released and came back with a Japanese officer, who boarded in our house for a few months. During that time, Father sent me to live with relatives in a neighboring village. When I would visit to clean the house, Father ordered the officer to make himself presentable; often he was wearing nothing but a white flap of cloth around his waist. Once, I overheard the officer explain to Father that Japanese troops were needed to keep the Vietnamese people calm. That sent a wave of anger through me.

As the architects of the Greater East Asia Co-prosperity Sphere, the Japanese occupied Vietnam to secure rice fields and raw materials and to control a strategic trade route to China. Japan coveted our rubber, tin, and jute and quickly drained the goodwill it had won in defeating Russia in the Russo-Japanese War of 1905, the first time an Asian nation had triumphed over a Western power. They badly needed rice for their troops. Before the Second World War, there were years when the South exported one to one and a half million tons of rice. We became the second biggest rice-exporting country after Thailand.

The worst part of the occupation came in 1944 when starvation gripped the nation and killed hundreds of thousands of people. Japan coerced peasants into planting crops other than rice and reserved stockpiles of rice for their troops. Japanese and French soldiers burned rice for fuel even as our people starved.

A period of awakening began after the Japanese invaded. After seeing the French bowing to the Japanese and witnessing French and Japanese soldiers callously contributing to the death by starvation of two million of our compatriots, it would have been impossible not to develop a firm conviction that things had to change.

The Japanese did provide one valuable lesson. The French—until now the undisputed, conceited, and fiercely proud masters of the country—were relegated to a subordinate role. This was one of the factors waking us up to the realization that, if the Japanese—Asians like us—could show superiority over the French, why not us?

In 1945, Father sent me to a nun's school in Soc Trang in the heart of the Mekong Delta but only for a few months. Fearing for my safety, he decided to send me to Saigon to be near my paternal grandparents, who lived on the outskirts of town. I was at their home when I first met members of the Viet Minh.

I had always heard that the Viet Minh were "pirates." People put out alerts: "Look out, the pirates are coming. Those people take all your belongings!" I was apprehensive about meeting anyone associated with the anti-French resistance. To hide their wealth, my grandparents and uncles stuffed jewels, gold, and all their fortune into large hand-sewn belts made out of thick cloth. After being warned of a visit by pirates, my uncles tied the stuffed belts—dubbed "horse intestines"—around their torsos under their clothes. When the pirates searched them, they found the belts and asked that everything be poured out on the floor. But they didn't take anything. They were not pirates. They were Viet Minh.

Girls my age often took jobs as nurses in Saigon's hospitals. I began this work, but in 1946, after the French reclaimed power and the Viet Minh lost again, I went back to school in Saigon. I didn't want to work for the French again. It is one thing to be welcoming and hospitable, to learn Japanese and French, to be friendly with foreigners. We like foreigners as friends—not as people who subjugate us.

Father resigned from his administration job for the same reason: he didn't want to work directly for the French anymore. He put me in the care of foster parents in Saigon and took a posting in the Mekong Delta province of Tra Vinh, where he collected money and medicines to supply the maquis and rallied support for petitions complaining about French authorities.

Why my father, who had enjoyed the glittering privileges of his status, took up the cause of the 1945 August Revolution stems from our history.

From the sixteenth century on, wave after wave of Vietnamese moved north to south to seek a better life. They left the poor, crowded provinces of the North for the rich opportunities offered by the South's fertile Mekong River Delta. As migrants, my family shares the characteristics of migrants: fearless, motivated by an unquenchable thirst to move ahead, prepared to work hard and show initiative. At the same time, like other migrant families, we are nostalgic for the homeland. To make up for this nostalgia, we cling to deeply ingrained traditions, like attachment to the village, to the tombs and ancestors, and to the community left behind. All these sow the seeds of patriotism and nationalism.

Spontaneously and secretively and inspired by the return of the French, politics became the topic of the day at school, in families, and among everyone. We hadn't talked about politics before; we were ignorant. Now, though, patriotic songs began to circulate, and people even dared to sing them. Tuyen's brother wrote some of the most inspiring songs.

As for me, one more factor that played a pivotal role was my education at Lycée Marie Curie. The classic divide-and-rule policy of the French was reflected in the two types of schools in their system. One, established for the majority, followed a curriculum for indigenous students. The other, reserved for a minority—daughters and sons of people with wealth or high standing and daughters of French colonialists—followed the curriculum taught in schools in metropolitan France. Lycée Marie Curie belonged to the second category. The goal was to shape us in the image of French boys and girls and for us to become citizens of Mother France. Since I attended primary school run by French nuns, it seemed logical for me to continue at Marie Curie, where we learned the same subjects as French boys and girls.

I reflected on the suffering of our people and drew the inescapable conclusions. We learned a lot and came to know as much as French boys and girls of our ages would know about the natural, physical, and social sciences. We even learned that the Gaulois are our ancestors! So my view of the world was that it was divided into those who are predestined to go to heaven and the rest, who are predestined to go to hell. Our people belonged to the second category because of the poverty, misery, and obscurantism in which they lived; for them, life was "nasty, brutish, and short," while the French and other people seemed to receive and enjoy all God's gifts and privileges. So I aspired to become a physician to help alleviate the sufferings of my people.

I harbored no fears in my heart about the future being in my grasp. I adopted a morality of hope, not fear. Only offspring of families of some wealth and social standing could attend Marie Curie. I studied hard. Because my family included a good number of dentists and physicians, I thought I could easily become like my uncles. I saw no obstacle to fulfilling my aspiration.

Thanh, Oanh, Le An, and I transferred to Lycée Marie Curie in 1947. I found it much freer than the schools run by the rigid nuns telling us, "Don't do this; don't say that." Oanh and Tuyen boarded, while Thanh and I bicycled back and forth from our homes. We received a liberal education. Teachers taught in a multidimensional, international way. We read classics by world authors. We read about world history. We learned a lot about Russia by reading Tolstoy and Chekhov. We became aware of the American Declaration of Independence in 1776, Jefferson, Washington, Lincoln, and even Benedict Arnold. We learned about the French Revolution and its ideals of liberty, fraternity, and equality. This was, in my mind, one of the main reasons we became patriots.

As we compared notes, we found the ideals of liberty, fraternity, and equality were not for our people. Why? As a people, inferior in no way to the French of the late eighteenth century, we decided we would see these ideals come true and translated into reality. In other words, we needed our own revolution.

At Marie Curie, we learned nothing about Vietnam. We only started studying Vietnamese after Mlle Lanh, a language teacher, came in 1948, and we studied it as a third language after French and English. Our relations with teachers at Marie Curie were distant. Most were French, who separated themselves in a world of their own, and their way of teaching offered little time for dialogue. In the French way, which my husband Lau saw while at the Sorbonne for his BA in letters, a French professor sits above and talks down to students. It's not like in England or the United States. You don't get near them; teachers arrive, give a lesson, and leave. They talk down to students. I witnessed scenes of teachers acting superior and assuming the role of *civilisateur* and *civilisatrice*. Culturally, we were taught to look at teachers as parents, so we maintained a respectful distance. And subconsciously—it was never taught in a systematic way, but we had absorbed it at home—we followed Confucius regarding respecting elderly people, parents, and teachers.

As students, we led hectic lives. We dashed from class to class, and in the little time left, we got together for visits to Saigon's parks and zoo. During this period, families tried to make sure their children did not have any free time. If you had free time, you would take part in resistance activities. So in addition to classes at school, families pushed us to take private lessons in all kinds of subjects.

At school, people said I led a life of privilege. I liked having time on my own. Thanh said I was soft-spoken and contemplative, a kind of *enfant philosophe*. She said I cast a calm and confident aura that some might find arrogant, but she thought it conveyed a sense of grace.

My father liked music and wrote books about traditional music. He made me take piano lessons. Though with the wisdom that comes with age I appreciate it now, I hated it then.

In July 1949, not long after Mme Ourgaud, our professor of French, gave an end-of-year speech urging us to go on vacation to "read, jump, run," I went into the jungle. I wanted to see the maquis, and I wanted to be among the first to go. My father didn't know where I went. A few girls at Marie Curie knew. I joined along with one other girl. I was unafraid.

I left with a few things packed in a bag: black pajamas, a black-and-white checkered scarf, a pen, and a watch. I brought something to give to the cause: a ring with three diamonds. The first day, we traveled by taxi about one hundred kilometers southwest to My Tho, a town occupied by the French. A liaison agent appeared and stopped the car. We got out and were taken to a pastor's home to wait. Early one morning, another agent led us to a sampan, and for a whole day we navigated streams and canals deeper and deeper into the jungle. We didn't know where we were going. We moved constantly until we reached the designated camp, which, we soon learned, also served as a base for printing pamphlets.

I attended the three-month training course for young people as well as students; there were students from almost every lycée in Saigon. No one expressed particular interest in us, the new recruits. No one asked me questions. During the day, we performed chores to make the camp self-sufficient in food and other necessities. At night, we attended readings on the resistance and its goal to rid our country of the French. They talked about the current situation and policies so that everybody, from every political current and walk of life, would know and accept them. They instructed only resistance politics, not ideology. They did try to tell you about nationalism and how everyone could use their own ways and means to help the nation. We also learned how to throw a grenade and shoot. We didn't think about killing people. We read pamphlets. We read writings by Ho Chi Minh. Most of us liked him. We didn't know anything about Communism; we just followed it because of him, because of a sense of nationalism.

After the lessons, some of us walked to a little market that was held at night for security. Women squatted by crude little wooden tables, lamps with pin pricks of light exposing their wares—fruits, vegetables, cigarettes, matches.

We split into groups and started classes. Soon after settling in, news spread of a high-level delegation coming by the Ho Chi Minh route from Hanoi led by the minister of health, Pham Ngoc Thach and Le Duc Tho. [Ed. note: Pham Ngoc Thach, 1909–1968, graduated as a medical doctor in Paris before returning to Vietnam and joining the Indochinese Communist Party in 1945. Le Duc Tho, 1910–1990, was a founder of the Indochinese Communist Party and political leader of the southern region of Vietnam in the war against the French.] They lectured about social economic developments and the course of the war against the French. A meeting was arranged with us, the young people. Pham Ngoc Thach made a little speech about his journey from Hanoi. I noticed a young man that evening. We did not talk at all. There were a lot of people. We only caught glimpses of each other in the dimly lit pagoda.

The next evening, at five o'clock, I heard the air alert. French fighter planes swooped in as part of an operation that I figured was targeting the high-level delegation. They came in full force. A group of us, boys and girls, had been working in the printing shop. Boys quickly hauled the printing machine and typewriters into sampans and rowed away. We buried the papers. And then we each tried to find a place to hide. The order given to anyone without combat duties was to run to the outer limits of the theater of operation. French planes flew so low we could see the faces of the pilots. Paratroopers hung in the sky, and the military planes swooping overhead fired guns to protect them. The planes did not drop bombs, but they shot at everything that moved. When a plane flew over, my heart skipped a beat, and I shut my eyes to the inevitable bullet, to the death that would follow.

Every few hundred feet, I fell into the mud, not sure I would rise again. After one fall, a hand helped me up. The man I had noticed a few nights earlier appeared out of nowhere and said, "Don't be afraid. Follow me." He led me far from the village to an area overgrown with trees and bushes, where we hid. I don't know how long it was before the planes left and we ran barefoot back to camp. I saw him slip behind a hut where there was a well. He filled a coconut shell with water and brought it to me, so I could wash my feet. I rolled up my black trousers, and his face turned red. He lent me his black-and-white checkered scarf and disappeared.

I didn't know anything about him. I didn't know where he lived or even his name—just his face. I kept his scarf, and that night, we had to decamp. We walked all night except for breaks when we rested, propped back to back against each other. There were no houses in the jungle, but we spotted a black dot in the middle of a rice field: a farmer's house. He and his family offered us rice, nuoc mam, and grilled field mice. Fattened on rice, the mice tasted delicious. We felt fortified and trudged on barefoot, sometimes wading in water above our knees. Walking, walking, walking, always in haste. During the night, we met *boi dois*, foot soldiers of the Viet Minh, who were ready to defend us.

After about a week, we came back full circle to our first camp. The land was burned and desolate. Huts lay charred, surrounded by swollen carcasses of buffalo, cattle, pigs, and chickens. A nauseating smell drifted from the dead animals. Thick smoke rose from the burning crops. We had to rebuild everything.

We returned to daily rituals of classes and learning how to throw grenades and fire guns. At sunset, we sang and reviewed events of the day. We took turns cooking with clay pots and plates. Rice and fish were plentiful, and we enjoyed eating together. To make water potable, we crushed white tablets that made the dirt drift to the bottom. We washed and bathed in a narrow river nearby. I used the checkered scarf as a shield against the sun, as a scarf around my throat, and as a towel. I jumped in the water with my clothes on, washing them and my body at the same time. The scarf made a handy screen behind which to change out of my wet clothes. Each person had a nop, a straw bed roll in the shape of a pocket. I wriggled down into it until my head was protected from the mosquitoes.

By burning homes and killing livestock, the French were able to cripple rice production. But they could not overcome a basic contradiction: to avoid attacks, they had to concentrate, and when concentrated, their troops were pinned down. Sooner or later, taking a stand in territory held by the maquis subjected them to guerrilla attacks, and they had to withdraw.

One day I spotted the young man who had helped me and told him I was ready to give his scarf back, but he said, "No, no, you keep it. I don't need it yet." The next day, he stopped by again. He used the scarf as an excuse to come back and

forth to see me. In the end, I gave the scarf back. But I still did not know his name—
just his face.

When the three-month course ended, I couldn't go back to Marie Curie. The
authorities knew where I'd been. Father moved me to a school about thirty kilometers away; I stayed at My Tho College for one term. Then I went to Pétrus Ky
College, where Tran Van On studied; he was the student who died in front of Gia
Long Palace where we demonstrated. We took his body back to school and held
a funeral a few days later. Although we attended a French school, we strongly opposed the French.

My father moved me to my uncle's house in Saigon. My uncle was a doctor
who worked at a hospital and had his own surgery at the house. Outpatients came
and went, providing a cover of activity. The atmosphere was tense. I saw fights
between Vietnamese and foreigners in front of my uncle's house every day. The
man who gave me the scarf came searching for me at my old house in Saigon, but
my cousin, not trusting a new face, told him I had gone abroad.

As demonstrations in Saigon multiplied, pictures of students began to appear
in newspapers, and police opened files on more and more of us. Suong, Sen, Trang,
and I lived near each other and met at student gatherings.

After one of our classmates, Tran Van On, was shot while demonstrating in
front of Gia Long Palace, we took his body to the hospital, where he died. His
funeral took place a few days later. My friend Suong's mother, Mme Tuong, helped
me collect money to buy the banner for the funeral procession. A flood of people
four or five kilometers long flowed behind Tran Van On's coffin on the road to
the cemetery. Once again, police took our pictures. They knew our names.

One day, the police called my father: "You had better send your daughter
abroad, or she will be jailed."

So I had to go abroad. Father took me to the special security branch of the
Commissariat to get a passport. On May 31, 1950, I was issued a two-year Union
Francaise Indochine passport signed by the police commissioner in the security
service. It described me as having "chestnut" eyes, "sunken" nose, "oval" chin,
and a "dull" complexion. Father booked a second-class ticket for me to depart
Saigon for France on June 10.

A trip to Marseilles usually took two weeks, but the *Athos II*, nearing its retirement, sailed slowly and had engine trouble at sea. The journey stretched out over
a month. I met a friend of my father's on his way to a congress of Buddhists in
England. He spoke no English and had arranged for a Vietnamese student in London to translate for him during the congress.

Reaching Marseilles, I met my uncle and his family. Before my father's friend
continued to London, I told him I did not like the French, I did not like France,
and I would like to go to London. England appealed to me; I had read novels by

the Brontës and others at Lycée Marie Curie. I said I wanted to study in London and asked him to help.

While still in Marseilles, I met representatives of the Viet Minh and of Bao Dai, a king in the Nguyen dynasty put on the throne by the French. When you met the Viet Minh, you were treated in a humble way; they had no money but tried to help in other ways and invited you into their homes. The Bao Dai representative took you to a restaurant or a big hotel.

I helped my father's friend by translating and mailing materials he needed for the Buddhist congress in September 1950. To help me arrange to study in London, he asked a Vietnamese student who turned out to be a friend of the man I had met in the maquis. The student was too busy but volunteered the young man whose name I still did not know. He sent a photograph, asking if I could pick him out among the students. I marked a cross on his head and mailed it back. He wanted to verify it was really me. His name was Lau. My father's friend was surprised when Lau explained he already knew me from the course we took in the jungle.

Lau started writing and introducing himself. My father was against our friendship and warned that I would be isolated if I went to study in a strange country like England. But I made up my mind and left everything, arriving in London on October 27, 1950. Lau and I had not seen each other since the maquis in 1949. He met me at Victoria Station. He had bought a pair of shoes the day before, and they were pinching his feet. Living in Guilford, he had woken up at 2:00 AM to buy a train ticket from Sussex to London. I had packed several colorful Vietnamese outfits, but the night before, the French staff at my hotel used bleach that dripped on and ruined the colors in my clothes. I dyed them all black; when I met Lau at the station, I said, "So we meet again in black."

Lau took me to Guilford and helped me rent a room in a boarding house. He rented one room, and I rented another. Enrolled in a general education course, I started studying at the college in Guildford. Lau did the same and then went to Oxford. I commuted to London to start music lessons. Lau suggested that, instead of medicine, it would be better to study music. I agreed, rationalizing the study of piano by telling myself that if medicine sought to soothe the wounds of the body, music reinforces medicine by soothing the mind and heart. I had no regrets for not taking up medicine. Father concurred with my decision. I never looked back. One does not live with regrets.

I went back to music and worked hard. I had not practiced at all in a long time. To make up for that, I played ten hours a day. I had to rent a room in a basement because my piano made too much noise.

On October 30, 1950, I registered at the Guilford Aliens Department, where they issued a certificate of registration listing my nationality as French, my "previous nationality" as Vietnamese, and my passport as French Indo-Chinese. A few weeks later, I visited the French embassy in London to get a *carte d'identité*. Signed by a French vice-consul, it listed my nationality as Vietnamese.

I took the exams at the London Royal College of Music. We had to pass an exam in writing that had three parts: piano performing, teaching, and accompaniment. Anyone could take the exams, even as an outside student. There were a lot of questions about teaching, musical analysis, harmony, and theory. I took private lessons with teachers at the College of Music. In 1954, I passed the oral test, teaching questions, and musicianship. Meanwhile, Lau studied at the London School of Economics, writing that studying in London was "nothing much."

Once we decided to marry, he wrote his parents. One brother had died, and his nephews who had joined the movement could not travel to London. But a cousin, a chief inspector of security, came to represent Lau's parents in asking for my hand. I asked this cousin where he lived, and he replied, "The Majestic Hotel," in Saigon. I was surprised since only rich people lived there. He reported back to Lau's parents, who sent a letter saying they did not approve of the wedding because my family was on "the other side."

We did what we thought best and went ahead and married since our first child was due in May. We went to the registry office in Kensington and married on April 4, 1952. We invited two women friends, from Finland and Sweden, as witnesses. After a simple ceremony, we four returned to the house for a meal of noodles and roast chicken. We splurged with a cake and a bouquet of tulips. I tell my kids it was that simple—and we stayed together our whole lives.

Meanwhile, the London Association of Students for the Resistance continued to meet monthly and discuss current events over a meal. Since meat was rationed, we ate the cheapest thing possible, such as curries made with horsemeat. We exchanged views, collected whatever we could to send home, and consolidated and strengthened our faith in our cause. A diplomatic delegation in Paris sent us bulletins and newspapers from home, though only at rare intervals. In 1954, Ngo Dinh Diem's ambassador in London tried to buy us off by providing an allowance every month if we would visit him at Tet and other events. We never did. They tried to work through the Foreign Office in an attempt to expel us.

When we joined the London Association of Students, the group had thirteen members, and the president was a friend who, like Lau, studied for an economics degree. Taking trains from the suburbs often made us late to meetings; each time, the president banged his cane on the table. It turned out he was working for Ngo Dinh Diem. [Ed. note: Ngo Dinh Diem, 1901–1963, was a Catholic nationalist who rose in the civil service under the French. He struggled to find a political path to independence that relied neither on the French nor the Communists. After Ho Chi Minh came to power, Diem met with Ho but refused to join the DRV. In

1951, Diem left for the United States, where he garnered the support of the Kennedys and Cardinal Spellman.]

The resistance against the French engulfed the whole nation so that the majority of other Vietnamese Marie Curie students took part in the movement, in one form or another. We rarely heard news of each other. But whatever scant information I did come across about classmates in the movement gave me real joy and happiness.

9

OANH

"I Did Not Become a Refugee"

Born in the Mekong Delta, Oanh attended Lycée Marie Curie because "most well-off people sent their kids to French schools." Her mother's family had land and wealth; her father, from a poor family, was able to marry her because he had earned a diplôme d'études in Saigon. During the revolution of 1945, her father was almost beheaded for being a landowner and collaborator but was spared at the last minute by a Viet Minh he had once helped.

Oanh admired her father for being like a father to the people and her mother for being educated, intelligent, and unconventional. She memorized literature, followed world events (like the rise of Hitler and Mussolini), and ignored fashions of the day. Oanh, who never married or had children, aptly noted she surely inherited her mother's straightforwardness and unconventionality.

Oanh took pride in being Vietnamese but did not have a strong political consciousness. She went along with student marches and other activities to "help make the crowd." Her parents wanted her to study in safety abroad, but Oanh did not want to study in France. Through a Belgian priest, she learned about a scholarship to study social work at Viterbo College in Wisconsin. Studying at Viterbo and living in the United States changed Oanh; she drew on lessons learned throughout the rest of her life.

Unlike most Vietnamese students she met in the United States, Oanh returned to Saigon, where she applied her degree to help young women affected by the social upheaval of the Geneva Accords. Even as her family tilted toward the Americans, one brother translating for General Westmoreland and a sister working for the U.S. Information Service, Oanh went her own way.

Oanh

I was born December 25, 1931, in Go Cong, once a province and now a district belonging to Tien Giang Province. I was born not just a twin of my brother Loan but also of Jesus, as my friends used to joke.

I attended Lycée Marie Curie because most well-off people sent their children to French schools. The most important government-run schools in Saigon were Lycée Marie Curie for girls and Lycée Jean-Jacques Rousseau, formerly Lycée Chasseloup-Laubat, for boys. During our time of war, schools faced a lot of challenges, especially a lack of teachers.

In 1945, I attended class at La Sainte Enfance, a French Catholic school run by the Sisters of St. Paul de Chartres, but the campus had to be moved from Saigon because of the heavy bombing of the navy headquarters and arsenal just across the street. In March 1945, I had to go back to Go Cong because the Japanese took over and because of the August Revolution. The Japanese were very martial and disciplined in their methods. They cut the fingers off robbers.

I stayed home and studied English by listening to the radio. When I came to Marie Curie in 1946, I made up for a lost year in a short time. I knew Thanh and Minh; Tuyen and I became close friends because we both boarded at the school.

Daily life as boarders was regimented but also fun. We had to do everything together: walk, two by two, up to the dorm; walk down for class; under the watchful eye of a surveillant, march from Marie Curie to Chasselou-Laubat for classes; sleep in a big dormitory, keep silent in the dormitory, though we giggled a lot despite being under the watch of a surveillant; get up with the morning bell; wash all together in the washroom while Tuyen always sang the same song, the first verse being about "the majesty of the sea"; recess together; eat together. In the dining hall, students sat on benches at long tables while, at one end of the room, the surveillants sat at their own table and monitored us even as they ate. What I hated most was that we did not choose our own clothes; they were distributed on certain days of the week. On weekends, sponsors who represented our families far away in the provinces came to visit or take us to their homes before bringing us back by curfew on Sunday evening.

Among the students were Vietnamese, métisse, and French girls. One of my best friends, Marguerite Axenoff, was Russian with French citizenship. Her father worked in My Tho, so the children—Yuri, Tamara, Marguerite, and another sister—stayed in Saigon to study. She and I had fun being little devils. I was one of the oldest boarders and acted as the leader in protecting little Vietnamese girls against little French girls. I led a group that protested when we were served lentil soup full of bugs with wings or rice stained with purple ink after somebody spilled a big bottle of ink on a bag of rice. We had to eat light purple rice until the bag was empty. When I refused to eat the soup, I was accused of a lack of discipline and told to look down when being addressed by the headmistress. For having led the protest, I was punished and could not leave on weekends, from Christmas to Easter. That headmistress was a real colonialist.

While the *surveillante générale* was a good French lady, those who monitored us day to day were not very educated. Many were French, others Vietnamese.

Most teachers impressed us by their dedication to our education. Of course, they were all French, except Mr. Nghia, our English teacher, who came back from France with a French wife, and two prominent Vietnamese figures who taught Vietnamese as a second foreign language. My French literature teacher, Mlle Hithos, followed the progress of her students one by one. Since I was a good student, we became quite close. She would anxiously look up our grades for the written part of our baccalaureate exam and be so happy when I got a high grade. She showed me how to prepare for oral exams. She took time to talk with me about my future. This relationship, with an adult who cared about my studies and guided me during those difficult adolescent years, made a very, very deep impression. I was literally shocked by this experience, and it was a positive shock.

In Vietnamese families, children and adolescents are cared for, but parents impose their ideas and don't pay much attention to the psychological needs of their children. My experience with Mlle Hithos and later with a sociology teacher in the United States strongly influenced my desire to work with people—particularly with youth, who need so much guidance and counseling.

Another teacher who did not stay long but made a major impression was a young Frenchman, a twenty-three-year-old who already had qualified to teach secondary school. He dressed in a sloppy way but was sharp and full of pep. We called him Anh Bi, "Brother Bi." He spoke Vietnamese, which was unusual for a Frenchman, and taught us to think differently. We liked him very much and asked him to give us private literature and philosophy lessons at the home of a student. Suddenly, he disappeared, and we learned that he joined the Vietnamese resistance and made an appeal on the radio to young lycée students to join. Quite a few students followed his call. This teacher was Georges Boudarel, nicknamed with an honorific as "Ong Bou," who became a prominent figure in the French Communist Party, which he later quit. [Ed. note: In 1993, the "Affaire Boudarel" erupted in the French media as he was accused of torturing French soldiers at a Viet Minh prison camp in the 1950s. Acknowledging he had been a commander at Camp 113, Boudarel defended himself claiming his work was political indoctrination, not physical deprivation. He died in 2003.] Another teacher who impressed us was Maurice Clergery. Years later, I saw his name in a French magazine as director of a French development studies institute.

It was at Lycée Marie Curie, where we ate French food and spoke French, that for the first time I became conscious of Vietnam as a nation. I am most grateful for my French education, which opened me up to world culture and, most importantly, gave me access to clear, logical, and systematic thinking. I learned to love books. The lycée provided the foundation for my studies and future work.

Although it was toward the end of the colonial period, many little Vietnamese boys and girls educated by their families spoke French, pretended not to know Vietnamese, or tried to speak Vietnamese with a French accent! We studied Vietnamese as a foreign language and a second one at that, after English. We could have considered it of lower importance, but the teachers succeeded in making us proud to be Vietnamese and helped us appreciate our culture and literature.

The political ambiance was that of a new push for independence, a discovery of Vietnam as a nation. High school students made up a dynamic force to back

FIGURE 9. Oanh (right) and a friend wear ao dais to go "Catinater" and be seen on Rue Catinat, old Saigon's main commercial street. From a wealthy family, Oanh was the only one of the Saigon sisters to study in the United States. Courtesy of Nguyen Thi Oanh.

up the revolutionary movement. Teachers during the 1940s played a very important role. Not just anyone was accepted as a professor at prominent French schools, such as Marie Curie and Jean-Jacques Rousseau. Two Vietnamese teachers were prominent figures on their own. The first was Duong Van Thoi, father of Dung Quynh Hoa, who was also a Marie Curieuse, as I liked to joke, in a class ahead of us. The other teacher, Mme Tran Thi Lanh, became—along with Mme Tuong—a mother figure to the Saigon sisters. With such teachers, how could we do other than we did? My brothers who went to the top school for Vietnamese boys, Lycée Pétrus Ky, often talk about their teachers Mr. Chi, Mr. Truc, and Mr. Thieu; all became future leaders of the socialist revolution.

I had a strong personality, felt proud to be Vietnamese, and enjoyed being the "judge" between Vietnamese and French children. But I had no political consciousness.

The Binh sisters, Tuyen, Sen (and her husband, Nhieu), Le An, Suong, and others were in an organized group under the leadership of the revolutionary movement; I was not involved but "made up the crowd" for them. Despite our different political views, we were very good friends at Marie Curie.

Thanh was a terrific leader. As a student she was more than outstanding, and as a political leader she was sensitive and accepted by everybody. One day, she came to me and suggested in a casual and friendly way, "Hey, tomorrow is Uncle Ho's birthday; let's wear white." I did not care much for the event but could not resist her suggestions. I also marched in the funeral procession for Tran Van On, the student killed by the police during a demonstration. It was a happening when Luu Huu Phuoc and Tran Van Khe came to Saigon on break from university in Hanoi and staged their musical presentations.

In my family, we are fifteen, with six miscarriages. I often said my mother was the founder of family "plan . . . ting." French authorities used to award medals to big families, but—too bad—another mother had sixteen live births! When my father said he had fifteen children, French visitors often asked: "Do you have only one wife?"

My mother came from a well-off family of the province. Although my father's family was poor, he was able to marry her because he got a diploma in Saigon. During the revolution of 1945, he was almost beheaded for being a landowner and collaborating with the French. He was a clean, honest man and kind to people. Once, he was spared his life at the last minute thanks to a Viet Minh member he had once helped. Father had been a teacher and then took on administrative work as a *chef de canton*, *chef de district*, and assistant *chef de province*. He accumulated all sorts of honorary titles. As an administrator, he was like a father to the people. He advised them in agricultural techniques, played the role of judge, and visited the villages at all times of the day and even at night if there was an emergency, like a fire or an attack by thieves. We accompanied him to the villages to see traditional theater performances and to participate in village festivals.

One day, we heard father shout very loud in his office in our house. We rushed in to find out what happened. The day before, Father had judged as not guilty a poor peasant he knew had been falsely accused. The next day, to thank my father, the peasant brought him a pair of ducks. Father exploded with anger at what he saw as bribery. My mother liked to joke about that story, but I think, like us, she was proud of Father's honesty and moral principles. We were also afraid of his hot temper, but as he got older he became more and more kind and patient. We loved him very much. Being a teacher, he knew how to play with us. He taught us, one by one, how to ride a bicycle. He took us swimming and watched over our homework.

Father liked to farm. He had a big piece of land far from the house but also a small farm nearby. After work hours, my father walked over there, gave instructions to the caretaker, and fed the animals that followed him wherever he went: pigs, ducks, geese, chickens, goats, sheep. It was always funny to see the animals trailing behind him like old friends. He won quite a few awards for raising the biggest pig in the province or for the new rice breed bearing his name. He dreamed of modernizing agriculture and expressed interest in stories we read about countries where farmers sow seeds from a plane and other experiments. We enjoyed accompanying him to the farm and playing in the fields during harvest season. My mother loved to garden; we all do.

While my father was a humble, disciplined, hardworking man, my mother—in something of a contrast—displayed an unusual intelligence and expressed deep pride in her family origin. Her family was one of the biggest families of Go Cong. By the standard of her time, she was educated, in that a tutor came to teach her, her sisters, and her cousins about poetry, music, and painting. While still young, she became an assistant to a French principal in a nearby school. Mother enjoyed literature and liked to cite proverbs and verses from classic literature. She had an unusual memory and knew many literary pieces by heart. She paid attention to world events and politics, telling us about the scary rise of Hitler and Mussolini. This, too, made her unusual for an Asian woman of the period.

Her most unusual trait was being unconventional. She said and did what she thought right and never submitted herself to the standards of others. One small example was her disregard for fashions of the time. When I was small, all little girls pierced their ears. I was the only girl my age who did not; people teased me, calling me a boy. My mother asserted that something fashionable in one country meant little in another, pointing out that "women in the West don't pierce their ears anymore, they wear clips. When my daughter gets in her twenties, people in Vietnam will also wear clips." I surely inherited my mother's straightforwardness and unconventionality. I believe these helped me adjust to new situations.

My parents named us all after birds. My father's uncle named all his sons after trees and his daughters after flowers. Of my sisters and brothers, only ten of us grew to adulthood. Brother number eleven—really ten, but we start with eldest sister as number two—and number fifteen were sent to France in 1947. Many families sent their sons to France so they wouldn't get involved in politics. Otherwise, these youth joined the resistance or were thrown in prison. Father placed a high value on academic performance. My brothers attended Lycée Pétrus Ky. Only two of his daughters—an older sister, who studied at the Couvents des Oiseaux in Da Lat, and me, who attended Lycée Marie Curie—were sent to French schools. We all spoke French but were not at all "Frenchy." Of the two brothers who went to France, one graduated in law, and one returned to finish his studies in public administration. We were the only siblings to graduate from university.

Each sibling took a different path. Sister number two, the eldest, attended Collège Gia Long and, like all pupils in high school in the 1930s, participated in a demonstration for Phan Boi Chau, an ardent anticolonialist the French had put under house arrest in 1925. Expelled from school, she returned to Go Cong and worked in public relations for a pharmaceutical laboratory after her husband, a brilliant doctor and politician, died early. She was like a second mother to us. She decided everything for the family. Brother number three studied English in Shanghai and was a rarity in that he came back around 1936. He worked for Shell Oil. When the French mobilized the youth for military service, my parents made him go back to Go Cong, where he worked as a village notable. He had innovative thinking. But he made the mistake of listening to foreign broadcasts on the radio and told people that, despite the expansion of the Viet Minh, the French would again return to Go Cong—which they did. In 1945, for having communicated with foreign forces, the Viet Minh executed him.

Brother nine finished high school but only because, while he hated math, he was brilliant in languages. He spoke perfect French and English before going abroad. He worked for the French army and the U.S. Embassy in Saigon. Sister ten did not finish high school but was very clever. She was the first to attend Marie Curie and then worked at the U.S. Information Service library and then Viet-My, the Vietnam-American Association, until 1973. Brother eleven, a professional administrator, held important positions in various ministries during the former government and then left for Australia. Brother sixteen worked in real estate and as a court translator in the United States; before he left, he was in the Vietnamese army, where he served as an interpreter, including for General Westmoreland.

Given this family, I could easily have been on the other side, accepted positions in the former regime, and been a refugee in the United States after the war. But life oriented me, step by step, to a totally different road. The deciding event, it turned out, proved to be going to the United States.

I was studying philosophy in the last year of my baccalaureate when people began talking about the marvels of the United States. Until then, studying abroad meant going to France, but I heard the first Vietnamese students were going on scholarships to the United States, and I wanted to try something new. The United States started expanding their embassy and the consular service, and my older sister was among the first local employees working for the U.S. Information Service (USIS). She worked as a librarian in the first USIS library. I enrolled in evening English lessons at the consulate and, along with hundreds of others, applied for a scholarship.

My father warned, "I don't have power or money like other parents to help you. Be careful." I told him this was my personal business and to let me try. Applying on my own may be one reason I won a scholarship, as I learned that most other youth were backed by their parents, who interfered in the application process, which did not go over well. I saw this firsthand when I returned in 1956 and was invited to help interview other applicants, who nearly always came with their parents, usually the father. Or the father came alone first to praise the qualities of the applicant, as well as of their siblings!

Called to my interview at the consulate, I spoke English but couldn't understand something that was being said. Finally, the interviewer and I had to communicate in French. In the meantime, my father worried more and more because the United States was known as a place where people live too freely and without morals. Even with money and family backing, how would I fare all by myself in this dangerous country? He was scared since we were still very traditional. He feared I would lose my soul. At that time, my oldest sister played cards in a group where she met the father of a student on scholarship who suggested, "Why not send Oanh through the Catholic scholarship program; it would be better." I applied and won a scholarship before hearing back from the consulate. My father expressed relief that I would attend a school run by nuns.

I was one of the first two students from Saigon to go on this program to the United States and among the first dozen students anywhere in Vietnam to go on scholarship to the United States. In May 1951, I flew to Viterbo College in Lacrosse, Wisconsin, a school run by Franciscan nuns. A few months later, I received a call from the Institute of International Education in New York informing me that a U.S. government scholarship was available. As far as prestige was concerned, that offer made more sense, but by that time, I was several months into one of the happiest experiences of my life.

I was thrilled to be chosen for the Catholic scholarship and did not know what I was getting myself involved in. Only later did I understand the role played by a Belgian priest, a missionary who worked in Phat Diem, a diocese known as a haven for nationalist-minded Catholics. This priest came to side with the

FIGURE 10. In May 1951, Sister Theodine, the president of Viterbo College in Wisconsin, welcomed Oanh to campus, accompanied by Louise Gerardy of Crossroads Student Center, Chicago. Courtesy of Nguyen Thi Oanh.

Vietnamese against the French, who expelled him. To help Vietnam from the out-side, he proposed to the Vietnamese Council of Bishops a scholarship scheme to send students—Catholic and non-Catholic—to Belgium and the United States to be trained and become future leaders of an independent Vietnam. Quite a few scholarship recipients later did become eminent personalities, on one side or the other.

This wonderful man is Father Emmanuel Jacques Houssard, who retired years later as a pastor in a small parish in Brussels. He may be old, but he stays young in his political and social views. In 1987, I saw him in Brussels after we had been separated nearly thirty years. He took me out to lunch and ordered two ice creams for dessert. When the ice cream came, he gave both to me, saying he was on a diet. All of a sudden, I remembered: one of the things I had liked a lot when I had arrived in the States was ice cream. Father Jacques thought of me as that fan of ice cream from thirty years ago, not the old lady sitting in front of him.

Father Jacques was dedicated, attentive to everyone's needs, and devoted to so-cial causes and to the independence of young countries. He did this all with hu-mor and an absentmindedness that made us laugh. Father Jacques inspired us, young students eager to serve our country. He was a mentor and a friend. He changed us. Without Father Jacques, there probably would be no Oanh; I owe him so much. Vietnam owes many of her brilliant intellectuals to him.

I ended up studying in the United States in part because I was not among the core members of the revolutionary group. I had no political consciousness at all. I followed students like Thanh just because of friendship. Going to the United States reflected a desire for a change from the French. At the time, some of us did not see the United States as the big imperialist, not yet. Some of us thought the United States could be a friend and that, at a minimum, we wanted to look there, too, for practical solutions to develop our country.

Father Jacques and a woman with the scholarship program were assigned to work with foreign students and prepare them to help lead their country in the future. Four of us from Vietnam came to the United States together. Arriving at the Viterbo campus, I saw that the school had hung a welcome sign in my dormitory. I was one of the first three foreign students—a black woman from the South, a Puerto Rican woman, and me. The three of us made a good family. We cared about each other. The young woman from the South was like my little sister, so I learned about problems facing people of color.

I studied sociology. My father wanted me to study medicine—the best profession to make money. I said no, and he counterproposed, "How about pharmacy?" "Oh no," I said. "How about agriculture?" Again I said no. My dream was to go into international relations as I excelled at languages. I planned to study English, French, and other languages to work in the Foreign Service. But on my way to the United States, during a stopover at Orly Airport in Paris, I met a Vietnamese man in charge of the student program in France. He asked, "What will you study?" "I will take languages and foreign relations," I replied. "No," he urged, "to serve the country, you have to be inside the country, not out. Why don't you take sociology?"

On this stopover, I also met Father Jacques, who was then president of the Catholic Student Association in Paris and in charge of the scholarship program. He helped me transfer to another airport to carry on to the United States. I had a chance to see two of my brothers studying in France.

Sociology was a completely new subject for many of us. The idea intrigued me.

At Viterbo, I had to take general education courses the first two years but completed them in one year because of my French baccalaureate. After passing a test, I started the last semester of the second year. The main choice was between education and sociology, but I chose sociology right after the first six months because I was profoundly influenced by the sociology teacher. My dad was so unhappy and lamented, "Social work is the work of nuns and priests!" I had little to do with social work at that time but felt drawn toward human services. I had a wonderful

French teacher and sociology teacher and thought young people need teachers like these who care deeply about young people.

I took a course on social problems in which the teacher gave an introduction, and each student had to choose a problem, read about it, and lecture to the class. I cried because I just could not understand such a strange role reversal. Why didn't the teacher do her work? And how could I get up there and teach in her place? Much later, I got to the point I could not teach any other way than through participatory methods.

The whole atmosphere at Viterbo struck a chord in me. In our Asian civilization, the care for the person is not concrete. It is not a down-to-earth thing. I was touched to be so well received and cared for, and I found the nuns kind and content in their dedicated life. It almost made me want to become a nun. I was thrilled and quickly determined to work in some kind of human service. I had benefited from the service of counseling through my French professor at Marie Curie, Mlle Hithos, who took care of me. At that time, I had many ideas that I could not share with my family. Nobody can talk about this kind of thing to a young girl. Some teachers helped so much I told myself: there must be a profession that helps young people, guides them. Father Jacques talked of service, of dedication, of building up the country. In one letter, he wrote, "The country will need you." Nobody had ever told me that; the eighteen-year-old in me became a different person. I was completely seized by this prospect.

In the winter, I tried to ski but fell all the time. A camp for Vietnamese students was organized near Chicago, where we attended a study session each summer. We all wore Vietnamese dress. I had my own room but shared a common bathroom with my friend Xuyen. We had a lot of fun together. I paid to have a picture taken of me wearing a cowboy outfit and smoking a pipe.

The women in this group wanted to return to Vietnam, and the majority did at first but left later because of their involvement with the previous regime. Some stayed in the United States because they didn't like the regime. All these students are in the States or France; one is near my sister in Virginia, one in California. They went before or after liberation. After 1975, the government did not trust those who had studied abroad, especially in the United States and especially on a Catholic program. I was the only one who did not have a big title, which is why I could stay. Scholarship recipients also included men who became priests and supported the Diem regime. Many became instruments of Diem's regime.

A new movement started to promote indigenization of the hierarchy. There was a Belgian father, Father Lebbe; I wouldn't be surprised if he is canonized one day. As a missionary, he went to China, where he saw awful things under the English domination. Foreign missionaries dominated the whole church. It took a long time for a local priest to be ordained; Father Lebbe thought the bishops should be locals. In 1926, he traveled back to Rome and lobbied for the first ordination of Chinese bishops. He urged the church to start a society of priests who would be completely separate from the ordinary missionary and submit themselves to the local hierarchy. He initiated the Society of the Auxiliary of the Mission (SAM). Father Jacques happened to be one of those and was sent to Vietnam because of his love of Vietnam, his nationalism, and his hope of building Vietnam's future through a scholarship program.

In the church, laity is repressed by the hierarchy. So they started a society of lay auxiliaries, Société des auxiliaires laïque des missions, known as LAM. These were lay people, not nuns. Members of LAM formed international teams to serve the local people. They learned local languages and became acculturated. St. Paul would say, "You have to be Greek with the Greek, Roman with the Romans." One had to integrate culturally into the country.

One of LAM's activities was to start international student centers to serve students coming from those countries. Centers called Crossroads sprang up in Lausanne, Paris, and Chicago. During summer vacations, Father Jacques sent us to the Crossroads in Chicago. I worked during the summers to assist foreign student associations. This is where I learned to be international, to accept all kinds of cultures. Otherwise, I could not be who I am. When I saw all those people, highly dedicated university graduates of different nationalities, I joined them. I was eager to get hands-on training before going back home to work in the mission country—that is, Vietnam. The group of LAM workers influenced me a lot in terms of their progressive views of Catholicism, the world, of working for international peace, dialogue with the Communists, and so on. I wrote to several of them for years.

I was one of the leading students and fostered cooperation among other students. We planned regular conferences and exchanges to discuss international issues of the day. I learned a lot. Running the Crossroads Student Center from eight in the morning until three in the afternoon taught me a lot about work. [Ed. note: In 1991, Denise Snyers, who worked with Oanh at the Crossroads Student Center in 1953, explained over the phone: "The center was more like a home than an institution. The staff welcomed everyone, listened to see what they needed. Student associations used Crossroads as their base since Chicago was a convenient meeting place. Students came and stayed on vacation, cooking their own food. Oanh came several times as a participant and then as staff in 1954–1955. She met regularly with students. She was obviously committed to service. Oanh is a very dear friend."]

One of my teachers was a nun who earned her PhD from Catholic University. She took a train to Chicago each week to attend a class with the eminent social psychologist Carl Rogers. Early on, in 1951, I had the chance to learn about Rogers's spirit and nondirective method in counseling and case work. I later introduced it in our society. Rogers took a radical approach to problems; teaching meant discussing and sharing—a kind of free learning. At first, I was lost, even angry at the unstructured learning process, but later I realized it was one of the most precious things I have received in life.

As I was the first foreign student, the nuns at Viterbo focused a lot on educating me. I became the exotic attraction in town because, besides a Chinese family running a restaurant, there was only a lonely Japanese war bride who spoke no English. I studied English with the head of the English department. I was coached by the head of the Sociology Department and dean of women. I even took home economics classes from the head of that department so as to become a well-rounded person. To introduce Vietnam, they made me sing a song and arranged for the head of the Music Department to help me rehearse. They made me talk on the radio; they made me write articles—all so that I learned as much as possible. I joined a debate group and competed with teams from other universities. They did everything to try and make me a smart person.

I won the 1953–1954 Catholic School Press Association writing contest on creativity. That year, a pastoral letter criticized the lack of creativity among American Catholics. They deplored the new "mechanical brides"—people acting as if programmed by advertisements, to the point they would not bother to think anymore. I found it funny and wrote about a related experience I had after coming down with malaria. I came down with one of the first cases of malaria in Chicago, and the nuns helped me find a doctor with experience in South America, after which I convalesced in the home of a Mrs. Sullivan.

One day, Mrs. Sullivan went shopping and bought an angel food cake mix to show me how Americans cook. When she came back, we opened the box, poured the contents into a bowl, and mixed it with milk. But we came up several spoonfuls short. No problem, I suggested, let's just add water; she didn't dare and insisted we go back to the store and buy more milk. I found that funny. I started my article with my mom making cookies, never using the same recipe twice. I wrote about what I saw as a lack of creativity in the United States. My article, "Getting Back to the Roots," dealt with the great uniformity in thinking in everyday life as a result of mass production and commercials. One time I bought a dress, and when I went for a walk, I met three people wearing the exact same dress. It was a big surprise to me when I became the national prize winner that year. The nuns were happy for me. They had worked hard to train me, and they really loved me.

Back home, we mainly took care of—and were devoted to—family and relatives or close friends. But in the lives of the nuns at Viterbo and the Catholic community in general, I saw that kind of dedication extend to a wider community, to humanity. That was new and inspiring.

I graduated from college at the end of 1954. I was going to continue with social work studies, but then the Geneva Conference caused a lot of refugees to flee as Vietnam was being divided into the North (under Communist control) and the South. That changed my life.

Part 2
WAR AND AFTERMATH
Geneva Accords to Today

French rule in Indochina ended with their decisive May 7, 1954, military defeat at Dien Bien Phu. The Geneva Accords, concluded shortly thereafter, called for a temporary border at the Seventeenth Parallel and a three-hundred-day period for people to migrate north or south, with national elections to be held within two years. In the West, concern grew that Ho Chi Minh would win a national election and add Vietnam to the list of "dominoes" to fall under Communist control.

In 1955, Ngo Dinh Diem, a nationalist and ardent Catholic supported by the Vatican, the United States, and others, deposed Bao Dai, the last king in the Nguyen dynasty, and became president of the Republic of Vietnam. Ngo Dinh Diem launched an anti-Communist offensive that was brutal and repressive and alienated many outside his powerful family and Church circles. His harshest anti-Communist legislation, issued in May 1959—Law 10/59—enabled special military tribunals to imprison and execute anyone for nebulously defined revolutionary activities. Having gained power as a nationalist, Diem was turning into an autocrat. In 1960, the National Front for the Liberation of South Vietnam, or National Liberation Front (NLF), was established to galvanize resistance to the repressive Diem government.

Ngo Dinh Diem was assassinated in 1963. In August 1964, two U.S. destroyers were conducting reconnaissance off the coast of North Vietnam when there were confusing signals of a possible attack by DRV boats. President Johnson was persuaded he needed congressional authority to address Communist aggression. On August 7, 1964, the U.S. Congress passed the Gulf of Tonkin Resolution authorizing military action in the region. U.S. troops poured into Vietnam, reaching a peak of 554,000 within five years. The 1968 Tet Offensive, an assault on U.S. positions by the Viet Cong and the North Vietnamese Army, was a turning point in the war. A military victory for South Vietnam and its Western allies, the offensive exhausted the resistance, and it exposed the depth of opposition to the government of the Republic of Vietnam.

To reconcile a divided Vietnam, delegates from the Republic of Vietnam, United States, Democratic Republic of Vietnam, and National Liberation Front gathered in 1970 for the Paris Peace Talks. A ceasefire agreement was signed in 1973 and the last U.S. troops departed in March. Two years later, North Vietnamese troops infiltrated South Vietnam, culminating with tanks rolling onto the grounds of the Presidential Palace in Saigon. The Socialist Republic of Vietnam was proclaimed in 1976, the same year Saigon was renamed Ho Chi Minh City.

During this tumultuous period, the sisters were scattered and lost touch. Thanh became a diplomat and the right-hand aide to Mme Nguyen Thi Binh, the National Liberation Front's delegate to the Paris Peace Talks. As a reward for her work as an agent in Saigon, Trang received a scholarship to study music at the Tchaikovsky Institute in Moscow. Minh continued to care for her family and juggle teaching and resistance activities. Le An and her artistic troupe split each year between being based in Hanoi and on the move to perform for soldiers wherever needed. Sen and her U.S.-trained husband, a vice minister of health in South Vietnam, steered a complicated course to help people without committing to a political ideology. Tuyen also remained in Saigon, immersing herself in family matters while running a pharmacy and, after 1975, organizing friends and colleagues into associations of health workers and other groups. Lien An lived and taught in Hanoi until 1975, periodically moving her daughters to a rural school to escape U.S. bombing raids; after 1975, she served as headmistress at one of the most prestigious lycées in Ho Chi Minh City. Xuan returned to Saigon from London to teach piano and raise a family, sympathetic to her husband, Lau, as he risked everything as a spy for the Viet Cong. Except when she studied for a master's degree in the Philippines and other training opportunities, Oanh rooted herself in Saigon and found myriad ways to apply her social work experience and skills to help people, especially the disadvantaged.

10

THANH
"We Are, After All, Human Beings"

Drawing on talents she polished at Lycée Marie Curie, Thanh used her love of French and English to serve the National Liberation Front (NLF), the Democratic Republic of Vietnam (DRV), and eventually the Socialist Republic of Vietnam (SRV). Soon after the Geneva Accords, she worked with the foreign relations office in Hanoi and was assigned to escort journalists like Wilfred Burchett and Madeleine Riffaud. Thanh advanced to become the translator and assistant to Mme Nguyen Thi Binh, on the Central Committee of the NLF, founded in 1960. They traveled the world to meet with women's groups, peace groups, and women's peace groups. Highlights included a gathering in Indonesia of Women Strike for Peace, led by the American Mary Clarke, and meeting Betrand Russell in Stockholm.

When Mme Binh, who became the foreign minister of the NLF, arrived at Le Bourget Airport in Paris in 1968 to lead the NLF delegation to the Paris Peace Talks, Thanh was at her side as a crowd heralded their arrival. Thanh was eventually assigned to the Vietnam mission to the United Nations, where, aside from official duties, she recorded old American movies she loved as a child.

Throughout her diplomatic career, Thanh made immense personal sacrifices. Her husband stayed behind in Hanoi, and they divorced. She feared for her daughter, who had to be sent to school in the countryside to avoid U.S. bombing raids of Hanoi. She felt inadequate in caring for two sons with serious medical conditions; she did arrange to be assigned to East Germany in hopes of getting medical help for a son's schizophrenia, but it made no difference.

Dubbed "Political Mother" by the sisters, Thanh rarely second-guessed her utter devotion to the revolution.

Thanh

Those of us who regrouped from the South to the North were given special courses. Since we were having our first encounter with winter, we were given wool clothes. We wore padded clothes. The first time we passed through Hanoi at night, I caught glimpses of Bach Mai Hospital and the Lake of the Sacred Sword. On January 1, 1955, a big demonstration took place to celebrate the victory. It combined militants, youth of the North, and the *tap ket*, the united contingent of those regrouped from the South. Wearing rubber sandals, those of us from the maquis practiced marching the day before. We paraded in front of Uncle Ho in Hanoi for the first time.

Father had spent many years doing his part in the fight against the French. In the 1930s and early 1940s, while working with the Public Works Department in An Giang, southwest of Saigon, Father had been put in charge of sabotage activities—cutting electric wires, blocking water pipes, finding ways to impede boat traffic on the rivers. Whenever French authorities came to inspect his office, he had to hide. The French suspected him and put a huge bounty on the head of Nguyen Van Duc. At this time, the future president Ton Duc Thang became a close friend. When Ton Duc Thang was imprisoned on Poulo Condore, Father took care of his wife, children, and friends. [Ed. note: Ton Duc Thang, 1888–1980, started out with the French navy before becoming a revolutionary and being imprisoned by the French in the 1930s. Elected to the Party Central Committee in 1951, he went on to become president of the DRV after the death of Ho Chi Minh in 1969.] They met again in 1945, after Father vanished into the bush to hide. Ton Duc Thang came to inspect the base where my father hid and told him: "You should not go into the maquis. Someone like you is needed in town. The information you can lay hands on—maps, roads, arteries—is invaluable." Dad put on a black baba jacket, disguised himself as a fish vendor, and rowed a canoe away from the bush and back to Saigon.

Upon release from prison, Father resumed his activities. He got a map of the Saigon sewer system for the resistance to use to chart escape routes after attacks on urban targets. When the resistance targeted the Ben Luc Bridge, a vital passageway between Saigon and the Mekong Delta, they asked him to help sabotage it. Only he could pinpoint the weak spots in which to place the dynamite. As his granddaughter Autumn observed, "Grandfather built bridges by day and blew them up by night!" Police arrested him after the bridge bombing and jailed him again for three months. They had no proof, and he never admitted to the sabotage. They warned him: "Even if you didn't do it, we know you have two daughters in the Viet Cong."

Back in Saigon, Father started a school in 1955 called Duc Tri (morality, intellect). He had found a job for at least one son of each of his brothers. Placing relatives and friends in jobs was known as *caser les gens*. In 1956, he approached the authorities in Saigon who had sought him out because he was a good engineer; however, An Giang Province police alerted their Saigon colleagues about his earlier resistance activities, and he returned to An Giang in handcuffs and spent fourteen months there.

Mother, meanwhile, faced her own challenges. With me in Hanoi and Trang working for the resistance in the South, she decided one year not to list our names on the city census report. On the birth certificates of Trang's daughter and my first son, she wrote, "Father unknown." For an upstanding, conservative family, this was hard. It looked bad, and it pained Mother to do it.

Soon after arriving in Hanoi, I volunteered to work in the international relations service to receive foreign correspondents. Though I had not spoken French in three or four years, I remembered it. I liked English very much. As a schoolgirl, I always came in first in my English class. At times of great upheaval, including the arrival of the Japanese, when schools closed and we stayed home—not even at home but at a friend's house that was safer—Minh and I read *Alice in England*. I would cover a word with my hand and practice how it sounded in English. Even without a teacher, I learned a lot of new words. I liked learning on my own.

The first two foreign correspondents to visit liberated Hanoi right after Dien Bien Phu were Wilfred Burchett from Australia and Madeleine Riffaud from France. I was assigned to escort Riffaud, the first Western woman journalist to come to Hanoi in 1955; she wrote for the French weekly *La Vie Ouvrière* (Life of the working class). At twenty-two, I had my first experience as a guide and interpreter. I quickly recouped my French. The work was successful; she appreciated my work and liked me.

I later learned that Riffaud had fallen in love with Nguyen Dinh Thi, a writer and officer whom she had met in Berlin in 1950 at a youth conference. He was the youngest member of the National Assembly of the Democratic Republic of Vietnam and wrote and composed well-known songs for Radio Vietnam. After he left Hanoi for the maquis, they met again. The party told him their love was not feasible. When Riffaud came to Hanoi in 1955, I visited her hotel room and saw his picture on her nightstand. He had married a doctor he didn't love. When I worked in Paris in the 1960s, Madeleine told me she thought of the morals of revolutionaries as puritan and moral, not the kind to have love affairs. She found Thi beautiful and elegant and said she knew no other militant like him. He would become secretary-general of the arts. After Thi wrote a novel in 1972, Madeleine visited Vietnam again, and they translated it together. I think it is a touching story how the two of them created literature together.

Other foreign delegations, especially from socialist countries, followed. I interpreted at meetings arranged for International Women's Day in 1955, when I was

assigned a delegate from India. I did the work of guide and interpreter at countless conferences.

I also worked as a translator in the foreign languages publishing house in Hanoi. While my French was better, I chose to translate in English to perfect my English. Two Australian experts, a husband and wife, came to help correct translations of texts and stories from Vietnamese into English. I ended up working at
the publishing house for ten years.

The struggle against the Americans was already intense in the South. [Ed. note:
In 1956, the United States took over training the Vietnamese military from the
French. Diem announced the Geneva-mandated elections would not be held and
converted the State of Vietnam into the Republic of Vietnam, with him as president. Under Eisenhower, U.S. economic assistance to Diem resulted in a depen-
dent South Vietnamese client state.] The NLF had been founded on December 12,
1960. I knew there would be a lot of diplomatic work to carry out, and in 1965, I
was called to work in the front. It made sense to travel for work from Hanoi
because if I left from the South and had to travel back north each time with a bag
on my back, it would be impossibly hard. It took too long and caused a lot of
fatigue. For most of the time, I was based in Hanoi.

It made me happy to participate directly in the liberation of South Vietnam.
The first time I left the country with a delegation was on a trip to Jakarta to meet a
group of ten women from Women Strike for Peace, headed by Mary Clarke. I accompanied a delegation of ten women from Vietnam—five from the North and
five from the union of women for the liberation of southern Vietnam. Mme
Nguyen Thi Binh, a member of the Central Committee of the NLF and vice president of the Union of Women for Liberation, led the southern delegation. [Ed. note:
Binh, born in 1927, traveled the world from 1962 to 1969 as the face and voice of
the NLF. She became the chief NLF negotiator at the Paris Peace Talks. She would
become minister of education and vice president of the DRV.] Sukarno, Indonesia's first president, who had led the struggle against the Dutch colonialists, was in
power. Hosted by the Women's Union of Indonesia, this gathering allowed us to
discuss issues together over five or six days. We described our long history of struggle for liberation and the way women have participated in this tradition of struggle. Women Strike for Peace members appeared sympathetic and said they would
campaign to bring U.S. troops home and demonstrate to end the war.

Among the group, I met a young woman with Students for a Democratic Society who asked, "What do the people of South Vietnam think about Ho Chi
Minh?" [Ed. note: Students for a Democratic Society was started in 1960 to support civil rights and organize the urban poor and became the leading campus-
based antiwar organization. It established four hundred chapters on U.S. colleges,
organized teach-ins, and ran a draft-resistance program.] I was so moved I could

not speak. My throat was tight. I cried and could not answer. The Diem government was terrorizing and repressing all patriots, even children who felt love in their hearts for Ho Chi Minh. Those who dared voice their patriotism were even executed. A story circulated about a young boy in prison, where his guards put a picture of Ho Chi Minh on the floor and told him to walk on it: "To be set free, you must walk on the picture; otherwise, you will stay in prison." The boy refused, tip-toed carefully around the picture, and was kept in jail. I also remembered when bank bills in liberated zones were printed with the photo of Ho Chi Minh. After the puppet administration came and controlled everything, they burned the bills—but old peasants hid them, even buried them, just to hang onto an image of the revolution. All at once, I thought of the young boy and old peasants and how much they loved Ho Chi Minh; I could not talk. That's why I cried. Asked that question on my first trip out of the country, I found I could not answer. After calming down, I explained myself to the young American woman.

From 1965 on, I served as Mme Binh's assistant as she attended women's congresses all over the world, starting with the Congress of the International Federation of Democratic Women held in Austria. We represented the NLF and the Democratic Republic of Vietnam, which sent a delegation of women from Hanoi. We received a warm welcome and expressions of support for our struggle against the Americans. At the end of 1965, the French Women's Union invited us to attend their congress. We landed in Paris to a triumphant welcome.

Mme Binh and I visited most of the socialist countries in Europe. Four of us—Mme Binh, Mme Ma Thi Chu, Mme Dung, and I—traveled on many diplomatic missions in Western countries. We met with organizers of peace movements in London, Switzerland, and Belgium, among others. We all spoke French, which proved a big help. Women in a French youth movement welcomed us, and we visited French families to talk about the struggle of women in South Vietnam. These groups often provided aid, medicines, and warm clothing to send to the maquis. A movement of solidarity seemed to unite around the world.

In 1965, when I was asked to go on diplomatic missions to other countries, I had the sense that I had a gift; I spoke English, I spoke French, and I found it easy to talk about our struggle. Mme Binh was very satisfied to have my assistance, saying she would be unable to find anybody better. It continued like that: each time I returned, after a month or so, it was again time to pack a suitcase. [Ed. note: In her autobiography published in 2012, *Gia Din, Ban Be, Dat Nuoc* (Family, friends, nation), Mme Binh recalls meeting Thanh, "an excellent Lycée Marie Curie student who was very active and became my assistant on diplomatic missions." Thanh appears in many photos, including at the microphone during Mme Binh's heralded arrival at Le Bourget Airport for the Paris Peace Talks in 1968 and with Mme Binh in front of NLF offices in Verrieres-le-Buissons in 1973.]

Unlike when I went to the maquis and my asthma stopped, living in humid Hanoi triggered many attacks because Hanoi winters are extremely humid. But then, after travel and many plane rides, my asthma disappeared again. I was happy about the trips.

I still wrote poetry. I had to travel far on work trips and missed Saigon. I had been gone from Saigon since when I went into the maquis at the age of fifteen. I wrote a poem about my hometown, how I remembered the tamarind trees and being a schoolgirl riding my bicycle along the tree-lined streets, remembering all the names of the streets—even the numbers of houses at each corner of the streets. While traveling for the National Liberation Front, I witnessed moving scenes of people in solidarity at various conferences and wrote about them. When I returned from trips, Radio Liberation asked me about them, and I wrote short stories that they broadcast and newspapers published.

My work felt natural to me. In 1968, I was quickly designated to be part of the delegation to Paris for the peace conference. Even before I left to be stationed in Paris, the bombing of Hanoi started. [Ed. note: In 1965, the United States had deployed 3,500 Marines to Da Nang, and President Johnson authorized an air campaign called Operation Rolling Thunder, which continued between March 1965 and October 1968. About 525,000 Americans were serving in Vietnam by 1968.] I sent our children to the countryside, where each family in a village took in two or three students from a class that had to evacuate. Students wore thickly woven straw helmets and coats for protection from bombs. Peasants stitched and braided the straw tightly to avoid tiny pieces breaking off during explosions and piercing the skin. They knotted long rows of plaited straw tightly together.

On Sundays, I bicycled thirty or forty kilometers to see the children. I left at four in the morning, in the dark, to avoid the bombing. Reaching their village around nine, I bathed them and cooked, and we ate together. I tried to prepare something different from their strict daily diet. Around three or four in the afternoon, I rode back and reached Hanoi at seven or eight. All mothers did this; that's what Sundays were for. Sometimes my husband came; sometimes he had work.

While I worked in Paris, my husband took care of the children. He lived in Hanoi and visited them on weekends. Colleagues and I received letters from our children that described life in the countryside and their friends. Whereas we city girls had known nothing about the countryside when we joined the maquis, my daughter knew about it and proudly shared the life of peasants. She marched up to the master of the house where she lived and offered to help harvest the crops. She carried two baskets attached to a pole that stretched across the back of her neck. Despite being so little, she was able carry the load, and it made her feel proud. She caught crabs in the rice paddies and learned to swim and cross rivers. Sharing the life of peasants inspired pride. At the end of her stay, the peasants gave her a few sweet potatoes that tasted delicious; when we have little to eat, everything tastes delicious.

One of the children who continued their studies in villages during the bombings was Dang Thai Son, the pianist who won the Chopin prize in 1986. People and instruments from the conservatory he went to were dispersed into the countryside. The piano was lowered into a trench for protection. He learned to play the piano in a trench! He was so talented, as was his mother, who continued to teach piano in the countryside.

Traveling to Paris with Mme Binh, we flew from Hanoi through Peking and Moscow. In May 1968, following the Tet Offensive, the Americans agreed to negotiate with the North Vietnamese. The early days were spent debating the shape of the table: Should it be square or rectangular? Cyrus Vance is one of the U.S. diplomats I remember at this time. Finally, it was decided the table should be round! The Democratic Republic of Vietnam always told South Vietnam their adversary was the NLF, and they should speak directly with them, the Viet Cong. In the end, the Americans had to accept to talk with us. The DRV and the NLF sat on one side, and on the American side, they were joined by the fantoches, the puppet government in Saigon.

The arrival in Paris of our delegation, led by Mme Binh, caused a sensation. A huge number of journalists waited at Le Bourget Airport, swelling the crowd that included Vietnamese living in France who detested the American intervention in Vietnam and supported an independent Vietnam. While still en route, in Moscow, the head of the North Vietnamese delegation wrote to warn us, "When you arrive, hang on to your glasses, so they aren't broken, and be sure to wear sturdy shoes." A security cordon had been set up to manage the crowd, which included people curious to see a woman leading the Viet Cong delegation! People wanted to see this NLF delegation: this faceless force, these phantom figures. Mme Binh read her declaration in Vietnamese, and I read it in French. It was a moment of triumph. The declaration recognized the sacrifice of our comrades that helped lead to the Americans accepting the NLF presence at the conference; it refuted those who always said we were lackeys, the "tail of the North." Instead, here we stand, representing a real force that waged a war of liberation.

The press printed a big photo spread of Mme Binh. People seemed stunned to see this photogenic woman, so beautiful, so noble. Journalists admired her.

We stayed in Paris until the final signature in 1973. [Ed. note: Thanh used the pseudonym Pham Thi Thanh Van while working in Paris.] One of the difficult periods was in 1972 when Kissinger put pressure on us to sign statements that would be harmful to our side. Throughout these years, many people invited us to conferences in their countries. Groups came from the United States to see Mme Binh, such as Cora Weiss, her husband and children, and Barbara Fuller, with

Clergy and Laymen Concerned. We talked about how the struggle was organized in the liberated zone in South Vietnam.

I wanted to bring my children to Paris, but they stayed back home for security. We had heard about the dreadful My Lai massacre. [Ed. note: The My Lai massacre, on March 16, 1968, was the most notorious atrocity of the war; U.S. troops killed approximately five hundred unarmed civilians. The military initially covered up the slaughter.] Even in the North, the bombing was continuing. I worried constantly about the children attending school in a village. One day, I read a big newspaper story about villages destroyed by bombs in the area where my children lived. I lost my head. I became crazed with grief, knowing there was nothing I could do. Colleagues consoled me, urging me to calm down. "Maybe your children weren't there at the time," they said. "Parts of the village were not destroyed." Everyone worried they had lost a family member. Among the twenty or so of us in the provisional revolutionary government, each and every one of us worried. Then the bombings ceased. Many B-52s had been shot down. It was called *DBP en l'air* (the Dien Bien Phu of the skies). Antiaircraft weapons fired back. Finally, a cable arrived saying no close relatives had been killed.

It was a miracle. Everyone breathed.

Later, I asked my children how they had survived. My daughter said there were cold December nights when there was no heating and she had to wear padded cotton clothes. Teachers alerted them when to go into the trenches, and she would dive into the bunkers. Some nights she resisted, shouting, "It's cold!" and ignored them, saying, "I am staying under the covers; if we go into the trenches, it will be too cold." She was an innocent.

Sometimes, the children saw the defenses shoot at planes that plunged to the ground. The next day, children ran out to see the planes, as though it was a show. They were just children. After two years in Paris, I went back for one month of vacation. Just one month in four years—but it was more than the others who could not return at all. An exception was made for me as Mme Binh's translator; it was too hard to go four years without seeing the children.

Once, a colleague at the Paris talks had to leave suddenly. She thought she was being assigned an important mission back in Hanoi. What she did not know was that her husband had been killed in a bombing in Hanoi. Nobody dared tell her; everybody knew but could not tell her because they liked her so much. We went to see her off at the airport. People broke into tears, and she suspected something. People tried to hide the news at any cost; they struggled to stay strong, firm. It was only back in Hanoi that she learned about her husband's death.

During periods of intense bombing, the Voice of Vietnam radio station kept airing to encourage people to stay strong. One the most famous *speakerines* (announcers) for the Voice was our friend from Lycée Marie Curie Suong. I lost sight of her for a few years, but she returned from London to Hanoi and started broad-casting on the Voice. She had excellent diction and knew how to speak naturally on the radio. During the worst of the bombing, it was dangerous to stay in town, and many people working at the Voice fled to the countryside. But Suong stayed. She was very courageous. The Voice did not go silent.

Suong's mother, Mme Tuong, could not know much about her daughter's years in Hanoi because it was hard to receive news from the North with the border closed at the Seventeenth Parallel. Suong was given an award for her broadcast-ing work during the war, though posthumously.

In 1967, I visited Stockholm with a group of young people from South Viet-nam. We went to meet Americans and others exiled from their countries for be-ing draft resisters. Sweden, as a very democratic country, welcomed the exiles. Several young men told us they were on the side of the liberation. I was touched by meeting a young American who did not want to fight, who refused to go to war and accepted living in exile in Stockholm. I was so moved that, as at other touching encounters, I cried. He was surprised to see a woman in her midthirties be so emotional, but I could not restrain myself. I thought of this young man far from home and friends, self-exiled to resist the war. I collected myself, and we talked.

The Swedish government, led by Prime Minister Olof Palme, advocated for progressive ideas. The Swedes organized large congresses and conferences to sup-port Vietnam. A delegation came from the United States for the Bertrand Russell Tribunal, and I had the chance to meet Russell and other major figures who de-nounced the crimes of the United States in Vietnam. Judges from different coun-tries participated. [Ed. note: The British lawyer and activist Bertrand Russell, who wrote *War Crimes in Vietnam*, organized the 1967 International War Crimes Tri-bunal that took place over two sessions, one each in Stockholm and Copenha-gen. Twenty-five participants, from eighteen countries, included Jean Paul Sar-tre, David Dellinger, and James Baldwin. The tribunal condemned the United States for war crimes.]

Around the time I became known as a specialist in the antiwar movement, Czechoslovakia offered to host a meeting between the Americans and the Viet-namese. A dozen of us met with forty Americans, including Dave Dellinger, a leader in the antiwar movement. We met with those involved in the Mobilization to End the War, formed in 1967 to oppose the war.

Between 1965 and 1975, I continued working in diplomacy for the NLF. Over and over, I traveled on missions and returned. I spent the duration of the Peace Talks, four years, in Paris. I participated in weekly press conferences that followed each session; over 140 sessions were held. There were occasional scenes worthy of the theater! Viet Kieu, Vietnamese living in Paris, would stand waiting from five in the morning—NLF flags fluttering in hand—just to see Mme Binh drive up and step out of the car or, at Le Duc Tho's last press conference, journalists starting spontaneously to clap. One of the exchanges at the negotiating table I can't forget is the Americans playing their last card, more bombing, and our side responding, "*This* is how you negotiate?" The Americans could never admit that, while their army had a good image after helping the Allies defeat the Nazis in World War II, their army played a different role in this war. Now it was the contrary.

We were part of the provisional revolutionary government formed in 1969 and recognized by many Communist countries. During the Paris Peace Talks, we rented a house next to a small lake in the suburbs of Paris. For four years, I looked out on that lake, home to a family of swans. I was witness to quite a few generations of swans.

After the Paris Peace Treaty was signed in 1973, I returned to Vietnam and worked in the foreign ministry, first in Hanoi and later in Ho Chi Minh City. I had my first assignment in New York at the United Nations General Assembly (UNGA) in 1978. Each year, the ministry sent four or five of us to help out; we arrived in September and left when the assembly ended in December. I worked at UNGA in 1978, 1979, 1980, and 1981. In 1985, I started a three-year assignment as counselor in our UN mission. At UN committee meetings, delegates from the United States attacked and insulted us. The United States was bitter about failing and wanted to punish us with all measures. I may harbor a sense of betrayal by Americans because of my three years at the United Nations and their primitive response, as reflected in a widely circulated joke: Vietnam should have declared war on the United States and, twenty-four hours later, quickly declared surrender so that maybe then, as with Germany and Japan, the United States would engage and be forthcoming.

While living in New York, I used a videocassette recorder to tape old movies. I looked for classics like *Waterloo Bridge*, with Robert Taylor and Vivian Leigh. It is a romantic story. I could not get it because it ran so late on the classics channel. I did record *Gone with the Wind*, which I loved very much. I waited for *A Song to Remember* to show again but could not find it; maybe it was too old. I also looked for all the films about composers, like one about Beethoven.

I had just come home from the United Nations one year when my son died. His sister and I are marked by his death.

By 1989, I had returned to Ho Chi Minh City and worked with the Union of Friendship Organizations that is based in Hanoi with a branch in Ho Chi Minh City. The union is officially charged with receiving aid and hosting delegations from nongovernmental organizations. The union groups friendship associations from different countries; we have the Vietnam-USSR association and associations with Laos, Kampuchea, Cuba, Philippines, Thailand, India, and others. A friendship association with France was initiated, in addition to one with the United States that will be with the people of the United States because we believe people need to understand each other. We need to conduct normal exchanges. The union president is my old boss, Mme Nguyen Thi Binh; she has been my boss for decades! I thought that had ended after she became minister of education and was elected to the National Assembly.

I try to make time to write and read. The director of the Museum of Women wants to bring women who participated in the resistance together to compile a history of their activities; they asked me to write a chapter on women in diplomacy that was aimed at gaining the support of people around the world. Only Mme Binh, I, and two or three others had time to work on it.

I used my French while with the Institute of Cultural Exchanges with France that invited French guests to a presentation of traditional Vietnamese music and theater based on mythology and legends. This kind of theater is highly stylized and hard to explain to foreign audiences. Mr. Tu, a colleague, and I edited the text and explained the gestures and movements—each of which conveys a lot of meaning. We managed to do it, and everyone involved got along well since we liked French and we liked theater. [Ed. note: In an interview, Mr. Tu observed: "After a long political career, Thanh still kept her artistic sense. She could have lost it; to sustain and protect that freshness and openness to artistic endeavors, one needs to be sensitive. It is a matter of heart. Politicians often imitate others and appreciate art in a superficial way. But you can see Thanh is from an intellectual family with an extraordinary musical and cultural background. She is animated and motivated by artistic works. She appreciate arts—not for appearances but because she has the temperament of an artist."]

If I have time, I would like to write for the theater . . . screenplays . . . literature. But I still have a debt to pay in writing a chapter on women diplomats. There is always a duty before you can do something for yourself, for your own enjoyment.

I also like to translate books, but it's exhausting because I get caught up in the characters! I can only translate about ten pages a day. One of the French writers who made a deep impact is Marguerite Duras; she was born in Vietnam and grew up in a poor family. She understood so much. I was glad a translation into Vietnamese of Duras's *Un barrage contre le Pacifique* (*The Sea Wall*) was published in 1995. It was a revelation to read it and realize that whites, too, were exploited by the French and that layers of society existed within the French community. It's the story of a family struggling to live off the land that is being mercilessly devoured by the sea. Duras wrote about poor children left to take care of themselves who ate green mangoes or drank from a lake and died. It is an unvarnished sketch of the crude living conditions of poor whites.

I had some gifts, certain abilities, others do not have. Generally, my talents have been well matched with my career. I was able to use them in the service of the country. Of course, I also paid a price.

My father built our house in 1933 and kept it, so his children would always have their real home to return to. Trang and I returned in 1975. My daughter, after training to be an architect in the USSR, also came back to this house.

In 1994, forty-four years after the fact, I traveled west toward Tay Ninh on the same road I took to the maquis in 1950. This time, I rode in the luxury of a car and found the green of the countryside relaxing. Seeing the straight lines of rubber trees reminded me of two students in the maquis, married just two months, who took part in an ambush on a French rubber plantation. He escaped, but she was wounded and taken captive.

Continuing to drive west, I saw that the site of our old base was flooded by a lake formed by a huge hydroelectric power project. The area used to be thickly forested! After 1975, people in the province cut the big trees down to sell. It makes me angry to think of tourists at nearby Cu Chi, the Viet Cong tunnel network outside of Saigon, paying a dollar to pull a trigger on a target. It's no good for Americans to fire guns on Viet Cong, or vice versa.

I've done a lot of things for the revolution, especially diplomatic work in Paris, through 1973 and the signing of the Peace Accords ending the American war. I witnessed historic moments.

I inherited a sense of duty. In the struggle for liberation, many people gave their lives and the lives of their children. They have not known what it is to live in peace. Many courageous intellectuals from Saigon were imprisoned, tortured, and killed. After the return of peace, there were temptations around money, which brought some of them down. Most people in the struggle did not accumulate wealth. They remained simple. We owe them a lot. When my father was put in prison, he wrote to my mother: "All is lost, except honor." Mother remained strong. They agreed they could not give up. In our family, we don't have a taste for money. We stayed very simple.

When we went into the resistance, it was for the people and for the cause. It is hard to talk about our own needs. If you go to the Museum of Women in Revolution, you see women who survived terrible torture and made unspeakable sacrifices. How can we talk about our own tiny sacrifices? I lost little compared to others who lost their lives, their children, and never knew what it's like to live in peace.

Of course, we all had private lives and emotions but had to suppress them. But we are, after all, human beings.

11

TRANG

"Prepared for Any Sacrifice or Risk"

At the time of the Geneva Accords, Trang was pregnant and did not join her husband when he boarded a boat to the North. Communication between north and south was cut. In 1956, the resistance asked her to take an alias and live with another agent and serve as a liaison. At first, her daughter, Autumn, lived with her. But after Trang was arrested and jailed for nine months, Autumn moved in with Aunt Minh at the family compound. For years, Trang caught only glimpses of her daughter, who came to think of Aunt Minh as her mother.

In 1961, to reward Trang for her sacrifice, the government in Hanoi arranged for her to study music in the Soviet Union. But the Sino-Soviet split deepened as both competed to be the leader of world Communism; as a result, Asian students were expelled from the USSR, and Trang traveled by train to Hanoi. As Sino-Soviet ties mended, Trang was able to complete her studies and graduate from the Tchaikovsky Institute in 1968, the only Vietnamese in her class to complete a degree in conducting. Back in Hanoi, she learned her husband had died in the fighting during the Tet Offensive. His friends gave her his diary.

Trang

When my husband, Tan, and I parted after the Geneva Accords, we did not know how long we would be separated. He disembarked at the port city of Haiphong and took charge again of a military song-and-dance ensemble, which regrouped in Hanoi. He told me he scanned the ships along the docks, searching for a familiar figure among the lines of people coming ashore or huddling on the quays. As the end of the three-hundred-day period for people to resettle approached, he calculated the arrival date of the last ships bringing combatants from the South. But I was not on any of them.

Beginning in October 1954, contact and communication between people north and south of the Seventeenth Parallel were cut. Our daughter, Autumn, and I lived together in the family compound from November 1954 until June 1956, when the struggle for independence forced a change. I was prepared for any sacrifice or risk even as I assured authorities that I had no involvement with the resistance. I decided to try and live in Saigon inconspicuously and resumed activities with the inner-city tendrils of the resistance. My alias required me to live as a couple with another agent with whom I shared a house in a quiet neighborhood. This haven provided the security I needed in which to copy proresistance documents to distribute throughout the city.

I had a second child, a son; occasionally, my baby boy and Autumn spent the night with the agent and me in the suburbs. I knew it was risky as our clandestine work meant the children could not live with us. One evening the police raided the house, entered the bedroom, and arrested us. I quickly made up a story, telling the police the children belonged to the neighbors and would know their way back home. I whispered in Autumn's ear that I hoped to avoid the worst; she stood in the road with her little half-brother as I disappeared in the police van. [Ed. note: Autumn later described this scene: "The last time Mother 'borrowed' me and my brother overnight, she was arrested. She whispered Grandmother's address in my ear and told me to run to our neighbors. Shock turned into fear; being only old enough to begin to talk, I forgot the address. After a few days at the neighbors, I remembered a clue. Mother said something about the 'house with the coconut tree.' The neighbors took me to residential areas, so I could identify a familiar coconut tree. Eventually, I picked it out. Ten days had passed. I reached home looking scraggly and dirty. But the family was so glad to see me."]

The other agent and I were released after several weeks. I remained high on the list of suspected resistance agents, and the next time I was arrested, they put me through starvation, solitary confinement, and interrogations that ended with a hail of baton lashes that left fist-sized purple welts. Through everything, I defended myself, saying my life revolved around a new beginning with my family.

Meanwhile, Autumn—after months of living with my parents and my sister Minh—began to think of them as her parents. Minh and my mother once brought her to the prison to see me. Autumn says she remembers the visit for two reasons: it was the first time she saw her grandmother cry, and for years to come, the jingling of prison chains rattled like a soundtrack in her nightmares.

I spent nine months in jail, including the Tet New Year of 1956. As soon as I was released, I planned to resume resistance activities. Autumn stayed at the family compound. I arranged to stop by the house for an hour or two to see her, until my police tail required more inventive arrangements. Our friend Le An's villa was right around the corner from our house; I gave Le An a message with a specific time she should put Autumn in a baby carriage in front of her house. At that time, I would stroll down Rue Léon-Combes—a short street made narrow by tall trees lining both sidewalks—and casually stop at the crib. I smiled at my girl and coaxed a return smile from her. I held her pudgy hands and stroked her round cheeks. I slipped a camera out of my handbag and took several photos. I saw her like this— five or ten minutes on my way to work—before walking on, my pace quickening as I approached the bustling boulevard Rue Verdun.

In November 1957, I made a plan to attend Autumn's third birthday party. On occasion, it was considered safe enough to have a daylong reunion or even spend the night at the family house. The family called it being a visiting mother. I also passed written notes home via trusted friends and colleagues. I constantly inquired about Autumn.

The government arranged for me to study in the Soviet Union. My natural talents lay in music, and officials understood the usefulness of cultivating the arts. I traveled to the Soviet Union in 1961. The day I left, Tan appeared at the train station with a present: a box of candied tangerines. I did not open the box. Boarding the train to the Chinese border, I dared only snatch glances back at him.

I arrived in Moscow and enrolled at the Tchaikovsky Institute to learn how to conduct choirs. To relieve my homesickness, I strolled under the birch trees draped in snow that lined the Moskva River. Outside of class, other Vietnamese students and I explored the city, taking pictures of each other in front of statues of Tchaikovsky, Pushkin, and Rimsky-Korsakov. I spent half of my seven years in Moscow living in a dull gray apartment building near the music institute. I made friends, including with my Hungarian roommate, Chinese students, and a Greek sculptor who played the piano. Another colleague, who had been in the jungle with Thanh, studied music in Sofia, where he wrote a symphony dedicated to South Vietnam's struggle against invaders called *Que Huong* (Homeland).

In the fall of 1962, Thanh transited Moscow en route to a conference in Guinea to interpret for Mme Nguyen Thi Binh. We carved out time to visit Red Square and catch up on family news.

As students abroad, we liked to organize excursions. One day, we took a bus out of town to picnic in the sprawling gardens at Peredelkino, Tolstoy's home. For vacation in 1963, a group of us traveled to Kiev, where I rowed a small boat down the willow-lined Dnieper River. I wrote a letter to the family, enclosed a picture of me rowing, and gave it to a friend going to France so that the letter would not appear to have been mailed from the Soviet Union. A friend in France served as our family's mailbox. Outside of Kiev, I joined a handful of students who dared to go skiing, which I found tiring but fun.

I did not receive any written news from Saigon until early 1964 when a letter arrived from Autumn. It was in French, which made me worry she wasn't learning Vietnamese. I admonished my family for not sending Autumn to a Vietnamese school.

After the Sino-Soviet split, Asian students attending Soviet schools, especially those of us studying the humanities, were expelled. I flew to Peking and took the train to Hanoi in the fall of 1964. Thanh and Suong met me at the station and tried to whisk me away from the attentions of a suitor who had come to greet me. [Ed. note: After she had lived with an agent in Saigon and then studied abroad, Tan had found someone else.] I ignored their warnings that he had a reputation as a playboy. Thanh and Suong wanted to protect me; they worried I was vulnerable after moving around so much and being separated from my children. They feared that "at the sight of open arms, you will be swallowed up by them."

I moved in with Suong and fell into a period of seclusion. A friend told me she would find me sitting alone knitting, bundled in a sweater with a scarf covering my hunched shoulders. On some days, Suong told her, I barely moved; if a friend walked in the apartment, I murmured, "Ah, it's you," buried my chin back in my chest, and kept knitting. Only two topics sparked my interest: news of the army moving south and teaching music.

When ties between China and the Soviet Union were bandaged, I was among the Vietnamese students able to return and complete our studies in Moscow. In 1968, I graduated from the Tchaikovsky Institute. In a class of hundreds, I was the one Vietnamese who became a conductor.

A year later, I heard about Tan's death as he came south in the Tet Offensive and vowed to collect and compile everything written by and about him. I had diaries and a handful of belongings. He wrote poetry and short stories using the pen name Nguyen Thi. He described things he saw on the front lines of the fight against the Americans. Many of his works won awards, such as *A Woman with a Gun*, about a mother of five who is pregnant but goes to the front, where she is killed in action. His books are read in public schools. A friend of Tan's told me he built a small table and chair for Autumn and placed a single item on the table: her picture.

I returned to Saigon two months after the Communists took control in 1975. I discovered many changes in the cityscape; buildings were destroyed, damaged, or newly constructed. Streets seemed far more crowded. Many places and streets were renamed. A lot seemed transformed except our family home, which stood back from the hubbub of what had been Rue Verdun, later to be renamed Cach Mang Thang Tam after the August Revolution. Parc Maurice Long was renamed *Cong Vien Van Hoa*, Public Park of Culture. After being away fifteen years, I had trouble recognizing members of the family, especially my daughter.

Autumn was twenty years old and had graduated from Lycée Marie Curie and studied at the Institute of Foreign Languages, where it showed she inherited our family's gift for languages. Friends say she is a mirror image of me. By this time, the situation had been clarified: Minh was her aunt, not her mother.

After 1975, a group of Tan's friends who were writers in the army brought his diary from Hanoi and gave it to me. Time had gnawed at the borders of the yellow pages; I couldn't be sure if the onionskin paper had been yellow, tan, or even pink. I keep a black-and-white photo of him, hardly bigger than a matchbox, marked, "Tan departs Cao Lanh, November 1954." I have a picture of Thanh and me in the jungle when I'm six months pregnant and Tan made me hold a towel in front of my stomach. Near the beginning of the diary, Tan wrote:

> Something has happened in my life.
>
> I have someone to whom I can pour out my feelings. With warmth, and with strength.
>
> I have known Trang since 1950 when we were in the countryside of Ben Cat. As usual, on the eve of every major attack on enemy outposts or convoys, the company performed an artistic program with artists from the High Command. Very inspired, I shared one of my poems and sang, "I think of you, my loved one." Maybe it's because Trang played her accordion so well. Fascinated by her music, I suddenly felt a vague feeling for her, unknown until now . . . the natural feeling of a young man hungry for love. . . .
>
> Time passes. I see her from time to time in meetings before or after battles. Each time, Trang and her music seem more beautiful than ever. But these are still just the joyful emotions of a young adolescent.
>
> After the battle of Ben Suc, during the artistic evening celebrating the victory, I see her again. Accompanying herself on her accordion, she sings a song she composed herself. The music is so beautiful, so melodious, that I think I've never heard anything as beautiful before.
>
> Last year, in July, Trang came to our company with her artistic group. I noticed that she hardly pays any attention to her physical appearance. She dresses very simply, without any coquetry, like a young girl of her age should.
>
> One day, by chance, I heard that Trang had been cited as a Combatant to be Emulated for Production. Suddenly, I spotted her in short

culottes and sleeveless shirt under the burning sun, working the charred ground where sweet potatoes and manioc were planted. I felt a sudden admiration for this Saigon schoolgirl who joined the Resistance, who could do everything as well as the boys!

July 10, 1953, Trang came to my battalion again with the artistic ensemble. The same feeling came back to me. But Trang is still silent and indifferent toward me. I stifle this feeling.

I was grateful to Tan's friends for bringing me his letter.

I began teaching at the Ho Chi Minh City Conservatory, the former National School of Music, which stands less than a kilometer from the house. I taught and directed both the traditional and symphony orchestras. I eventually became director of the conservatory. Each year, I helped organize the two concert seasons that enrich Saigon's cultural life: one season with the traditional orchestra and one with the classical orchestra.

Throughout the eighties, I worked long hours, teaching by day and conducting at night. Besides the concert seasons, I conducted special performances for Independence Day celebrations and fund-raising concerts for schools and social projects. I conducted from the podium three or four evenings a week, whether at the conservatory or the old Opera House, where Tran Van Khe and Luu Huu Phuoc once performed rousing patriotic songs and plays.

Life has taught me to be wary of human relationships. For someone who is introverted like me, going to big public soirées each week was draining. Only the passion of conducting music helped me overcome my antisocial nature.

Since officially retiring from the conservatory in 1990, I participate in different activities. Every few weeks, a nephew drives the family Volkswagen bus to a church in Bien Hoa, where the nuns ask me to rehearse with the choir. They give me a token payment, but I am satisfied just knowing the nuns are serious about learning the music. The priest is grateful. I receive many requests to guest conduct. At one event at the conservatory, a photographer took a picture that captures my focus when I'm on the podium. My eyes are half closed, and my head tilts as if my soul is floating somewhere with the music. The photographer submitted the picture for a contest at the workers' union newspaper. He won first prize.

12

MINH

"I Led Two Lives"

Faithful daughter, wife, and mother—and "adopted mother" to nieces and nephews—Minh also endeavored to find ways to support the resistance. She led an external life as a teacher, while building networks and arranging activities among teachers and other intellectuals sympathetic to the revolution. She welcomed into her home liaison agents who carried letters for the resistance and bought and packaged supplies needed from town. Despite taking precautions, she was arrested and sent to the jail in which Trang had been held.

After the war, Minh welcomed Thanh and Trang back into the family compound on Cach Manh Thang Tam. Having remained at home as the family anchor, Minh tried to make up for lost time to satisfy her curiosity about the world beyond Saigon. She took jobs that allowed her to travel and explore other cultures. She poured her boundless energy into teaching piano and French. With time, Minh observed it would be all right to slow down: "In retirement, it's good to think a little about one's private life."

Minh

While secretly working for the resistance, I studied law at night and taught during the day. I was a militant in the movement that based its *comité de direction* (steering committee) outside Saigon; after the burial of Tran Van On in 1950, the steering committee also organized a network in the city. Having participated in the funeral, I was among the first students in the network. I helped print and distribute leaflets. The police had arrested me and come to our house to look around but found nothing.

Intellectuals and others in the resistance who returned after the Geneva Accords in 1954 found they could do almost nothing in society under Diem. All we could do was go into education. So I worked at Duc Tri secondary school and hired professors in all subjects. Duc Tri was set up by an anonymous association of intellectuals, including my father. My husband also taught at Duc Tri. It was private, so we could hire people who had returned and help regularize their situation. I could help them get official papers; otherwise, they had no papers. They taught classes as a cover, but everyone knew we still worked for the resistance.

I joined the association of teachers of private institutions to help friends make a living and to militate, each in his or her own sphere. We did not do so openly in class since some students were the children of policemen. We had become teachers again; we needed a normal career to help us earn a living and show a public face. We kept out of each other's business, but when we saw each other, we felt like kindred spirits. We knew we worked for the same cause. This was the spirit at Duc Tri; teachers shared a strong sense of sympathy and warmth. You could not find that atmosphere in the state schools or even in other private institutions because people were afraid. At the same time, people were not foolish enough to propagandize publicly.

By 1954, after the Geneva Accords, my sisters came back from the jungle. In 1955, the front was organizing student activities; demonstrations in Saigon continued, and Trang and I played the accordion and piano at student reunions, camp outings, and other gatherings. Students were taking a stand against the wave of people coming from the North after 1954 under Ngo Dinh Diem. Being from the South and in the ranks of the front, we did not want people from the North to come because they were *téléguidé* (controlled) by the Diem government. We elected students to lead the association of students protesting this influx from the North and organized meetings of the Association Générale des Etudiants de Saigon (General Association of Saigon Students) in the gardens of the faculty of pharmacy and medicine, a building once used by the U.S. government that houses the War Remnants Museum.

I led two lives. I had my external life as a teacher, and, underneath, I had another face, the face of militancy. I worked with student and cultural movements. As a teacher, I joined the Association des Enseignants Privés (Association of Private Teachers). It was a revolutionary group under cover of an official association of teachers, without which teachers could not gather and organize. We worried about spies among us but followed all the official and professional regulations. A friend, Dr. Hoa, wanted me to play piano at an event organized by a group of doctors, but they refused to invite me, fearing I would play a revolutionary song.

In fact, I would have played something like Chopin; it would have been crazy for me to play something openly revolutionary! But they did not dare let me play. When Dr. Hoa told me that years later, I had to laugh.

With a law license, I could have worked in a law office and become a lawyer. But I was already launched in my teaching, and the resistance wanted me to be mobile and move around town to make contacts. I taught classes at public and private schools, including those run by French nuns.

In 1960, a liaison in the resistance was arrested in Phnom Penh; he had all our files with him. The resistance could only focus on damage control. Arrests were made in the order of names found in the files. The French wanted to strangle the movement. They wanted to bludgeon it. Wherever we were, we had to stop our clandestine activities, especially in student and intellectual milieus. At this time, friends who had earned their bachots went to France, most of them intending to later return to Hanoi.

The atmosphere turned more tense. Having heard about arbitrary arrests, we never traveled alone. [Ed. note: This was the time of Ngo Dinh Diem's Law 10/59, passed in May 1959, giving tribunals full power to arrest, imprison, and execute people for undefined revolutionary activities. Between 1954 and 1960, about 50,000 people were jailed.] If someone was arrested while driving, the other person could at least follow the car to see where you were jailed. If you hailed a cyclo, the driver might take you directly to the police station, and you would drop from sight. Even Dr. Hoa took her niece or someone else in the car with her. Many of our friends had been detained. I knew the police had my name on the list, but they did not know my face. They drove one of my former students at Gia Long to my house to keep watch and identify me. I stayed in.

When I did venture out in the family car, I always locked the doors. One day, around 1960, I took the car to go administer exams, not realizing my sister had used it earlier and unlocked all the doors. When I left at one thirty that afternoon, assuming the back doors were locked, the police across the street began to follow me. I made a detour, taking a narrow lane by the side of the house to exit; they caught up with me at the railroad tracks and jumped on the car. Reacting by reflex, I made a U-turn to drive back to the house. A policeman was hanging on and got in through the back door; after I made the turn at the intersection near our house, he grabbed the ignition key and stopped the car. Luckily, it was right in front of the house of my former music teacher. He happened to come out and see what was going on and went to warn my parents about my arrest; with the alarm raised at home, they recouped the car and at least knew where I was.

At the prison, a policeman told me that capturing me was like chasing a gangster in Chicago. When he jumped from the jeep onto the back door of my car, had it been locked, he might have been dragged along and broken his foot. I was first held at a villa converted into a police station. After one day, they transferred me to one of the military camps at the time of Diem. They held me in Le Van Duy prison and demanded I tell them everything I had done. But they already knew since I was on the list. It did not describe everything but identified many acquaintances, especially the former lycée boys and girls in the youth movement who had already been arrested. Trang and I ended up in the same prison under different circumstances; Trang was arrested while in the clandestine resistance movement, and I was held while officially a professor involved in antigovernment activities. They arrested many people in that furtive way. Compared to others, because of our class and relative youth, we were treated better. We witnessed and heard the torture of others.

While I was detained in 1960, a coup d'état against Diem erupted in November but failed. During the coup, people in the youth movement organized to demonstrate, but things went wrong, and many were arrested by police and put in cells isolated from everyone else.

When I was released from prison in 1961, my husband and I married right away. I became director of a private institution located near the police station; it was so close that friends asked, "Aren't you afraid to organize a school right next door? Aren't you afraid?" For me, it offered a way to keep track of friends who were arrested and released.

I also used my license in law to work in a Vietnamese insurance company. With my background in international law and economics law, the company asked me to attend meetings in Japan and Jakarta. These are the only trips I made. It was my bad luck to be tied down; being trained as a geographer, one should travel!

But I was stuck. A big part of my work was to maintain contact among families, as well as among parents and children. If I left, who would do this? I had to stay. I had to be resourceful to learn to make liaisons and how to militate. And I raised the children.

One of my tasks while assigned to stay home was to welcome liaison agents who carried letters for the resistance. Each person dropped off a straw hat. First, though, they flashed a small picture of someone in our family, a parent or sibling or cousin, to signal we were in safe hands. I would then peel back the hat's outer layer of straw and find letters inside. I pried up the thread used to stitch in each letter and pulled back the thin skin of paper. Messages were written in invisible ink, or lemon juice, and read by the light of a kerosene lamp. Letters literally materialized as you read by the light. I read letters from Thanh, then in the North, who asked for news of our parents and the children. Other letters explained what supplies and support were needed. I also received letters with news of Trang's husband up north. I wrote replies at night in the privacy of a small room tucked away in the house. Maman and Papa knew nothing about it. I folded the letters tightly and sewed them back into the straw. At a prearranged time, the liaison came back to reclaim the hat.

In terms of material supplies, I made purchases and packaged them, so the contents were concealed. Thanh went back and forth to the countryside; nobody knew she carried supplies for the maquis. We often emptied jars of nuoc mam and filled them with supplies, such as medicines, carefully replacing the corks. We had money to buy toothpaste, soap, and other provisions to pass to friends desperately in need, like one family that returned to the maquis after being in prison on Poulo Condore. After receiving supplies, the liaisons thanked us silently; walking by, they moved their lips to say, "Cam on" (thank you). It meant the items had been received. You could not trust everyone. There could be traps. A climate of suspicion hung everywhere.

During the time of the Americans, everyone rented their houses to them. At one point, our finances came up short, and we proposed selling our house. Maman said, "No, we should not sell because *les petites*, the little ones will not know their way home."

It was common knowledge that many teachers were former militants, and people were afraid to associate with them. I had been in the thick of it. I had already been arrested and survived; otherwise, maybe I would have been afraid like the others. Periodically, I was warned the police were close by and could disrupt our activities. I managed to juggle the school, the students, and professors, all official activities nobody could reproach.

Hiding behind my music also deflected attention. At one point, the police arrested the head of the teachers association and questioned her, "What do you do for the resistance? Do you know Minh?" She replied, "Minh? I see her occasionally when she plays piano at the end-of-year musical gatherings."

We were in the generation at a crossroads: Thanh, Trang, and all our friends of the same age were the pivotal generation rocked by these events. Those in the previous generation lived through a different atmosphere whereas we were really at the crossroads. I told myself simply, "Here I am at the crossroads. Voilà." Many of the twenty-year-olds of our time joined the maquis, which meant they could not stay in town. They had to leave for France or stay in town as part of the movement and very likely spend time in prison as a result. Either way, one could not escape prison. There were three groups: those in the maquis, in prison, or in France. Again, I felt at a crossroads. Other friends were arrested for a second time and released only after 1975.

Two days later after the victory, Thanh returned as part of a foreign affairs contingent. She left a message at the house, signaling she would come soon. It was the return to the fold. Papa was still alive to witness the triumphal homecoming. We had waited for my sisters to return since the Paris Accords. At Tet 1972, we drank champagne and hoped *les petites* would return soon. We had to wait three more years.

Trang returned after June 1975 because she was teaching at the Hanoi Conservatory and stayed to administer end-of-year exams. She trained the accordionists who performed in the victory parade. Trang said people listened to the radio to closely track the march south. On the day of victory, she had tears in her eyes thinking about her daughter, Autumn. But it was hard to get south; people stood in long lines to buy train tickets. Everyone clamored to get back home. It was an incredible moment and made more special by being able to return and find one's parents still alive.

During eight years of study in Moscow, Trang did not once have a chance to see Autumn. From time to time, her letters to Autumn arrived, but we didn't know from where. Letters carried no return address, only a date. Friends hand carried letters from Paris, or travelers took them to mail while on a trip. Trang and Autumn were marked "unknown" on the Saigon census. Their names did not appear on the list of family members.

When Autumn turned twenty, I told her everything. She did not understand the whole story. We told her the truth. She had had doubts. While she lived with us, we treated her like other children in the household. She studied well and easily passed exams at Lycée Marie Curie. As an "adopted" child, she was used to calling me "Mother." We took her everywhere—just another child in the family. Vaguely, she knew there must be an explanation for her mother being absent. In 1968, Autumn's father died during the Tet Offensive. He had suggested ways to try and see her in person, but we didn't dare. It was too risky.

Autumn studied English and music at university. She was my piano student at the conservatory. When her mother came home in 1975, everyone at the conservatory was shocked. Nobody knew Autumn was Trang's daughter. They assumed she was my daughter or had been adopted.

After 1975, old acquaintances and friends regrouped and talked about the ways they participated in resisting: "I did this," "I did that." Some were active in the provinces, but we only learned about it after 1975; while they taught in Saigon, they also worked elsewhere. We talked about having to run out the back door at Duc Tri each time a protest brought police to the front door! You had to have courage and keep a level head. We also helped gain recognition for parents who participated in the common cause, so they could qualify for government benefits. While some had worked for the police, they also helped the resistance through inextricably complex activities.

From time to time, I look back on my life and think, "Life has to be fully lived." I drew the maximum out of life. I have been able to study and gain a solid foundation in the arts and sciences. I play classical music. I dove deeply into the sciences.

I did not let the resistance movement pass me by; I threw myself into the cause. I carried out my work as the daughter of the house. I profoundly believe I will never be without interesting things to do. I have ambitions that are not yet fulfilled. I want to see everything.

When I worked at the insurance company, for example, I spent three months at a training course in Tokyo. I studied the geography and culture of Japan before going, so I would appreciate the architecture and style of the houses. The Japanese managers said they were amazed at what I had already learned. I wanted to fill up every day and take in small events, not just big monuments. After attending a conference on insurance in Jakarta, I traveled to Bali with two colleagues and convinced them to break the return trip to Jakarta into three segments by plane, train, and car. Map in hand, I pointed out each town along the way. By plane, we would have seen nothing. It's to say, I always want to live with exuberance—*vivre des minutes* (live minute to minute)—to not pass by any opportunity.

I have lived a modest life. A small life. I mainly lived in one place. Thank goodness the education Father gave us was so complete; even compared to others who returned from abroad, my education is strong. I never went to France but people ask, "How is it you speak and teach French so well?"

People treated me fairly. In the resistance, each person managed their own sphere; each acted in their own way. Years later, when people see me, they smile. We feel a bond. I think that means I did things right. If I did bad things, people would stay away.

My husband helped a lot at home and with the networks that enabled Trang to come and go, risky as that was. Everything had to be done in a clandestine way. When we see friends in town now, we try to place their face in context: "We saw you . . . in prison . . . at the lycée . . . in a play on stage . . . as an insurance agent . . . on a trip."

In retirement, it's good to think a little about one's private life. With age, I need to be a bit wiser and put order back into family life and take time for my interior life. My children tell me I am out of the house too much. I recognize that. I stayed in one place so long; I feel the need to keep moving to make up for it. I have a strong desire and curiosity to see things. I also like doing things in the home, especially sewing. I make my own clothes. I don't like to depend on others for what I can do myself. I can spend hours making a dress; that is part of my feminine side.

Students today, without being in a movement as we were, don't share the same concerns or ideas. We were transported by the ideal. The patriotic spirit moved us. My sisters and I were drawn in the same direction.

We were in the generation at a crossroads.

13

LE AN

"The Theme of Our Work . . . Was Revolution"

Le An joined an artistic troupe that performed for military units and youth groups during the war. She spent over two decades living in the North, both based in Hanoi and moving with the military. Artistic troupes were brought together as one to prepare for the events of 1968, which were expected to end in victory. Le An also crossed a border with her troupe, performing in southern Laos in 1971, and survived a period at the Seventeenth Parallel that was punctuated by the heavy bombing of Binh Dinh and Quang Binh Provinces.

After liberation, Le An returned south by boat to reunite with her husband. He had served in the army in the North, but they could only rarely meet; they had not seen each other in so long that as she walked toward him at the rendezvous point in Can Tho, he did not recognize her.

Le An

During the war, I was in a group that performed for military units and youth groups. Members of the Vanguard Youth contributed to building roads, agricultural production, and other works. They did not officially belong to the army but did in the sense of being an army of *pioches*, pickaxes they put to use instead of guns. They constructed roads like the Ho Chi Minh Trail and repaired roads hit by bombs. The Vanguard Youth assisted the army as a popular force but one with the strict discipline of the army. Many of them died young.

My artistic troupe was made up of thirty people divided into three units that could serve three locations at the same time. The troupe did not live in a military camp; the army transported us by truck and jeep from one place to another. Given the need to evacuate quickly, we set up camp a little apart but did eat with the military. We used sheets against the cold and the rain. We worked mainly during the dry season, when there were not too many mosquitoes. Sometimes we had only a sheet to help repel the mosquitoes and draped it across a piece of string to make a protective "wall."

We performed under the sky. The countryside was beautiful. I suspended my hammock across a stream, stringing it between two solid tree trunks, and dangled my feet in the water.

I stayed in the North from 1954 until 1961, acting in plays about the revolution in the South. We no longer performed in the forest but rather in provincial villages. Plays brought to life the regional revolution of the early 1930s, the Nghe Tinh soviet revolution, in which peasants and intellectuals rose up against the colonial system and which the French suppressed. Other plays praised the heroism of laborers on the land. Overall, the theme of our work was revolution, whether in Vietnam in Nghe Tinh or in the Soviet Union with its October Revolution. Plays covered other themes: how socialism is organized, World War I, humanity, and, in 1970, the hundredth anniversary of Lenin's birth. With help from Russian performers, we staged Russian plays and short comedies that required only two or three actors.

For six months we stayed in Hanoi to stage plays and then spent six months on the move. We performed in the big theater in Hanoi. In 1959, one large troupe was founded that united young people from the North, the South, and the center. When on the move, we could not rehearse all together, so plays had to be ready to perform before the groups dispersed.

Before going out on assignments, costumes and props were prepared in Hanoi. Typically, we carried four portable musical instruments: a guitar to accompany solos in traditional cai luong, music of the South; a harmonica; an accordion to play during dances; and flutes to accompany emotional scenes, especially sad ones. Each person carried their things in a backpack. To get to places unreachable by car, we walked four or five kilometers at a time, all the while on alert to react as swiftly as soldiers. The soldiers liked us a lot. I was not afraid because they were ready to protect us. If they even suspected an enemy attack, they did not invite the troupe to come. The forest was dense, and the foliage shielded us well.

After 1963, we staged Chinese plays about revolution and, especially, the need to remain vigilant and defend against espionage. Specialists in theater from China came to help us. We only performed in major provincial towns because these plays required large stages. During the war, a play usually lasted half an hour or up to an hour; they had to be kept short to avoid drawing the attention of bombers. For protection against enemy airplanes, we performed in gardens overgrown with banana trees; their leaves provided camouflage. During periods of heavy bombing, we dug a large hole in the ground. It was not uncommon to have to perform in trenches. They dug trenches deep and big as a pool. Soldiers stood around us in a circle, and we performed in the middle. The same trenches were used to hide military trucks covered up with leaves. When our theater troupe arrived, they moved the truck for us to perform. Soldiers had few chances to see theater, so we moved around often, especially before big battles, when seeing a troupe perform provided encouragement. It made them happy to see beautiful girls and have a sense of being glorified.

A play might be as short as ten minutes; it would be preceded by other acts, whether songs, accordion playing, dances, or *jeux de dextérité* (magic tricks) that included tying rope into knots or hiding cards. Soldiers were grateful for any distraction, any little bit of fun. To perform magic tricks, the troupe enlisted beautiful, young girls.

At night, even a tiny flame could be detected. Like the soldiers, we moved between midnight and four AM. We performed plays at seven or eight in the morning. After an hour or hour and a half, we moved on to perform in two or three venues a day. Each unit had a hundred soldiers. After a play, we ate lunch and moved on. Everyone encouraged each other. Our superior commander liked to select plays that made people laugh. He did not think we should put on plays with sad scenes; he said soldiers should be able to laugh and be entertained. He encouraged us to sing and dance and dramatize scenes about friendship, positive feelings, devotion, and heroism.

From 1964 on, while living up north, parents had to send their children over one hundred kilometers out of Hanoi to protect them from the bombing. We made the trip by bicycle over two nights and a day. Each department was responsible for a camp for its members' children and for helping to raise them. During one of the twelve-day bombing runs of Hanoi, most inhabitants left, but I stayed and read communiqués in English on Radio Hanoi. I was chosen as announcer because of my accent. I spoke in Vietnamese, too. I read from eleven until midnight. I read each day, so I stayed in town and didn't even go to the suburbs. Our friend Suong read short sentimental stories; everyone liked to hear her read abridged stories. Thanh was in Paris at the Peace Talks.

After 1968, all the troupes were reunited in one that brought together all forms of art, dance, singing, and *théâtre rénové* (traditional theater). Twelve or thirteen troupes trained together; we were preparing for the events of 1968. We thought that year would end in victory, so troupes needed to be ready to perform, even for the inhabitants of Saigon. After six or seven months of training, each student performed a piece that showcased their training. It was something like an exam a student had to pass at the end of a course.

The campaign in southern Laos in 1971, part of the battle against Thieu's forces, ended in victory. [Ed. note: In 1955, North Vietnam had begun carving a supply route through eastern Laos to South Vietnam—later known as the Ho Chi Minh Trail. Because it proved a crucial transportation link for North Vietnam to attack South Vietnam, the United States bombed the area for many years. In February 1971, South Vietnamese and U.S. troops crossed into Laos to sever the trail, but Operation Lam Son 719 failed, and northern troops were able to occupy more towns and widen the supply route.] I received a medal for being part of a troupe sent to perform for the soldiers. Each actor received a gift from the military units. I have a medal dated 1960 that commemorates the fifteenth anniversary of our first independence in 1945 and a medal in honor of the one hundredth anniversary of Ho Chi Minh's birth.

I keep an insignia of the NLF flag. We saw this flag, blue and red, for a while after liberation, and then it stopped being used, and we put up the red flag with the star. They said, "It is now the unification, so we don't make use of that flag anymore." The NLF insignia does not have much value for the new generation, but for those who value history, it is precious. For others, it means nothing. I appreciate historians who are interested in the things we accomplished in our youth. But the masses can't see it. My children are not historians. These things can't be bought. They are contributions to history.

I was based for a time at the frontier between the North and South when there was a lot of bombing in Binh Dinh, Quang Binh, and other central provinces. Heavy fighting concentrated on the bridge at the Seventeenth Parallel; the president of the nearby Comité populaire gave our troupe a gift of a certificate.

I led a troupe of nine. During a particularly heavy bombing of the Seventeenth Parallel, half of one of the local troupes was killed. Since our troupe moved around, none of us died in that bombing. The Cu Chi tunnels suffered even more bombing as the Americans sought to devastate the region to stop soldiers from passing through.

The West was so mountainous! Our troupe climbed a mountain to perform for a handful of soldiers in the unit assigned there. All soldiers needed to be served. It was said that if you went up this particular mountain, you had little hope of coming down because of the intense bombing. My troupe divided into several small groups to climb. It turned out that a troupe stationed close to this mountain had been killed in a bombing. It was a matter of chance. When a bombing raid took us by surprise, we scattered in clusters of three or four. Some nights, the bombing continued till morning. Bombing stopped only a few hours during the day. From experience, we figured out which hours the planes did not fly.

FIGURE 11.   Le An and her artistic troupe were based in Vinh Linh, near a heavily bombed bridge at the Seventeenth Parallel between North and South Vietnam. Le An holds a certificate of appreciation from the leader of the local Comité populaire. Courtesy of Le An.

Planes deforested the land. We took advantage of local guides to move quickly through the ravaged area; some stretches had no trees, so we could make quick progress. That's how we made it up the mountain. Soldiers lived in underground shelters and tunnels, sprinting from one shelter to the next. They didn't stay in a shelter long, just long enough to eat and sing a few songs and move on. These men living on the mountain were very courageous. A-1 was notorious because of all the battles to control it. At the summit, only a few trees remained. Many soldiers died, and in the end, this unit was decimated. It was a heroic unit and duly decorated. Other soldiers moved quickly, between bombings, to climb up and bring provisions to the unit. Those of us in the troupe moved more slowly. We brought back a bit of dirt from the hill. Upon return, our troupe received a medal for heroism.

Later in 1971, we traveled to a provincial town to stage a play about a little boy who is a shoemaker. A woman played the role of shoemaker, and I played the mother who mends the shoemaker's clothes. A cadre, working for the people as part of a mobile force, comes into the old lady's house, and the two hide the cadre behind the house. The stage is set using a single sheet or mattress and a small table. An American soldier comes and asks if they have seen the cadre; the mother and son use clever words to send him off in another direction. The American soldier can't find him and returns and beats the mother and son. The soldier leaves. The cadre returns. It was a small sketch about the heroism of town citizens who help the resistance.

A Saigon author wrote a play about the wives of three ministers who quarrel over the portfolios their husbands have in the government. Officials changed ministries and positions all the time. The women argue endlessly about rank and position. While continuing to bicker at the end of the play, the wives fight over a chair and break it; each is left holding one leg of the stool. This play described the decadence of the puppet government. In the end, nobody holds more than one leg of the stool.

Another play portrayed a teacher in Saigon whose students don't like her. Over a holiday, the teacher organizes a gathering at which each student talks about what makes them sad. One is an orphan. Another is poor. One has a cruel mother-in-law. One shines shoes. Some go to school in the morning and scavenge for food in the afternoon. Each student talks about their life. Then the teacher talks about her own sorrows, and they come to understand each other. Many people are poor and miserable. That is life under the imperialists. Life is unfair. The students had been mean to the teacher, but in the end, everyone understands each other.

After liberation, I sent a telegram to my husband's sister saying I would return south by boat. She came to meet me. The next day, my sister-in-law and I took the whole family to Can Tho to meet my husband. I had been thirty-one when my husband left for the army; when we met again, I was forty-four. He had gained weight and become much more nice-looking. But when he saw me, he did not recognize me because I had lost weight and looked older. My small glasses from the North made me look like an old lady. I have an aunt who looks like me; my husband thought I was her.

In 1975, I came back to our old house. My youngest child was twelve. The state appealed to everyone to produce food, so I raised fish and chickens and pigs. Everyone needed to encourage family production to earn a little more salary. Tuyen observed that, after 1975, people did not understand each other; I agree that intellectuals became dissatisfied. They felt there was no confidence in them. One story told of an engineer who thought he was no longer respected and had no role to play. This, after he had helped build the first dam in the Soviet Union! He showed his unhappiness by going around selling matches.

I teach theatre renové and the theory of theater and train theater directors. Theater School No. 1 is up north, and No. 2 is here. We have about two hundred students. Trang helps teach traditional music. I attend meetings of charitable associations in my neighborhood. There is a society of charitable women that visits orphans and poor children.

I visit the Women's Museum to learn more about figures like Nguyen Thi Minh Khai, the first woman to participate in a congress of the Communists in Moscow in 1935. She was arrested in 1940 and shot at the age of thirty. Nguyen Thi Dinh served as a famous commander. Vo Thi Sau was shot in 1952 at Con Dao when she was sixteen. Nguyen Thi Ut, the "mother with a gun," had six children but still fought the French.

I like to travel and would like to visit more countries. I have traveled in Vietnam; now I would like to see Italy and Japan, and recently I have thought of seeing the United States and meeting friends there. But I have little money. Two things I want to learn are to play the *danh canh* and to speak French. I want to build on what I learned in school years ago, which should make French easier to learn than English, which I studied just a little.

I married in 1959. I am happy. My daughter, who studied in Bulgaria, works for a precious metals company. [Ed. note: The Soviet Union offered scholarships to students in communist countries to go and learn the language of one of the countries in the Soviet bloc.] My son is a chemical engineer who works for an electronics enterprise. I have close friends. At the French lycée, we participated in demonstrations and printed documents. Some old friends retired; one became a movie actor. One had a career in foreign affairs. Another studied in Bulgaria and is a stage director. All these friends are here. Others left with official approval; when they return and we meet again, I realize they do not think like us.

Le An's Husband, Le Minh

A tall man with a crew cut, Le Minh came from a poor family in Tra Vinh and joined the revolution in 1946, just before he turned fifteen. Two years later, he went to look for his family but found his village destroyed by the French. He found them taking refuge in a small straw hut in the countryside.

In 1957, Le Minh met his wife and, as "fellow southerners," found they shared an affection for their home region. Courting for two years, he saw Le An only twice. On one occasion, to visit her in Hanoi, he left his camp, walked fifty miles to a train station, took an eight-hour ride, and walked three kilometers to her troupe's headquarters, only to learn they had gone to Haiphong. By the time he found her, they had only a few hours together.

For much of the war, Le Minh fought in the South, "always the front." He believes he and Le An are lucky in marriage for having unity in responsibility toward the nation. With a hint of pride, Le Minh says that even in retirement, Le An devotes herself to others. "Le An and her Marie Curie friends, despite different social backgrounds, came together around this: they all love the country and agreed with the revolution."

Le Minh

I come from a poor family in Tra Vinh and joined the revolutionary army in 1946, not long before I turned fifteen. I left a mother and three sisters, the youngest being six years old. In the first years of struggle against colonialism, my family faced many difficulties. Their eldest son was away and could not help them financially; for the first year after I left, I was transferred around nearby provinces and could only visit my family from time to time. At the start of 1948, my duties took me farther from my home province. I saw my family once in 1949 and once in 1952. But that year, my native village was destroyed by the French, and I did not see my family there; instead, we met in a small straw hut in the countryside.

For the Vietnamese people, faithfulness is a tradition. You see it in legends and folk tales in which people sing about faithfulness. I am the only son and the eldest child. To have left the family as an only son and the eldest was out of the ordinary. Along with the tradition of fidelity, being part of the army and at the front of the liberation made me realize that, while sad to be far from loved ones, once we understand the goal—a higher goal—we get over the sadness and put all our energies into overcoming these feelings.

Shortly before I went north after the Geneva Accords, my mother and third sister came to see me at Ca Mau, the rallying point for forces taking boats to the North. I have strong feelings for my family, especially my mother and third sister. During my first years away,

I was young and missed my family so much it hurt. Especially at night, before going to sleep, I thought about my mother.

In 1950, because my family was among the poorest in our area, we received support and land from the government. Their class benefited from the revolutionary government. This land was taken from landowners who worked for the French. My family had no land before they were given a hectare and a half. Distribution of land to farmers is one reason workers supported the revolution. It was just. Laborers had nothing while landowners, lackeys of the French, controlled hundreds and thousands of hectares. That was unjust. Throughout the war, land was given to farmers, making it possible for farmers and workers to live comfortably, right up to now. The working class can live as it should.

When we compare farmers now and then, how they live, their level of education, and how they dress, they differ like the sky and the earth. Housing and living conditions have improved a lot.

Being young and part of the revolutionary army and knowing in my heart that my family could live comfortably, all this boosted my confidence in the revolutionary government. After I left for the North, I visited my family in Tra Vinh just twice: in 1964 and again in 1966 during an army movement.

I met Le An at the end of 1957, when she belonged to an artistic troupe that was making a film. She had come from Hanoi to Thanh Hoa and Sam Song, a beautiful beach about 150 kilometers south of Hanoi. My unit was stationed another 50 kilometers from Thanh Hoa, in the village of Nong Cong. I was a captain and head of a company of soldiers. We met, and, as fellow southerners, we shared a sense of affection for our region. I traveled to Hanoi periodically, and we became friends.

I decided to visit her father and ask for her hand in marriage. Two years later, in 1959, we married on March 8, International Women's Day. I had waited before asking to marry her since I am not of the same class. She comes from a rich family of intellectuals.

She was nearsighted, which was uncommon among peasants. I also hesitated because of her profession. As an actress, her activities differed so much from what we do in the army. Furthermore, my regiment was part of the force majeur of the region and relocated often, making it hard to live together.

While we courted for two years, I was able to see Le An only twice. It was hard to see each other; she was often on the move, and I had only ten days of vacation per year. To get to know each other, we wrote letters. To visit her in Hanoi, I traveled a long way on foot and by train. I saw her in 1958 on the occasion of the anniversary of the birth of Ho Chi Minh. I left my camp and walked fifty kilometers to the train station. The train took eight hours to reach Hanoi. From the station, I walked three kilometers to the neighborhood where her troupe was based. When I arrived, I didn't recognize anybody and was told the troupe had departed for Haiphong. Once in Haiphong, I could find nobody from the troupe and learned that, once again, they had been on the move. I walked at night until I finally found her at the troupe's encampment, at which point I could stay only a few hours. I made the trip back, on foot and by train, and arrived in Thanh Hoa after walking the last fifty kilometers.

After the wedding, we were together a few days, and then I returned to my unit. I saw Le An only during annual vacations. In 1960, the number of vacation days given to soldiers went up from ten to fifteen. I had a chance to be with her and take care of her only a few days a year.

At the end of 1959, Le An came to see me in my regiment. In August 1960, she gave birth to our son.

I was promoted in 1961 and worked for a division, which gave me a chance to visit Hanoi more often and see my family. When my son was three, Le An became pregnant with our daughter. At that time, I transferred south with my regiment. I knew my specific date of departure; most others did not know when they would be going south. My wife was able to accompany me to the National Defense Department, a military area to the east of Hanoi. I left early one evening in the spring of 1964. I keep a fresh image of that moment: Le An and I are sharing a bicycle, I am pedaling, and she sits in back. I jump off the bicycle and leave it with her before walking to the building where I need to attend a meeting. I looked back and saw my wife and the bicycle in the middle of the road; she looked stunned, heartbroken. She did not know where to go, what to do; she just stood there, in the middle of the street, watching me walk away. I was going to the front, in the South, and people were afraid because of all the bombing.

The second time I was so moved happened ten days after our marriage. I had to go to Thanh Hoa. At the train station, I looked back. Le An looked scared, emotion drained from her face—as though she was dead. She was the picture of a wife seeing her husband go away, toward a dangerous future.

These moments stay vivid in my mind. I have not told my wife about them. These memories are important to me: images of a faithful woman separated from her husband just at the start of their happiness. The image of a faithful woman separated from her happiness and of a woman separating from her husband, possibly for a voyage without return. It is for us, husband and wife, to understand each other, to love each other always, even when separated for long periods.

We lived apart from 1963 until I came south in 1975. Each year, we received one or two letters from each other. Often, letters did not reach their destination. If a letter did get through, it was often wet or damaged. Le An sent photos of the children, but the photos stuck together. When I tried to pull the pictures apart, little or no image was left. I held them up to the light but could hardly make out anything. We never knew how long a letter would take to arrive. It depended on the routing. Letters might be hand carried through Cambodia. Sometimes the courier encountered obstacles and dangers. Sometimes old women carried mail because they aroused less suspicion. The fastest a letter reached me from the North was at the end of 1967, and it broke the news of my father-in-law's death. He died in August, and the letter reached me in December. Letters arrived so rarely; Le An thought I had died at the front.

I came south again after a big battle at Binh Gia, where many Americans died. This was before the Ho Chi Minh Trail opened up, when small groups were sent south as reinforcements, not yet the major forces. I arrived at Ca Mau. From 1968 until 1975, Le An and I exchanged no letters. During this period, information was shared only by spoken word. When someone traveled north to make reports, he was asked about who was still alive. My wife also got news from the army about who was alive, who was not.

I was in Can Tho at liberation. Four months later, my wife came to Saigon. I stayed in an army camp, and my wife did not have the address. She did have the address of my third sister in Saigon, who guided my wife to Can Tho. They arrived around noon. I had finished lunch and just started reading the newspaper. I was sitting on the veranda and looked out on the street. I saw my sister, who I recognized right away, along with two children I did not recognize. When I left Hanoi, my son had been three; now he was eleven. My daughter had still been in the womb when I left. Behind the children stood my wife; I did not recognize her. She was so thin; she weighed only thirty-five kilos. Her skin was dark from the deep wrinkling due to all the weight she had lost. She had been on the first boat bringing combatants south from Hanoi. The boats were so full that people had to sit in the sun during the weeklong journey. Le An arrived on the first boat, the *Thong Nhat*, which means "unification."

Everyone wanted to come south quickly. They had suffered a lot under the bombing in the North. Children had to be sent to the countryside. Parents bicycled out in groups on Saturdays to see their children and returned at midnight on Sunday. They went to work

Monday morning after bicycling as much as eighty kilometers each way; that was another reason An was so bony and dark-skinned.

I did not recognize my wife at all. I waited for my sister to introduce this visitor. It was easier for Le An to recognize me because of my hair cut: I always wear a crew cut.

It's hard to emphasize enough that the tradition of our people is fidelity between spouses and ensuring that each person's responsibility, their most important duty, is toward family.

Throughout much of the war, I fought in the South. I was serving among the people in the South, where we were always at the front, the zone of combat. In the North, there were some periods without war, but we were constantly engaged in combat under tough conditions. I concentrated my mind and strength on fighting.

We are left with fewer days together as husband and wife. We are already old. But overall, we feel content and happy to be together. We have known happiness. Based on my experience, if our happiness as husband and wife is separated from that of the people, it is no longer happiness. We are only happy if all the people are happy as we are.

Love is only love after overcoming many obstacles. Marriage is just the beginning of happiness; it is not the culmination of love. Young people think marriage is the crowning of love, but marriage is the beginning. After marriage comes a new phase because life together brings complications that can't be predicted. We can't yet see that life together causes consequences that are hard to resolve. My wife and I are lucky to have this: unity in responsibility toward the nation.

What I love most about my wife is that she has a highly developed sense of responsibility. She is devoted to others. Even in retirement, she dedicates herself wholeheartedly to activities in the neighborhood. She is one of the people charged with resolving problems.

My wife and I also agree on the need to be sincere with our friends. We need to be sincere with everyone. We should not be calculating. We should be generous. This is our view of life. My wife asks nothing for herself. Even when it comes to meals, she makes sure her husband and children get the best part of the meal.

Under all circumstances, we agree on the need to live like everyone else—to live from one's labor, even under harsh conditions. One must learn to live honestly. After the war, we experienced the joy of finding each other in good health even though, in material terms, life was demanding.

Le An and her Marie Curie friends, despite different social backgrounds, came together around this: they all love the country and agreed with the revolution. That is the fundamental factor bringing them together as good friends.

Since the end of the war, we have worked hard but live happily. In addition to my government job, I work manual jobs to meet expenses. After the war, we encountered different challenges, but in terms of earning an honest living, we see that as an act of love for the family and for the country.

The people are not the same as their government. The American government is different from the people. Ideas differ based on material interests that influence those ideas. Power is in the hands of capitalists; those who have a lot of money influence the government. The government serves capitalists, but the people think differently. The government doesn't understand the people and works for the interests of capitalists. To understand people, one has to evaluate things according to one's own feelings. Everyone loves children. All parents love their children. The next generation also wants their family to live in peace. We all want families to be happy.

This is one way to understand how a developing country could fight for such a long time. Either be a slave, or be independent and free. That is how to endure such a long war. There is no other way. The path that leads to independence and liberty is strewn with struggles and sacrifices and cruelty. Now that we have independence and unification, we need to develop the country and bring the nation to prosperity. This is a difficult task that requires making sacrifices every day.

Rich people enrich themselves by the fruits of the labor of the poor. On our own, it is hard to enrich ourselves. We only enrich ourselves through the work of others. Even now, there are rich and poor, and the rich profit from the poor. There are people who do not live honestly. If everyone conducted themselves like Le An and me, they would not be able to do that. If we examine life, things are always complicated. But even if complicated, there is a straightforward side through which we should understand things. In human society, as in the society of a nation, one must look at the material interests of each to understand the attitude of that person.

What we know is that our country, every day, is making progress. Everyone is impatient and wants to speed ahead. We have to acknowledge we are trying to do something we have never done before. Before the generation of the Marie Curie girls, many generations participated in the revolutionary movement, and today, the work still continues. I started very young; now I have white hair. Everyone has white hair, but the work is unfinished; we carry on with the conviction that we are making progress. Every day of our lives, we should think about those who died for the revolution and how much we owe them. It is our duty to bring their contribution to fruition. We have to improve and enrich the country. That is our duty. What we think about and do in our lives may surprise others, but I firmly believe that anyone else faced with our conditions would react exactly the way we are.

14

SEN

"Working for the People, Not a Particular Party"

Sen did not care for politics as a student and grew to dislike it more as an adult. She and her husband, Nhieu, worked "directly for the people" through acts of charity. Nhieu studied public health at Johns Hopkins University before earning a diploma in pharmacy at the University of Saigon. His appointment as vice minister of health in South Vietnam provided cover for their clandestine actions: supplying food, donating medicines, arranging lodging for agents whose families disowned them or who came to the city to give birth.

After the revolution and reunification, many friends were afraid to meet Sen and Nhieu in the large home they managed to hold on to: being rich meant being guilty. She believes northerners and southerners are very different in how they live and share only one thing in common: patriotism.

Over time, siblings and children began to flee: a sister to Switzerland, children to France and Australia and America. A son tried to escape as a boat person and drowned.

Nhieu managed his pharmaceutical factories to produce medicines at a low price. Sen immersed herself in family and friends who remain in Saigon. She is happy that, despite different paths taken in the war, friendships formed at Lycée Marie Curie bring rare comfort.

Sen

Since I could not continue my studies after leaving Marie Curie, I went abroad and studied to be a beautician. I liked this profession. It made me happy to help someone look younger and more beautiful. I think of *l'esthétique* (aesthetics) as an art, along with music and painting. Physical appearance influences a person's spirits; throughout the bad situations I've survived in life, I always tried to take good care of myself. After the war, I no longer practiced my profession because making oneself beautiful was considered a luxury. Now we see another extreme: women and girls coming from Hanoi are more coquettish than Saigonese! At that time, too, beauty products became scarce due to heavy taxes.

When I studied in Switzerland, I found it utterly charming. The Swiss are neutral and open to visitors; they are not racist. They are welcoming toward foreigners. If I held an important position in the government, I would open Vietnam's doors to all the countries of the world.

I was living in Saigon in 1957 when I met my husband, Nhieu, a former student at Lycée Chasseloup-Laubat. Together, we did everything possible for the people. We thought of ourselves as working for the people, not for any particular party. We did not get involved in politics. We figured that, if everyone left the south of Vietnam, who would be left to help the people? Who will feed people in the resistance? It was the inhabitants of Saigon who fed them, who hid them. They came to buy medicines, to give birth, and to see family but did not dare stay at their homes since everyone knew their families were part of the resistance. So they stayed with us.

We had the sense that the gathering storm would burst. We knew the revolution would succeed. My husband was not in any resistance organization; he worked directly for the people. He and I helped the people by giving them medicines. When I left the maquis, I was no longer in any organization. I just helped friends on my own. I did it according to my conscience, without others knowing it.

I hid friends for as long as needed—a few days, a week. Nobody suspected us. Nhieu had a diploma in pharmacy from the University of Saigon and became vice minister of health in South Vietnam. He had also studied at the Johns Hopkins University School of Public Health. The authorities did not suspect us given his position as vice minister and the fact we lived in a nice neighborhood.

At one point, the comings and goings at our house did draw attention, and I had to leave. People in the resistance were bringing the wounded, blood flowing, to our house and laying them under the trees. My husband was in the United States at the time, and I had to take the children to a friend's house.

I remained in Saigon throughout the war against the Americans. We detested the U.S. government as we had detested the French colonialists. The Americans came because they were afraid the Communists were spreading everywhere. They did not want Communism to influence countries around the world. That's why they fought the war. It's different from the French, who had their interests: rubber, rice, coffee, tea—that is what drew the French here. One came for political reasons, one for economic; the two are completely different.

During the war, some people came to Saigon to give birth. Afterward, they left the children to be raised by their parents, just as Thanh and Trang left children with Minh. They had to do it: give birth and leave their child. How superhuman.

Minh stayed in town and worked for the resistance. I am sure she also hid friends in her home. I don't know the extent of what happened after she was arrested and jailed. The only one among those siblings who was not Communist, Minh did a lot for the resistance. If she had not raised Autumn as her own daughter, Trang could not have been at ease. Minh also cared for Thanh's boy, who became deaf and dumb. He did not speak. At four in the morning, he would go into the bathroom and stare at the light. He did this, without moving, from four until seven each morning. Minh was the pillar of strength in the house. She was so busy with nieces and nephews that she married very late. Minh is brave and kind; I like her and admire her.

Northerners and southerners did not get along. All we have in common, as Vietnamese, is patriotism. In terms of how we live, we are not at all the same. Life in the North is hard; people are toughened. Their character is also hard, unlike in the South. We live easily; we earn a living easily. We are more generous.

After the revolution and reunification, many friends did not dare meet me because they were afraid I was in the big bourgeoisie. Being rich meant being guilty. They didn't know there were rich people who earned their living honestly, thanks to their talents and their intelligence. Since my husband was a former vice minister of health and we lived in a nice house and neighborhood, we were considered bourgeois.

Even my friend Le An did not dare meet me. We had joined the maquis together in 1950, and I did not see her after I went south to Ca Mau in 1951. When I returned to Saigon in 1953, she and her husband went to Hanoi. It was only at the urging of Suong that she came to see me in 1977. I had my own feelings about Le An; I liked her and thought about her often. But she had reproached me about leaving the maquis, saying it was because I could not bear the misery. I did not want to see her unless she came to see me first. After Suong scolded Le An about not visiting, Le An came with her husband. Suong had explained everything to her about why I left the maquis, including that I had permission from the leaders. When she met me, Le An was very happy. We are good friends. We understand each other.

My daily activities revolve around my children and grandchildren; most are in France and the United States. We have a son who lives with us; he is mentally ill. He rides a bike in circles in front of the house for hours. Starting when he was two, he suffered up to ten epileptic fits a day. They damaged him forever. We lost a son in 1980. He was fed up with the political system and took a boat. The engine died in a storm. A buoy fell into the water, and somebody jumped in to get it, but he could not swim well, so my son took off his clothes, grabbed a rope and a lifesaver, and jumped in. Both people drifted farther and farther off. The rope proved too short, and my son was cut loose. After fifteen minutes, even with the help of binoculars, neither could be seen.

One sibling married a Swiss woman and worked as a doctor in Geneva. Another earned her diploma from the University of Paris and became a dentist. A third opened a Vietnamese restaurant in Lausanne but then got tired and sold it.

My husband likes running his pharmaceutical companies and other businesses that help him feel he is serving his country. I like to cook and sew. Even as a child, I made clothes for my mother. Mother was an excellent cook. My husband likes French cuisine; his father was a French citizen, and Nhieu was naturalized French but revoked that status. As a boarding student at Chasseloup-Laubat, he played with the young French kids; he was like a Frenchman.

When friends from Marie Curie and I had to scatter to the maquis, I never thought we would be able to see each other again. Bringing together the sisters from Marie Curie is the work of Tuyen. She set out to gather us one by one, and our first reunion took place at Le An's house at Tet 1983. Le An's husband strongly supports our friendships. My children encourage us to get together because it helps us relax and gives us a chance to share ideas.

Some of us are Communist; others are not. We get along well because we had the same goal and we pursued the same cause: to liberate our country from the yoke of the French colonialists and American imperialists.

15

TUYEN

"Everyone Was Wrong"

Staying in Saigon to care for her parents, Tuyen trained as a pharmacist, got married, and found her own ways to aid the resistance. After the Geneva Accords, her brother Luu Huu Phuoc worked in the North. They rarely dared sent letters for fear of what would happen if one fell in the hands of the police. Throughout the 1960s, as she raised a family, ran a pharmacy, and helped the poor, Tuyen harbored hopes a decisive event would "change everything, change life itself, and rid us of ills."

After 1975, Tuyen tried to help rebuild a better society. She observed social, economic, and political problems around her: inherent mistrust between people who had been on different sides, fighters who fought for the people who became seduced by the lifestyle of the bourgeoisie, jobs given to unqualified northerners instead of educated southerners, the corrupting influence of foreign aid.

She continued to take care of her family and pharmacy as siblings with medical training left. A sister in California asked Tuyen and her husband to come live with her. They declined. A French professor of philosophy at the lycée had introduced Tuyen to Communism, the first ideal she had heard of. She found it beautiful: "It is like religion, a search for justice, which is not yet achieved."

Tuyen

I graduated from pharmacy school in 1957 and married in April 1961. My husband is also a pharmacist and spent three months in the United States in 1966.

He is industrious and serious and was elected to the syndicated committee of pharmacists; we met at one of their annual meetings. When he returned from his studies in France, he started to teach. I was in my last year of pharmacy studies. We knew each other four years before we married. My mother liked him; after all, he was a teacher! His father was a teacher from the same social class, so he and my mother understood each other easily.

My husband and I lived in a large house. I worked at my pharmacy during the day and went to have dinner with my sister and mother every evening, getting back home as late as nine each night. I hired help to take care of the children, so I could work. I have always worked outside the home. I may have left my children too often, but I was attached to my mother. I was close to my father, too, but he did not talk much.

I love going out and being with my friends. I care about them. My husband took care of the house, so I felt at ease and could look outward and take care of my friends and people who needed me, especially my parents. My mother was severe, wanting this and that. My sisters didn't dare confront her. I was the only one who was patient and could keep my mother company. My brother Luu Huu Phuoc had already left, so it was my duty to stay with our parents. That's also why I didn't go to the maquis with Le An, who asked me to go with her. It was not such a hard decision because there was a lot of work to do here, too. Friends in the resistance came to talk about the mission. We could provide assistance to those who needed us.

If we really want to serve, we can serve anywhere. I did not commit completely to the struggle; I served as needs came up or money was lacking. I was afraid that, given our uncommon family name, everyone would know right away I was the sister of Luu Huu Phuoc.

When the Americans came, they gave out a lot of money, but many of those who received it were lazy, including people in the military. Very few worked hard with or for the Americans. *Les gens bien* (decent people) took part in the revolution. I saw that a majority of decent people joined, so I firmly believed the revolution would succeed, but I did not know when. Revolutionary militants would come to fight and then pull back. I thought it would happen that, bit by bit, they would destroy the army or break the morale of the people in power. You would have to be foolish to take power before you have enough strength, before you are ready. You might be able to take power, but not keep it.

A delegation from the resistance asked me to help. Someone from the CIA came to our house and asked my husband to send a letter to my brother in the maquis asking him to work for peace and a "better world." The CIA man told my husband he worked for world peace and everyone wants peace; he wanted to ask me if I would send words of peace to my brother. My husband refused, saying, "My wife does not pay attention to these things; she just does commerce." I would have told the CIA man the same thing. In contrast to my quiet husband, one of my brothers-in-law did receive these CIA people regularly because he liked to talk. The propositions these people made were ridiculous.

It was very hard to stay in touch with my brother Phuoc. From time to time, he sent a message, but I did not dare send him letters. We were afraid of what would happen if a letter fell in the hands of the police. I did not try to communicate with him at all. If someone from the maquis came to town, Phuoc sent along a note with a few words saying that he was well and wished our mother well. He wrote that he was fighting the imperialists and would return soon. He conveyed a lot on a tiny piece of paper.

It was hard to raise children at this time, not unlike when my mother gave birth to us. In the past, epidemics of cholera, yellow fever, and smallpox were terribly common. To fight diseases, we made medicines out of plants and anything we thought might help. We even used basic scientific methods to make an ointment out of goat excrement, spreading it on a slab of baked mud and putting it in the fire. The remaining ash contained minerals; once burned down, the excrement is good and clean. We added oil from a large grain that has properties to cure scars. We spread this oil, mixed with the ash from goat or horse excrement, on scars or swellings. We also relied on sorcerers, especially to treat mental illnesses; my mother told stories about them from her past.

We did not know what would happen leading up to Tet 1968. We expected something but did not know what.

When I was young, I thought I would go into teaching, but my family wanted me to become a pharmacist. If I could not be a teacher, I wanted to be a doctor to help people living in any circumstance, even in the countryside, where people were utterly deprived. My family told me I could teach after I became a pharmacist.

Working at my pharmacy from 1958 to 1975, I gave advice to those who needed medicines. Poor people came to ask how to cure different sicknesses. My customers liked me. Supplying my pharmacy was complicated due to irregular imports. I had to spend a lot of time stocking my pharmacy. We imported many types and brands of medicines from France, the United States, Italy, and Holland. All these choices confused people, and sick people had to spend a lot of money. I thought, if we are liberated, there will be just one brand of medicine, and it will be easier for people to know what to take.

Everyone thought that, after a certain big event happened, all our ills would be cured, but they were wrong—on their side as well as ours. We hoped one decisive event would change everything, change life itself, and rid us of ills. But in my opinion, everyone was wrong, including those who joined the maquis in the first place. Some were so far at the end of their strength that they believed if the liberation arrived, all the ills in life would end. But liberation was only a beginning.

In 1975, everything closed for a couple of weeks. In my neighborhood, three people from the maquis occupied a house designated for use by the popular committee. I helped them set up a dispensary and spent afternoons there after working at my pharmacy. I was asked to be president of the local chapter of the Women's Union, where I saw the communiqués from Hanoi on which actions were based. Unfortunately, the illiterates interpreted these weekly messages differently. Southerners and northerners had not communicated easily or often up to this point, and all they understood in common was political language. This constant misinterpretation of messages slowed any effort to bring order out of chaos. I was asked to organize and help women in the community, but no longer as president of the local chapter: I was disqualified because of the size of our house.

After a while, there was such a need for more cadres to help women; they decided to send me to a weeklong course. I was appointed president of the women's association in my locality, and my first job was to carry out a census of women. I made a list of women in the area, splitting them into groups and asking them to choose a leader who would know how each family was faring, so we would know right away who had problems with money, a job, or whatever. We met weekly to see what happened in the *quartiers* (neighborhoods), and we recorded the addresses of poor people to whom we brought rice. There was also an issue of security. The government was bringing together former officers to serve away from their homes and wanted to monitor their wives in case they needed something while their husbands were gone. Officers' wives had to learn to earn money rather than wait for their husbands' salaries. They were afraid of dying of hunger while their husbands were away. The government also worried that, if overlooked, the wives might panic and cause problems; we had to reassure them they would receive news and know the intentions of the authorities.

The groups of women were supposed to meet often to help each other. In some cases, they arbitrated in the case of family disputes. In my neighborhood, people were educated and behaved well; the women were functionaries or wives of ranking officers, which made my work easier. In poor areas, people lived so close together they had more problems.

We rallied the women's groups whenever we needed to celebrate a ceremony or attend an event. Each locality needed at least ten or twelve women who could be relied on to join a gathering; we were told when and where to send them. Committees who carried their duties out well got women to go; if the committee did not work well, people would not attend. There were many public events: ceremonies and memories of battles and historic dates. People participated because they were enthusiastic about the victory and the revolution. They did not know what they lost.

Public opinion was for the revolution. At the beginning, we knew almost nothing but kept working because everyone had some reserves of money. We were exhausted but kept on. Southern cadres who returned from the North also faced difficulties. Wives of officers, like Le An, were allowed to return south right away. Couples with a husband from the South and a woman from the North were also allowed to return right away. Many others were not.

It was only with time that the government, trying to set up social services, admitted they did not have enough trained and specialized cadres. They brought cadres from the North who arrived en masse: people who were poor, far from home, with no savings and no family to help them or raise their children. The cadres we had trained either fled, or the authorities did not trust them.

One of the difficulties northerners faced was not having grandparents to take care of the children or guard the house. The government decided that kindergartens had to be quickly established for children of these cadres. This job was given to the Women's Union, where I was assigned to organize kindergartens for kids aged two months up to three years. I was trained for two weeks. We were told to find staff by choosing young women, eighteen years of age and older, who were in good health and had their diploma. In the North, meanwhile, they put old women in charge of the *crèches*: women who were in poor health and could do little.

In the years right after 1975, parents left their kids in the care of young women who, despite a low salary, worked well. People received a small amount of money from the state. Nobody had any needs. There was a fever to consolidate power, which we saw as the work of each person. It was our turn to consolidate into one.

Everyone was thrilled to have independence, which during the time of Diem and Thieu had come tied to far too many foreigners. The aid that came into the country went into the pockets of the authorities. We saw officers and their wives become rich. We didn't like that. But the foreign aid did do a lot to develop industry in our country. People had money to spend, and the poor could earn a living. Everyone lived well, but we were not happy as the "independence" at that time was not real. And there was still the war. The war carried on, and every family had young men in the army; we didn't like the mobilization at all.

After liberation, there was peace and everyone was happy. Everyone was enthusiastic about following a Communist ideal: if everything came to pass as it was supposed to, in principle, it would be a paradise with justice for all. The cadres who had been in the maquis and in the camps were good people. They were poor, they had nothing, but they were ready to help. Everyone was ready to help. People who had been oppressed won everyone's sympathy; but once in power, they acted differently. Some cadres were honest and remain honest, but over time, those who were not sure of themselves went in another direction. First, they got a house. Some were satisfied with a tiny house and kept working. Others took on the lifestyle of the bourgeoisie and had a huge house with lots of furniture and vestiges of luxury. The original inhabitants of the house fled, and those who moved in learned the life of luxury. Bit by bit, living in a sumptuous home, they developed new habits and found they liked their new way of life.

The children of the nouveau riche started going to movies, watching football, sitting in cafés, and asking for money from their parents, who wanted to give them anything they wanted. Those children could corrupt their parents by demanding the most beautiful cars, the latest motorbikes, or expensive clothes displayed in storefronts. Parents who had had to live far away from their children for a long time wanted to give their children everything they wanted, even if such luxury spoiled them.

Children from the North listened to Western music and danced like it was a fashion. They imitated what they saw. They became much more spoiled than youth in the South, who were more used to such things and didn't fall for them all.

I worked in the crèches until 1979. We recruited nurses. We nominated older, experienced women to run kindergartens. In 1979, a woman selected as *chef de service* became my boss. I was more educated but could not be the office director since I was not a party member. The new director had almost no education; she was the wife of a revolutionary who had been imprisoned. While he was in prison, she had a stall at the flea market to earn something to send him, so he could eat. She could barely write, talk, or do math. She was often sent for training; to be somebody, one had to keep attending courses.

I had worked a long time, while this new director didn't know what to do. She had a complex and did not want me to go to meetings. One day, she went to a big meeting with representatives from many districts; each representative had been given orders each district needed to carry out. She did not know how to carry out the orders. As a privilege for children, the state allowed the kindergartens to buy things at low cost. Supplies were bought in quantity for use throughout the month. Thieves figured this out and entered the schools and stole the supplies. The director gave an order to assemble all these stocks in her bureau! She made a plan to resell the items on the black market. She did what she wanted.

In 1979, I worked with the health service, which was poorly organized. Production of medicine was emphasized, so since I knew formulas for medicines and chemical and plant products, I started producing medicines. I realized they paid me too little for this work. Normally, the more experienced one is, the more you are paid. I pointed out that I had graduated in 1957 and should receive 115 piastres, but they paid only 85. Younger pharmacists made twice as much though they were two grades behind; I asked why. They said the chef of the health service only made 85, so even if you were very skilled, you couldn't make more than 85. While in the Women's Union, I only made 55 piastres as secretary but did not complain because that was not my specialty. If I make less than those more junior in my field, that is different. I protested at the health service office.

The government created an association of doctors and pharmacists to build solidarity. They started looking for someone with experience who had lived in Saigon a long time and knew pharmacists from the former regime. The doctors and pharmacists in the new association brought different backgrounds: some had worked before the liberation; some came back from France, the United States, and Germany; others had studied in socialist countries. Most had gone abroad. We decided it would be best to have meetings and reassure and organize them as a group.

A group called the Medical and Pharmaceutical Association was formed in 1980 to serve as a scientific organization. One of my sisters and I, along with our husbands—all of us pharmacists—became well known in the association. This helped bring colleagues together to provide comfort, to evaluate each person's contributions, and to support those in need. Many professional colleagues did not hold the positions they should have. They were not valued.

The association planned meetings and elected an executive committee for each hospital and pharmaceutical venture or department. We did things based on professionalism. We arranged symposia and encouraged members to demonstrate their knowledge and skills. We urged them to read new documents and research and to exchange ideas about articles and issues. We ordered books and magazines. Compatriots in France sent us books and periodicals and bulletins, which we loaned to doctors and pharmacists. We established a small lending library, which differed from most libraries because we did loan out books since most colleagues could not spend hours reading in a library, away from their patients. We helped get approval for members to have a practice at home after working hours. Before, in the North, doctors practiced at home in secret.

Our association organized ceremonies to honor doctors with especially high moral standards from the past, such as Dr. Pham Ngoc Thach, who did so much during the war. He had studied medicine in France and married a Frenchwoman. During the 1945 revolution, he helped train the youth and was often found at the head of anti-French demonstrations. He became minister of health and then minister of foreign affairs. He went north in 1954, and his wife returned to France with their children. Dr. Thach returned south with the liberation army and died of an illness. He was proclaimed a hero of the workers. Dr. Thach had been active in health education for peasants in the North, invented medical treatments, and adapted to difficult conditions to pursue scientific research, especially on tuberculosis. A street in Saigon bears his name.

After the revolution, the need for talented, trained cadres first crystalized in the health field, because everyone gets sick. It was clear that good cadres were crucial. In other fields, like enterprise management or public service, people did not understand the importance of having qualified cadres. I don't think it's their fault because the needs were across the board. They took power without realizing the need for many different talents. They did not realize you must know the country well to govern it well.

While cadres from the maquis had everyone's sympathy, those returning from the North didn't know how to do things. They didn't know anything about whole regions of the country! All the orders come from the capital. In terms of talent levels, we were used to the old regime that included the Americans. There were complaints about cadres from the North but from our side as well. Poorly educated people came to power and imitated those from whom they seized power. Some say it is because "on a une complexe d'infériorite, on fait comme vous" (we have an inferiority complex, so we imitate you). People who are not from the peasant class are somewhat better off than they were up to the early 1980s, but many are discouraged and withdraw—called throwing a blanket over oneself. For years, many people wasted their skills or saved money to get out.

Bit by bit, intellectuals were the first to leave. They had diplomas that would help them live and work overseas. Later, others left—again, bit by bit—because they heard that life overseas was easier and did not require a lot of skills to survive. Here, even if people worked very hard, they could not make a living. It became *une mode de s'enfuir* (a fashion to flee). Even in the markets, fish and vegetable vendors talked about this all the time: "My aunt lives in such-and-such state and sent photos showing how well they live!" Poor people chose to go, especially fishermen on the coast who could leave more easily.

When men were being mobilized to fight the war in Cambodia in the 1980s, young people left too. We didn't like war.

For years, working in my pharmacy, I was at the counter to receive customers who were sick, poor, and illiterate. I took pity on them and served to my utmost capacity, while trying to earn a living. I watched the news but was always occupied with my customers, from early morning to night. When people asked for a certain amount of money, if I didn't have it, I asked friends or took up a collection.

Three of my siblings are in the United States, each in medicine: a doctor of oncology, a pharmacist, a nurse. A sister in California encouraged us to go there. My husband categorically refused. I would only want to visit. It will take generations to educate cadres who can help the country function. Meanwhile, uneducated cadres are given positions where their incompetence makes problems worse. A favorite slot for nonspecialized cadres who need a job is as head of personnel. There, they don't distinguish between categories, literally colors, of diplomas.

People are put into positions as favors. I am sympathetic to the fact that those in power were unable to pursue studies during the long war. The length of the war created generations of poorly educated cadres. But they squander resources by not encouraging those who do have training and careers. Northerners remain vigilant to keep the South from rebounding too quickly.

Even now, I take part in Communism, but the way of applying it varies greatly. It depends on each person's mind. A French professor of philosophy introduced me to the idea of Communism; listening to the professor, I thought I understood Communism. Before, I only knew about patriotism. I began to understand Communism is something that fascinates. It is a beautiful, idealistic ideology. Everyone has difficulties in life, so when we see something beautiful, we want to take part in an ideal. It was the first ideal I knew. I found it beautiful. We were young, with a lot of enthusiasm. I liked the ideas but felt it should not mean being told how to conduct every sphere of your life. Communism represented an ideal that had not yet been achieved.

Communism reminded me of Caodaism, a religion that talks about justice and liberty but was despotic itself. Its leaders believed only they can change the world. At the same time, religion is something like Communism: a search for justice.

I like to visit friends. I like to help others. I visited camps the government set up for thieves, drug addicts, and prostitutes, to sing for them at evening musical soirées.

Now that my children are grown up, I enjoy traveling. I like seeing parts of my country as well as going abroad. I realize I don't know the geography of my own country; when I was young, I learned the geography of France! When I visited a friend in Tay Ninh, I was embarrassed after offering her oranges because I thought the area was arid, but it is actually very fertile. I think travel can translate into better understanding and less likelihood of war.

My brother Phuoc died in 1989. I know many of his friends, but they hardly know me since I was so young when we met. Some died during the resistance; they were shot or died from illness. A hundred days after the death of my brother, friends and colleagues organized two soirées to sing his songs, each one introduced by Professor Tran Van Khe.

With only a few of us having been together at Lycée Marie Curie, our bonds of friendship tightened. Many friends who came from smart and wealthy families ended up leaving; those who studied in Vietnamese schools mostly stayed in the country. In every family, one or more students, especially boys, chose to go north or join the maquis. Some returned and looked me up after becoming officers or heads of a department. One after the other, they retired. I greatly respect the generation that is now retired.

My life does not include as many adventures as do the lives of my schoolmates. I am neither daring nor courageous. I content myself with being patient, with an average intelligence, and possessing the spirit of aiding others. I am drawn to beauty, by which I don't mean outside beauty. We have a saying: wood is better than paint.

The Music Professor, Tran Van Khe

Tran Van Khe came from a family in the South known for actively participating in the anticolonial movement and for extraordinary musical talent. His musical and academic genius ensured him a seat at the University of Hanoi in 1942, where he met Luu Huu Phuoc. Together, they wrote and performed songs that awakened youth, from north to south, to join the revolution. The Saigon sisters recall going to their concerts at the Opera House in Saigon and being awed and inspired.

Tran Van Khe went to study in France in 1949, earning his doctorate from the Sorbonne in 1958. While he remained based in France for the next five decades, he also traveled the world researching, teaching, and performing traditional Vietnamese music. Among his academic accomplishments, he came to the United States in 1988 as a Fulbright scholar. With each prize and scholarship awarded to him, his reputation as the premier ethnomusicologist of Vietnamese music soared.

For the first time since 1949, he visited Vietnam in 1976, landing at Hanoi's Noi Bai Airport as the guest of his friend Luu Huu Phuoc, who had become minister of culture after 1975 and followed a strict political line. The only common ground left to these old friends was the need to preserve Vietnam's musical tradition.

Tran Van Khe described visits to Vietnam that are poignant and wrenching, obstacles to helping his people while trying to avoid politics, and glimpses of his philosophy of life. He returned to live in Saigon in 1989, occupying rooms at the back of a villa he transformed into a museum of traditional music.

Tran Van Khe

When Phuoc decided to dedicate everything for the Liberation, he destroyed all his precious belongings: childhood photos, family photos, love letters. He burned everything, admitting later: "I was a fool—what a stupid thing I did. I made a complete rupture with the past, but now I miss the beautiful things I burned." This gesture was typical of him, and indeed, by early 1944, he was giving his all. He went into the resistance zone and wrote a song for Ho Chi Minh and a song, "Dong Nam A Chau" (Southeast Asia), about how everyone in the region supports the battle. Few of these songs were good; they were songs to mobilize and drill followers. I think his heart was in the struggle, not in making beautiful music. Throughout this period, he produced many marches for the maquisards, but I did not find one song that touched the people as before.

During the years Phuoc was minister of culture in the provisional government, the National Front, he sent his articles, publications, and lectures on music but not any compositions. Starting in 1951, I devoted myself to researching traditional Vietnamese music to prepare my doctoral thesis at the Sorbonne and was uninterested in new songs. Phuoc focused on ideological issues more than music composition.

In April 1976, as minister of culture, Phuoc received me on my visit to Vietnam at the invitation of the Union of Vietnamese Composers. Phuoc hosted me in 1977 and 1978 as president of the Parliamentary Commission for Culture and Information, with the rank of minister and as director of the Institute of Vietnamese Musicology.

As a friend, Phuoc had not changed. He was the same affectionate and passionate person I had known before. But in his thinking, he was different. He thought like an official; he followed the political line. I avoided talking about a lot of things with him. We agreed on needing to save musical tradition. That is why we were able to work together from 1976 until 1989. He defended me whenever I was attacked, whether by subordinates in different ministries or by people who did not understand my position. He did not hesitate to defend me. I did not ask him to, but he often did.

In 1976, people were full of hope. When my plane landed, I closed my eyes and thought, "I am back on the soil of Vietnam!" We landed at Hanoi's Noi Bai Airport and drove into town. It still looked mutilated: roads riddled with potholes caused by bombshells, bridges destroyed. Each time I saw these things, tears came to my eyes.

For the first time, I saw police agents in Vietnamese uniform who did not have a foreign power behind them! In the South, military police used to be everywhere; here, I saw only Vietnamese. It was a strange feeling. Finally, we were masters of our own destiny. But at the same time, I was afraid. The Communists used such violent means. At the airport, they thrust a big sack at passengers, and, instead of saying, "Show your passports," they shouted, "Collecting all passports!" I had a Vietnamese passport and threw it in the bag, thinking, "I am done; I am nothing; I have no identity; I can't travel." They looked at everybody with suspicion, as if each of us was a spy, and repeated: "Collecting all passports! It is forbidden to stand. Everybody sit!" I was both moved and upset to be welcomed to my country like that. At the exit, I quickly forgot everything thanks to a warm welcome and bouquets of flowers brought by musician friends. The local police returned my passport. All was forgotten, but my first impression remained a painful one.

Years ago, Luu Huu Phuoc and I had been arrested at the same time by the French and imprisoned at the Catinat station, which now served as his office.

I met many people who harbored a lot of hope. Finally, maybe we can rebuild our country and do what we want. I also felt full of hope. It was a few years later that I became disillusioned. Things did not unfold as I hoped. From the cultural point of view, I admit that I did not worry or suffer because the line given was the right one: culture should reflect the national character that is clearly recognizable, even from abroad. Culture should not be reserved for a privileged class but for all the people. But while the line given was the right one, its implementation was not.

They tried to create all kinds of difficulties for me, even in how they hosted me. Ignoring the international regard given to my profession and my place in it, the ministry of culture claimed it could not make a car or any transportation available. I went to give lectures by cyclo: my son on one pedicab, me alongside on another. That's how we went to meetings. People stared and said, "But this isn't possible. It can't be!" But it was like that.

People accused Phuoc and me of selling music documents to foreigners to make money. Who would buy them? People making the claims were crazy. They thought these were popular songs people would want to buy, but nobody wanted them, not even to make a record since royalties were tiny compared to songs that were in fashion. But they made the claims. They even put accusations in writing to the government, which set up an investigation committee. After six months of inquiry, the committee concluded there was nothing there. Phuoc was thrilled and said, "Khe, we are cleared of any suspicions; I am so happy." Even the head of the committee, Prime Minister Pham Van Dong, said the same to reassure me: "This is all finished now; we are sure of the pureness of your feelings, the pureness of your honesty."

I told Phuoc:

You are happy, but I am not satisfied. I am hurt because when there is an assertion like this and a committee of investigation, it means the government thinks there could be something shady. If the inquiry finds nothing at all, he who made the accusations faces nothing and is pensioned off. It means there is no law. If there were any law, I would file for defamation. I would not do this to be mean or take revenge but to bring out the truth and prevent people from committing the same stupidities. We are in a country where we have no rights. You may be happy, but I am mad.

I told him that. He understood. It was essential that people know we did nothing wrong, which was a relief. But deep inside, I was mad. The fact they organized a committee meant they had once held doubts.

At the end, in 1989, Phuoc arranged a gathering that meant a lot to me: a festival of lullabies. There had never been a festival of lullabies anywhere. I gave a talk on the importance of lullabies as what a child absorbs in its subconscious; at the moment the mother gives milk to nourish the child's body, she sings a lullaby that introduces into the child's memory a popular melody or popular poem. Phuoc organized the festival; women and men sang ancient as well as modern songs from the center, north, and south of the country. When asked to address the closing, I said,

> I feel great joy. Ideas I planted here and there are bearing fruit with this event. Lullabies still endure. Where we thought the fire had gone out, I see embers from once-hot coals now covered with the dust of time; it takes just a breath of air to lift off the ashes and let the embers glow anew. I hope this fire will not be one of straw that leaps up, only to flame out. I hope it will be a fire that you light always by your love for the homeland, your love for the people. By that dedication, this sacred fire will never die out. Never.

I spoke these words while looking at my friend Luu Huu Phuoc.

In March 1989, Luu Huu Phuoc composed "Loi ru chim lac," the lullaby of the *lac* bird. The word *lac* can also mean "to stray." When he first composed it, Phuoc was not satisfied with how the song was sung. I made a suggestion, but he smiled: "We can't have all the songs I compose arranged to be sung only by you!" Luu Huu Phuoc left us forever in June 1989. When I sang this, his last song, friends cried. From start to finish, it is about our national character: there is nothing of the West, nor of military marches. It is a lullaby about a bird crossing great distances to go home and, ultimately, find the country ravaged by fire. This, his last song, moved me to tears.

I knew his mother and siblings, including Tuyen, who thinks of me as a brother. One of his sisters loved him very much but had to leave the country before he came back. They met once in France: she flew from the United States; he came from Vietnam. Of all his siblings, only Tuyen stayed to look after the spirit of her father. As the youngest, Tuyen was close to Phuoc. She loved music, the arts, and the sciences.

In one sense, I live through my interior life. I reside in France, but I live as if in Vietnam. I read in Vietnamese; I talk and write in Vietnamese. I sing Vietnamese songs. I play Vietnamese music. But it does not keep me from having a bicultural life, two things at once that I live in a deep way. I speak French as fluently as Vietnamese, while some speak French fluently and forget Vietnamese. I speak Vietnamese at conferences and don't mix in a single word of French. I have composed many poems in Vietnamese. I do not feel far away. My research requires me to reread the historical works of Vietnam; every day, I come across a Vietnamese record or meet a Vietnamese musician, and it's exactly as if I am returning to Vietnam and gathering these flowers, one by one, to make a bouquet.

This is to say, while living in France, I did not feel far from Vietnam, even though it was terrible when I was unable to visit. Until I went back after twenty-seven years, each time I flew over Vietnam, my heart tightened. When I visited Thailand, I saw banana and coconut trees, and memories filled me with joy; but when I touched a tree, I knew it was not a Vietnamese tree. It was only in 1976 that I could return and touch a Vietnamese banana tree, stand under Vietnamese rain, meet Vietnamese people, or talk with Vietnamese on the street. At that moment, I made up for time lost. It gave me not only a source of extra energy, but from then on, I played music better than before.

Plunging back into Vietnamese society, I felt something completely different. It was a renaissance. I played instruments with more breadth, more innovation. I rediscovered the breast at which the infant is nourished. I found my roots. I drank again at the ancient spring of musical traditions.

Many Vietnamese abroad think I am Communist or pro-Communist. They hung onto false information that I was in the

Communist Party in the early 1940s. I was never Communist. I am not now; I never will be. When one of Phuoc's nieces asked me about it, I explained: "What differs for me is that I am not Communist, and I am also not anti-Communist like you who have a hatchet out for everything." I didn't accept certain ideas and things that were done, but I had to recognize that during the resistance the Communists played an important role. That is certain.

Many refugees think I work for the Communists. I say nothing. I have pure feelings about my people regarding culture; everything I have done has been neither for one political party nor one government but for the whole people. And where the people are, I am there—whether they are in Vietnam or live outside. That is why, wherever in the world, when asked to come and talk about our music, I do it. I am neither poor nor rich; I have enough to eat and live simply. I don't have needs like others: I don't drink; I don't smoke; I don't play cards; I don't spend a lot. I eat, and I work. That is why I do not play for money or honor but for a love of culture and music, for a love of people. I want to share what I have learned and experienced, not just with students, not just with friends, but with all people who want to know.

In 1979, I visited prostitutes and criminals kept in "prisons without walls." They thanked me for coming and speaking in a language they understood. The only thing they had with which to thank me was a song. I visited drug users where I met a Western-trained doctor who specialized in traditional music. To detoxify patients, he had no Western medicines, just herbs. The withdrawal is terrible. During an attack, he had only one way to help. He used medical plants as a calmant, acupuncture, and especially love: the love of a doctor for the sick.

I like to be anywhere I am needed, not just for the music. Several times, I told Phuoc: "When I see a house destroyed, in utter ruin, I am unafraid. We can rebuild a house. We can repair a bridge. But when I see the mentality of the Vietnamese people completely distraught by a situation, I am afraid because these things are invisible and I don't know how to restore all that. I don't see it. These things are beyond my understanding. They exceed my imagination."

I suffer a lot because I see children no longer sing children's songs; they shout insults on the street. I see people no longer give something for nothing; they give to get something. Naturally, there are many who continue to give freely for nothing. Thank goodness. I am among the happiest because I have met many who still give out of the goodness of their hearts without wanting something in return. I have also met people who were extraordinary before but who, seen up close, changed once they started to have a little money. I have seen education deteriorate, and that affects the future generation. I have seen the quality of medical care deteriorate. Doctors don't seek to cure and save, as I wanted to do when I studied medicine. They do it because they are paid, and they try to get paid as much as possible. Some still have good hearts, but in general, people are obliged to be like this. All of this causes me great suffering.

I am not at all Buddhist in the religious sense. I never had a sacred name given by a bonze. I did study Buddhist philosophy and music, and I have a lot of respect for Buddhism, as I do for Catholicism and other beliefs. I do not consider religion an opiate of the people but a refuge for the unhappy who don't know what to do anymore, who are unable to change the course of their destiny and find refuge in religion—perhaps to find a little peace. I respect that and how the precepts of religion are always good works, doing the right thing. I do not believe in the existence of Jesus Christ or Buddha or whatever it might be; I see them as human beings who reached a degree of enlightenment and understanding.

16

LIEN AN

"We Understood What We Had to Do"

In 1954, Lien An left her family to answer the call of the government in Hanoi, where she launched a long career in education by attending the school of pedagogy. During periods of U.S. bombing, she transferred her two daughters to live with a peasant family in a village sixteen kilometers away. Back in Hanoi, life revolved around her studies, political training, and standing in long lines for food rations.

In 1975, the ministry of education organized the return of teachers to the South. She visited her sisters still living in their old house, arriving exactly one year after the death of her father.

Lien An became principal of Le Quy Don, formerly Lycée Chasseloup-Laubat, where she worked from six in the morning until seven or eight at night. Reliving the many hardships—classes with over fifty students, constant staff turnover, chronic petty theft—she stops to remind herself, "But after all, we did have peace."

Lien An stayed at Le Quy Don from 1977 until 1986, when she welcomed a chance to retire. Not long after, she answered another call and found herself director of a different kind of school.

Lien An

I did not expect to become a teacher, though we played school at home. At the time I passed my baccalaureate, some classmates pursued law; others, medicine or pharmacy. Few people thought about becoming a teacher. At first, I chose law.

When I went to Hanoi and met Professor Tran Van Giau, who had studied in France before joining the resistance, he said it would not be like before. With socialism and a new society coming, we were encouraged to enter the pedagogy university of Hanoi. I had not planned on this.

In the North, we figured sooner or later there would be bombings, so we moved our children out of the schools and into villages. I took my girls to a village about sixteen kilometers away, where they lived with a nice peasant family. My daughters were happy to ride on the back of a buffalo. One day I came back from school and saw my five-year-old riding a buffalo. I was afraid because buffaloes can kick people in the head. She and a little herd boy, also five years old, had taken the buffalo to the field, where she easily climbed onto the beast and sat pleased with herself. I asked, "How did you get up there, and how will you get down?" It turned out the little herder boy had only to make a grunting sound, and the buffalo got down on its knees, and my daughter could easily slip off his back.

At first, it was not easy, but the little ones adjusted quickly. They went to the village school and acted like little peasants. They ran in and along the rice fields, played with the peasant children, and fished for tiny shrimp used in cooking. Where there were no village schools, we built them. Few people could stay in town, so most of us had to choose a rural district in which to stay. Parents and children left the city at the same time; a few parents entrusted their children to a peasant family while they stayed in town. I taught in a school where 90 percent of the students were originally from Haiphong but had to leave to avoid bombing of that port city.

When the bombing stopped in 1969, we returned to Hanoi. The twelve days of bombing in 1972 showed us we should expect more. Long periods of bombing followed under President Nixon. We read about Americans going to the South and bombing. We talked about it every day. When bombs hit the train station and the French embassy very close to us, we went into the basement.

We paid attention to everything related to our country; we kept current on what was happening and what we needed to do. We accepted this because we could not do anything different. If we wanted to be independent, we could not do differently. We also reserved time for our private life.

We believed in the party and in the government and in what we did being just. It is a matter of loyalty. It is what needs to be done. There is no other way. It is not only for our people but for all oppressed people. This was well studied and communicated among cadres and the youth, in the schools and in the education of the youth who accepted the need to leave and participate in the movement. We were taught three things to be prepared to do as the youth: study, carry a gun if necessary, and produce supplies. People accepted the need to help liberate the country. We had to take care of the family because that affects the nation. We had to produce food and other provisions, especially when a father was absent. There were just old people left working in the rice fields, almost no young people. And in the North, unlike the South, it is hard to grow rice. I had students who at age eighteen or nineteen went to the South to fight.

Through the education we got in the North, we understood and realized what we had to do. When I had left Saigon, it was still vague. We were going to participate in something important, in reconstruction, in the life of a country where there would be independence and justice and equality. But it was still unclear. When we went north, we realized what we had to do, what we could do, and what we thought we could do. That education was a whole program. In our little household, my husband and children got along, as it should be in a good society that follows the right path and helps our countrymen. We take on sensible careers. We can contribute to the development of the country.

It must be said, the North did demand a lot from us. Compared to life now, it was hard. At the same time, we found it completely natural. We had to make long lines to redeem ration tickets for meat, rice, and petrol. Everyone did it. My little ones, at ten and twelve, became expert at standing in line. We lived together, so if someone suddenly had to dash, we would call out, "Hey, little one, come stand in line for me." And they'd run over and stand in line and bring back vegetables. It was natural since everyone did it. In youth, we adapt easily.

Sunday was reserved for standing in line for rations, so we woke up early. We made lines for staples but also for meat, nuoc mam, fish, chicken—everything. My children started the lines, and I arrived later with money to pay. We had the basics. We got used to it. We were not hungry. In the North, life is more difficult than in the South. Fruits are harder to find and more expensive. The most satisfying thing about returning south was we did not have to stand in line anymore.

The government organized our reentry to the South after the war ended on April 30, 1975. The government needed cadres and groups of educators and doctors. We left Hanoi at the end of May. The Ministry of Education organized each leg of our return. We took a train from Hanoi to Vinh, where we climbed onto trucks and drove to Hue. Something went wrong, and we stayed a week in Hue. We got back on the road and arrived in Saigon on June 18, 1975. We jumped down from the trucks in front of the education ministry.

I came south alone, and my daughters joined me a few months later. My husband stayed in Hanoi until 1980. I had not seen Saigon since November 1954. I recognized the streets right away; they had not changed. The cathedral was the same, as was the education ministry. Everything around my house, however, had changed. Before, rice fields had extended along the road on both sides. All that had disappeared.

The atmosphere was quiet. We were warmly welcomed by our parents and friends who had stayed. I telephoned others who had come back earlier. It was exactly one year after my father's death in 1974. I went to our house with my sisters.

We organized a group of teachers. I was one of the older teachers, with years of experience. For two years, I worked at Vo Thi Sau High School, named after the first woman who had fought the French and been executed at Con Son Island, formerly Poulo Condore prison. I didn't really like administration; I had not done it since 1957. I liked teaching history and being with students! But after two years, the teachers at Vo Thi Sau asked me to be the director. It was a school for girls. They wanted a teacher with experience. Parents did not want to entrust their children to someone too young.

My next assignment took me to Lycée Le Quy Don, formerly Chasseloup-Laubat. These were difficult years. Le Quy Don is a big school. Internal conflicts festered between older teachers and the longtime director, who could not deal with teachers who did not accept her. The male students fought all the time. Some days, I worked from six in the morning to eight at night. Students arrived at Le Quy Don between quarter to seven and quarter after. Something always happened at the end of the day, so I had to stay late. I worried about things if I wasn't there. The job tired me out.

Education reform took hold in several ways. There used to be too much talk about politics and time spent teaching Marxism-Leninism and philosophy. There was not enough teaching about morals. Bad influences came from society, where parents were busy working all day, looking for money to normalize life. There were good students who behaved and were eager to learn, and others who did not study. Even the children of the rich, who have an easy life, turned bad.

At Le Quy Don, we divided classes into two shifts, one in the morning and one in the afternoon. I had to stay all day. I don't know if it's my fault, but I had little luck with vice directors. With huge classes, we needed staff to be monitors. We had classes of thirty-five students, but also of fifty and fifty-five! Teachers were tired. For each topic, there would be a *chef du groupe* (group leader), but these key teachers sometimes left and had to be replaced. The student population increased so much that even the dormitory on the first floor was converted into classrooms. Because the school sits on a busy corner, the street noise was deafening and made it hard for teachers to teach; they had to shout, especially during rush hours and when loud honking motorbikes passed.

We faced three basic challenges at Le Quy Don: the biggest remained the size of classes, followed by turnover in personnel and the management of materials at the school. During the tough years, people committed petty crime, pocketing

FIGURE 12. Lien An in front of one of Saigon's famous high schools, Le Quy Don, where she served as headmistress after 1975. Many future leaders attended the elite school, built by the French, when it was known as Lycée Chasseloup-Laubat and later as Lycée Jean-Jacques Rousseau. Courtesy of the author.

school supplies and so on. Boys would take apart a fan in minutes. Guards constantly chased after students. We lacked money to buy materials.

But, after all, we did have peace.

Compared to the war years, things got better as we overcame difficulties. One of the hardest situations in Hanoi had been housing two schools in one building! In the morning, one administration operated the school, and in the evening, another. Many Hanoi schools were organized like that: one school, one building, one classroom, except that two schools used them. The schools had two separate names, in the same building! In the morning, teachers did one thing, like plant a little garden, and in the evening, others ripped it out. Constant conflicts arose between the school administrators in the morning and in the evening. We asked that, in the South, we organize as we had before liberation: one school, one administration. It means more work, and we have too few staff, but at least we have a unified organization.

Every month, schools organized events to observe historic anniversaries. On January 9, students sang and commemorated the anniversary of the death of Tran

Van On. February 3 was the anniversary of the founding of the Vietnamese Communist Party in 1930; March 8, International Women's Day; Liberation Day, April 30; Workers' Day, May 1; Uncle Ho's Birthday, May 19; the fall of Dien Bien Phu; International Children's Day. Only October did not have a particular celebration! November 20 is Teachers' Day. December has a lot of anniversaries: the nineteenth is when the resistance began against the French, and the twenty-second is the day of the popular army. Young boys prepared at eighteen to enter the army, so we organized trips to army camps. Every month, you had to think ahead to arrange these events! It was hard to maintain order. Tet tired students out, not least because the fire crackers make it hard to sleep.

During the first years after liberation, parents did not have to pay any school costs. Now we find that the government does not have enough money, so parents pay some tuition.

The parents' association was represented by a committee of a dozen parents. Each month, school leaders met with the committee to share results of the students' work and discuss what we needed parents to do. We were constantly in contact with parents. This was our government's way of doing things: school contact with parents and school contact with society. If a district needed something, the school, the parents, and the society responded.

Lycée Le Quy Don maintained a high level of academics. Students scored well in exams and won prizes, and a high percentage of graduates entered university. Lycée Le Hong Phong, the former Lycée Pétrus Ky, and several others in District 3 also produced good results.

I worked at Le Quy Don from 1977 until 1986. I did all I could. Women have to retire at fifty-five. I worked continuously for over twenty-five years; by the time I reached retirement, I had worked almost thirty years. I believe in letting the youth come up; as long as we are still in place, they can't. So I thought it was better to retire. It hurts your head to always try to find new ways to organize students, staff, and programs. I found some things hard to overcome. I think the young do better than the old, so we need to make room for them. Nobody is irreplaceable. There are those who think they can't be replaced, whereas I think there is always someone who comes along and can make things happen.

My husband retired in 1980. He likes to stay engaged with society. He visits friends all day. Recently, he has had health problems, so he stays home more.

When I retired, I did not expect to work again. I thought I might give French lessons or teach history, but teaching is tiring, and I can't talk for a long time now. At a meeting of the Communist Party at the district level, the parent of a former student at Le Quy Don recognized me and persuaded the district party secretary to ask me to help establish a school for handicapped children. I went to look at the school that had been set up in a house. He reassured me, "Each day you only have to help the teachers out for an hour or two." So I started. I also helped in the evenings. I soon found myself the new director; I promised to stay for a year. That was several years ago. The school for handicapped was known as Ecole d'Avenir (School of the Future). It's all new; in the past, there were no schools like this. I go almost every day. My office is in a garage attached to the school. At first, three out of five teachers of the deaf students left; other teachers left to teach at a school in Chinatown, where parents are wealthier. We still had difficulties with staff, but the situation became more stable. Parents readily paid the tuition fees. Kids started learning faster. The mute children learned to talk more. Parents wanted their children to be able to conduct themselves in society. Some learned how to respectfully address people: "Chao co" (Hello, sister), "Chao ba" (Hello, older sister).

Things got better; this is the kind of result I find very satisfying.

I have no passion for writing memoirs or such. I take care of my little ones at home. Things happen that we have not thought about, just as I had never thought I would be a teacher. I remember being very young and chatting with a classmate about what we wanted to be when we grew up. I said, "I'd like to be a doctor, so I can help the sick and make them better." She said, "I don't want to do medicine; that means you are always around people with complaints. I'd rather be a teacher because we are always with the young and we feel young." At that time, I still thought I'd rather be a doctor.

When I was a child, my father told me the fortune-teller declared I could be a nurse or a teacher. I was afraid to be a nurse; I'd rather have a different profession. I went to Hanoi thinking along those lines and took an offer to enter the professorate. Things happen randomly: *l'homme propose, dieu dispose* (man proposes, God disposes). I never thought I would become a school principal. At Vo Thi Sau, I knew others who would be a good director, but the teachers said, "No, it should be you. This is a school for girls; you have the age and experience to be the director." That's how I became a principal.

When I returned in 1975, I found classmates who are very precious to me. Not many old lycée classmates had stayed. At Marie Curie, I knew Minh first and Tuyen only in the last year of lycée. Sen and Trang were in class with my sisters. Our families knew each other. While not all in the same class, when we returned, we started to meet up. When I came back, the first person I saw was Minh. Tuyen came looking for me after Minh told her I was back. One day, by chance, I caught a glimpse of Oanh from afar but could not call to her. The next time I saw her, she was walking along Pasteur Street, and I called out and was glad to see her. Tuyen suggested we all get together, and a few days after Tet, we met at Le An's house. I was not in her class, but our parents know each other. When I went to Hanoi, I saw Le An again, and we knew each other there.

After our first reunion at Le An's, we liked the idea of getting together from time to time. We built on that plan, with Tuyen as intermediary. Each time a meeting is planned, it's easy to reach those with phones, but some do not have phones, so Tuyen goes in person to make contact. She always remained young and youthful in character. Sen does not age. She is so young.

It is easy for us to be together. As Mme Tuong said, we had the same education, we had friends in common, and we had parents who knew each other. And we shared the same goal.

17

XUAN

"We Could Not Stay Indifferent"

Xuan's path led her from the jungle to London and back to Saigon in 1956. Having first met Lau in the maquis, serendipity brought them together in England, where they married. Members of a group of Vietnamese students in London, she studied piano at the Royal College of Music, and he attended the London School of Economics and studied the bar at Oxford. Of thirteen Vietnamese students, eleven left to serve the government in Hanoi. Xuan and Lau returned to the South.

Keeping a low profile teaching piano and raising four children, Xuan despised the rule of Ngo Dinh Diem, "a dictatorial regime whose injustice the people had to bear daily." Lau worked undercover for the Viet Cong and published an English-language newspaper, the *Saigon Daily News*, to counter Diem's newspaper, the *Times of Vietnam*, and to be a voice in any coalition government. One night in 1969, he hailed a pedicab to go home but never arrived. Xuan found out he was arrested. He remained in jail until late 1972. To survive, Xuan taught piano, cared for her children, and drew on her "hope mentality" to give her the courage to overcome.

Xuan

In 1954, my father came to visit me in London with Suong and her mother. They found a convent in Cambridge where Suong could study; her husband lived in London and brought her there on weekends. Suong's parents had once lived in the same town as my parents, so we were more than casual friends.

Of the thirteen Vietnamese students in London, eleven went to the North; only Lau and I went to the South. Another member we didn't know well became a minister of economics under Diem. Most in the student association went to serve in the North. One, Nguyen My Dien, a student at the London School of Economics, became Ho Chi Minh's translator on travels to Indonesia and elsewhere. Suong became the English-language radio announcer in Hanoi, where she had the name "Lan huong" (scent of an orchid). She read abridged versions of sentimental Vietnamese stories over the radio at night. She read each day of the week and did not go to the countryside, not even during bombing raids. Everyone, north and south and along the length of the Ho Chi Minh Trail, listened to her on the radio.

On May 1, 1956, I landed at Ton Son Nhat with two children and pregnant with the third. I had to go to the home of Lau's parents in Hue to wait for his return. He stayed in London until 1957. Then we all traveled to Saigon, and I started teaching at the national school of music.

The regime of Ngo Dinh Diem was at this time trying to consolidate power by launching a bloody campaign in the countryside against former Viet Minh resistants and by conducting a kind of McCarthyite witch-hunt in the civil service to find those supposedly supporting the other side. This was the anti-Communist movement that culminated in inquisitions and the guillotine stalking the land, its length and width, to claim the heads of former resistants and to strike fear in the hearts of the people. During these years, I kept a low profile, teaching music and rearing my children, limiting our relationships with former Marie Curie students to the minimum.

Minh, Thanh's sister, also lived in Saigon, but whenever we met, we made it as coincidental and brief as possible for fear of arousing suspicion that we, who must have been on the government's blacklist, would once again get together for subversive activities. We had to keep each other at arm's length and took the precaution to meet seldom.

I taught piano from 1957 up until now, doing that one thing for over thirty-five years. I am emotionally simple. This is perhaps an exception rather than the rule with artists, who are generally known to be highly emotional and complex. I cannot bear the sufferings of others. Sociologists and psychologists nowadays would attribute this to my social dimension being "transcendent." Until the fall of Ngo Dinh Diem in 1963, we lived under a dictatorial regime whose injustices the people had to bear daily. I felt unhappy although economically and socially I had nothing to complain about. I continued to teach at the conservatory and to give private lessons at home, and Lau worked for Esso as a senior executive, earning a very good salary. I shared with him the passion, simple but overwhelmingly strong, of the unbearable pity for the suffering of all.

We did not, however, play an active role in the campaign led by Buddhists to topple the Ngo Dinh Diem regime. As former Viet Minh and sympathizers of the resistance, we were more or less under surveillance, not until the last stage of the campaign, that is, when, one night, a Buddhist friend, attuned to where our sympathies lay, knocked on our door and brought in three fugitive monks seeking shelter to avoid arrest. We lived in an apartment complex that also housed Americans who worked as pilots for the national civil airline, Air Vietnam. Our small flat was already overcrowded with my mother living with us. But it was unthinkable, inhuman, against our conviction, and below our dignity not to welcome the religious men in. We made them sit still and keep absolutely silent, to the astonishment of my children. In the meantime, we discussed who in the apartment complex was likely to help: Who would be courageous enough not to fear the police and compassionate enough to provide temporary sanctuary in their home?

We decided on an American pilot, a bachelor who lived alone. I went to ask, and without a moment's hesitation, he accepted, and the three monks stayed with him for three days before evacuating to a safer place. Three days were long enough for them to become a heavy burden on our good quiet American. Not content to send the pilot on errands, including as a courier to mail and even deliver their antigovernment letters, each morning the monks ignored their status as fugitives and, draped in their yellow robes, spent time on the balcony doing physical exercises. They exposed us all to the danger of arrest; when they left, we and our American friend heaved a deep sigh of relief.

After the fall of Ngo Dinh Diem, the war escalated rung by rung to such proportions as to engulf our whole country in fire and fury. The war was everywhere: in the streets with grenades exploding and on television and radio news. There was so much hatred; I was ready to go back to the maquis. We could not stay indifferent; something had to be done. We answered the call of the resistance.

My husband published the English-language *Saigon Daily News* with a view to winning support for peace. I helped him in every way I could. In April 1969, the police found out that he was a Viet Cong and picked him up. He was arrested and given a five-year sentence. The newspaper closed. After that, people avoided me, but it did not affect me. I still had good friends. [Ed. note: Nguyen Van Threu, president, Republic of Vietnam, 1967–75.]

An uncle of Lau's had married Thieu's daughter, and he and two other friends tried to get him out before the full five years. Political prisoners could be released after serving half a sentence. During my husband's time in prison, I worked hard to rear my four children, to take courage and live to wait for Lau.

Lau was released on Armistice Day: November 11, 1972.

Lau, Xuan's Husband

Lau is tall with silver hair and twinkling eyes. His flawless English and background in business and law prepared him to be an executive with Esso, a journalist and publisher, and a spy. He was also a keen philosopher and a historian. He lamented that the Vietnamese, steeped in revolution, are afraid to express any doubts about it—perhaps, he mused, in fear of concluding it is not worth the cost? Lau often quoted Shakespeare—"my nation, right or wrong"—and attributed his schooling with Jesuit priests as the greatest factor in his awakening to nationalism.

Lau

As schoolchildren, we awoke to the revolution. Our first love is revolution. To our own amazement and pity, it remains so. Revolution was our first love.

My family came from the North; perhaps my ancestors lost courage and stopped in Hue, the ancient imperial city. We are considered more traditional, but I am not sure about that, as Xuan's family is even more so. When her cousins who settled abroad, many in France, marry off a daughter and take in a son-in-law, they carry out the ceremony in which the bride and groom prostrate themselves before the parents. This is a phenomenon about which I am still curious. In my family, we reject all this kind of ceremony and paraphernalia. Perhaps my family suffered too much from feudalist traditions and wants to be rid of them quickly.

I went to a school run by Jesuit priests. I attribute the schooling as the greatest factor in my awakening to nationalism because the curriculum was the same as that taught at French lycées. Staffed by Canadian Jesuit priests, the school was run democratically. They did not distinguish between us and French boys. When a fight broke out between Vietnamese and French boys, for instance, they asked if we were willing to put on boxing gloves.

We became Marxist in part over ownership of land and status. There is the general context and the particular. The general context is that, as Vietnamese dominated by the Chinese for a thousand years and by the French for a hundred years, we are fanatical about not being a servant. The particular context is that I come from a family of revolutionaries, even radicals. I say radical because my father and his brothers rejected education in Chinese characters and embraced French education. That was quite something at the end of the nineteenth century and start of the twentieth century! My relatives are intelligent, and many earned high degrees in Chinese, but they found that with those degrees, at the turn of the century, they could not make a living. They switched.

The royal family owned a lot of land and redistributed it to members of my family and to people who were more deserving— that is, people who served in the war. We received a gift of land given by the king. The majority of people live on the fruits of the land. My father taught high school, and my mum taught primary school in a French lycée. We lived off our own earnings. We are a laboring people. My mother was like Florence Nightingale. That is the economic explanation. The social explanation is that there was inequality. Some people were more equal than others.

On the side of my mother, the stereotype held that all kings and queens are traitors, Benedict Arnolds. The Nguyen dynasty is not that bad; of thirteen kings, research shows that only four collaborated or had anything to do with the Vietnamese people losing their freedom. Officially, this is still only timidly discussed in articles. The official line remains that royalists are bad and kings are traitors. A poet with a good reputation did a study based on poems by Nguyen kings—after all, they had nothing to do!—and advanced the theory that if they could write such beautiful poems, they could not be traitors. Now the ball is rolling. A serious study put forth the thesis that the Nguyen dynasty was not too bad. At least three kings who fought the French were exiled abroad, including on Reunion

Island. The remains of one or two kings have been returned for burial in Hue; my great aunts attended the funerals. This is very unusual for a socialist country!

When I came back to Vietnam, I had read my PPE (philosophy, politics, and economics) at Oxford. I spent two years at the bar specializing in international economics law. In Saigon, I worked as an executive for Esso. When I thought about what was needed in the fight for independence, I left Esso. I was asked to publish an English-language newspaper, the *Saigon Daily News*; the strategy was, if a coalition forms, we will have our own newspaper in English.

I went to my general manager in Esso to tell him I planned to leave. He happened to have studied with me at the same school at Oxford and was flabbergasted that I wanted to quit. He kept repeating, "Why, Lau? Why? You are highly placed, and your future is assured!" In 1963, during the regime of Ngo Dinh Diem, I traveled to many places as the Esso representative. I acted as Esso's delegate for a refinery project that brought two sides together, the Vietnamese government and three oil companies: Esso, Shell, and Caltex. Esso invested the most capital, so we would manage the project. At the stage of building the refinery in Nha Trang, President Diem and his brother Nhu asked us to provide more information. To gather relevant details, I was asked to travel to the Philippines, Japan, and other countries, where I saw how other refineries had been built. I was a VIP, and my future was bright. I flew all the time; they called me the "Flying Dutchman." But I told my colleague I had to leave. I could not tell them the real reason, so I said I was tired of flying all the time.

By then it was in late 1963, after the fall of Ngo Dinh Diem. There was the urge to have a newspaper of our own, by which I mean the Viet Cong. My boss just said, "I don't understand you people."

Xuan and I sold off our car, jewelry, and other property to start publishing the *Saigon Daily News*. It was to be distinguished from the *Saigon Post* run by Bui Diem. The *News* reached a circulation of fifteen to twenty thousand in Vietnam and abroad. Twenty thousand

Americans alone lived in Vietnam. The short-term goal of the paper was to influence opinion in a subtle way by adding pieces favorable to the Viet Cong that demonstrated their strength and appeal, counteracting official efforts to downplay support for the Viet Cong.

Volume 1, number 1 of the *News* ran on Thursday, November 1, 1963, with the banner "The Nation's March toward True Democracy." It sold for ten piastres. Each paper included its purpose, to explain to its readers "the reasons and meanings of developments in Vietnam." Readers were informed it "has no link with the Government either directly or through association with any particular member of the Government" and is "a free paper, treasuring freedom, and respecting freedom." Nor would the *News* be an "opposition paper; it will give credit to the Government . . . where credit is due . . . criticise where criticism is deserved . . . The aim is not to destroy, but to construct." The introduction to the *News* ended on a humble note: "Being a human undertaking, the *Saigon Daily News* will naturally have its failings."

In the long term, the *News* was to be a voice in any coalition government that would be formed. As Saigon fell quickly, this did not prove necessary. The paper also sought to counterbalance Ngo Dinh Diem's personal project launched shortly after the Geneva Accords in 1954, the *Times of Vietnam*. Diem had used the *Times* to sell himself to the United States at a time when the U.S. Congress was unsure who to support. To woo Catholics from the North who moved south after the accords, Diem financed the *Times* to help elicit U.S. funds to defray the costs of resettling close to a million refugees from the North. When Diem launched the *Times* in 1956–1957, English was uncommon in Vietnam, but Diem relied on his entourage of U.S.-educated aides to produce it. Read by a small number of Vietnamese, the paper was aimed at congressmen and VIPs in Washington and needed subsidies to continue.

Many but not all of our acquaintances knew we led double lives between 1965 and 1969. Xuan helped make editorial decisions in the *News*. We moved in circles of power, including elites playing tennis on Diem's court. I rarely traveled because the printshop could not be left unattended. I did meet a lot of American journalists. Walter Cronkite once asked, "How can the Viet Cong vanquish the Americans who are a thousand times better equipped than the French had been against the Viet Minh?" I replied that the Vietcong were 1,001 times better organized than the Viet Minh had been against the French.

After the 1968 Tet Offensive, the Viet Cong asked me to be minister of information for the National Liberation Front. In the enthusiasm of the time, we were prepared to go to any lengths. Xuan and I worried about the social effects of taking the job, especially on the schooling of our children and ties to family and friends. But we started packing to leave Saigon and take up the post in the jungle. Xuan prepared to return to the maquis because she hated the treatment of the people. Then an agent communicated an urgent message: a counterorder.

If we had gone back to the maquis, I would probably have spent my best days insulting myself, because of the impact on the children, especially their education. It is one thing for us to have gone; as schoolchildren, we awoke to the revolution. Our first love is revolution. To our own amazement and pity, it remains so. Revolution was our first love.

Having sold our car, I commuted back and forth to work by cyclo. One evening, I stopped at a store to buy meat for dinner and hailed a pedicab for the ride home. A military police jeep pulled up behind us; I figured the cyclo driver was being picked up as many Viet Cong worked in town as cyclo drivers. But I was the target. They took me to a special interrogation center where I soon realized they knew I was a spy.

Xuan waited without word from me until 4:00 AM, when a friend called the police station and confirmed my arrest. She claims it was a relief; the expected had come to pass. Having lived dual lives for years, we always felt that one day the game would be up.

In line with Viet Cong instructions, I did not reveal my network. Over three months, I did not reveal a single name. But on a weekly visit by Xuan and our eldest son, aged fifteen, he walked into the prison and asked me, "Where is Mr. Hien?" In the presence of numerous interrogators, he had innocently asked about my main Viet Cong contact.

The government shut down the *Saigon Daily News*, and a military tribunal sentenced me to five years in jail for "actions detrimental to national security." In my deposition, as reported in *Time* magazine, July 18, 1969, I said: "Although I oppose Communism because of its inhumanity and because it contradicts the basic values of Asians and Vietnamese, I wonder if our people should continue to kill each other over an alien doctrine." [Ed. Note: The *Time* article on dissidents calls Lau a "soft-spoken, London-educated journalist and member of South Vietnam's elite who part with President Thieu over 'peace and how to achieve it.'" The article adds that Thieu closed thirty newspapers for publishing unpatriotic pieces. One of Lau's lawyers assailed Thieu for jailing opposition and creating a vacuum "into which Communists may be able to move." Intellectuals in 1960s Saigon rallied around *attentisme*, waiting rather than acting, in the face of two bad choices: a U.S.-supported Thieu regime or the Communists. The article indicates Lau sought a third option: "using the side opposing Thieu . . . with the goal of establishing a nationalist, not communist, government."]

I was imprisoned from 1969 to late 1972 and released early, prior to the Paris Peace Talks.

Vietnamese have long been highly educated, but since 1975, many in power fought in the jungle starting as children, running barefoot to deliver messages against the French. They are not educated. But the deep roots of respect for education surfaced even in

FIGURE 13.   Xuan and Lau—who met in the maquis in 1948, studied in London, and returned to Saigon to fight for Vietnam's independence—were considered *the* love story among the sisters. Courtesy of the author.

how interrogators showed respect for me in prison. It is status not claimed but given. Even in the 1980s and 1990s, when friends who are intellectuals saw me ride around Saigon on my old French bicycle, they cringed. When people see an educated person treated lowly, they suffer. It is the intellectuals who have suffered the most since 1975. And yet, Ho Chi Minh's own father held the highest academic degree attainable in imperial times.

Looking back, we haven't had any stability in our lives. Growing up, we had to quit school to fight against the French. Even families in villages had to leave home to come to town. My family had to leave Hue. I moved from Hue to Saigon, to Paris for study, and from Paris to London. It's not surprising that in our system of values, stability ranks very low. Also because of that, we do not fear the future. Tomorrow, if something happens to us, and we have to move out of this house, we are prepared.

Throughout the vicissitudes and upheavals in life, we find ourselves to be all right.

Xuan and I have what we call a hope morality, not a fear morality. For her, this is very significant. Otherwise, she would not have been able to sustain my years in prison. It gave her the courage to overcome.

18

OANH

"French Are Very Nice in France and Very Colonialist in the Colonies"

After the Geneva Accords in 1954 triggered a flood of refugees, Oanh returned to Saigon and put her social work training to use. The accords had called for the soldiers and administrators of the Democratic Republic of Vietnam and the Associated State of Vietnam to withdraw from their adversary's zone and gave civilians three hundred days to move north or south. The meeting also resulted in a tenuous agreement to hold elections within two years to unify the country under Ngo Dinh Diem or Ho Chi Minh. Approximately 800,000 people moved south, over half of them Catholics, and roughly 120,000 DRV personnel moved north.

In 1955, Oanh helped run a women's hostel for students, including refugees and girls from the provinces. Her political baptism came when she saw the Diem regime "impose Catholicism on a Buddhist country and use religion as a tool for political domination." With excellent English and experience in the West, Oanh affiliated with foreign and local priests, the Catholic Action Movement, and other groups focusing on social problems in a war-torn society. Along the way, she gained a master's degree in social work in the Philippines. Offered jobs by UNICEF, the UN agency for children, and other donors, Oanh chose to never work for an agency that was not Vietnamese, and in Vietnam.

After 1975, with a degree from the United States and siblings aligned with the U.S. government, Oanh found herself out of work. The new government viewed people like her with suspicion. With a foot in the West and one in the East, Oanh looked for ways to bridge the two. She was equally unforgiving of faults observed in the capitalist and Communist systems.

The one sister not to marry, Oanh devoted herself to young people, the disabled, the unemployed, the abused, and others in need, as well as to old friends from Lycée Marie Curie.

Oanh

I was going to continue with social work studies, but then the Geneva conference caused a lot of refugees to flee south, including many high school students who arrived without their families. A group of lay missionaries was started in 1937 by the Belgian priest Vincent Lebbe, a missionary in China who pressured the pope to appoint the first Chinese priests, and known after 1947 as the Auxiliaire Feminine Internationale (AFI). AFI assembled an international team of Vietnamese, Belgians, Italians, and others to build a hostel for refugee girl students who migrated from the North without their families. I attended AFI training for six months in Montreal and flew back to Saigon in the middle of 1955. This hands-on way is how I came to social work. Rather than continue for a master's or PhD, as others did, I returned with my BA and started running a hostel named after a female poet, Thanh Quan.

I started working at the age of twenty-four. At first, I had a lot of problems managing groups, so every time I went back to Europe and the States, I tried to get training in how to work with groups of students. Between 1958 and 1960, I traveled to Brussels for training in the spirit of the Inter-Cultural Association, formerly the AFI, and took courses on philosophy, religion, and sociology. It was not yet social work per se but the study of how to get along with groups of people and how to learn sociopsychological skills. That's why I am good at this kind of thing: I had a lot of training on how to organize people and how to communicate.

The women's hostel for students, either refugees or from the provinces, started in 1955 and continued until 1968, when we gave it back to the government. I thought I had helped the rich people enough at that time. In fact, an ex-minister of finance, Mr. Phuong, gave us the house to start with. I worked there until 1960 as assistant director.

At the same time I was managing the hostel, a leader of the Christian Worker's Movement, also started by a Belgian priest, approached me and said, "Oanh, the students don't need you anymore; you should work with the workers." I was a consultant to the Catholic Student Movement and the Catholic Intellectual Movement, so I knew a lot of people.

I had become politically conscious because it was the Diem regime, and we were all against the fact he tried to Christianize Vietnam. He wanted to impose

Catholicism on a Buddhist country and use religion as his tool for political domination. We withdrew from groups who supported him in this work. At the same
time, priests studying in France awoke to a similar consciousness of needing to
Vietnamize and get away from politics in that sense; we formed a group of pro-
gressives working for all the Vietnamese people. We opposed the way Diem used
the church. I was approached about working in the women's association founded
by Mme Nhu. I refused. Of course, we did not make a lot of noise because we
would have been in big danger.

My involvement in politics became more and more radical, in step with the
situation in the country and what I saw happening to people I worked with.

Father Jacques and I knew Mr. Phuong, a Catholic who joined the Diem regime to help the country. He became minister of finance. Diem's family forced
him to do all sorts of awful things, like import wine for mass free of tax, which
the church turned around and sold. Phuong refused to do such favors and was
appointed director general of the national bank, where Mme Nhu forced him to
make illicit money transfers for her. Again he refused. One day he went mad, actually mad, and broke a thick windowpane in the bank with his own fists. They
brought him to the hospital. Realizing he had made the wrong choice, he felt betrayed and disillusioned. After the Diem regime, he recovered and was elected
senator and joined a group of Catholic senators. A few years before 1975, his wife
and daughter left him. He again went mad. He sometimes begged near my house.
He died a few years later—one of the most intelligent, dedicated intellectuals of
that time. Phuong was an honest man, so he didn't enjoy the glory and the feeling of wielding power. People like him became too deeply involved with the Diem
regime.

Father Jacques made one mistake in his life by supporting the Diem regime at
the beginning. He lived too far away from the situation and did not realize how
bad things were under Diem.

One of the women in the women's association approached the bishop of Saigon and said, "Why don't you ask Oanh and her group to do something with the
workers?" Monsignor Binh had a parish, a little out of town in a mango orchard,
led by a progressive French priest who had studied sociology. I went there and
started a community center for girls left at home when their parents had to go off
to work. Half the families came from the North, half from the South. They were
not refugees, just poor.

Meanwhile, the political situation was boiling over. Diem had been killed. Radical lay Catholics started taking stronger and stronger positions. We took positions against American imperialism, but not a very strong one—yet.

Three priests who came from France were so radical and Marxist that the diocese in the province that was supposed to take them in dared not. They came to

Monsignor Binh, who sent them to our center in the "Mango Orchard Parish." Our little cluster of progressive laypeople and priests started a chapter of the Young Christian Workers movement, which later played a leading role in progressive youth movements. Headquartered in Belgium, this movement was started by a radical cardinal named Cardijn, who came from a family of mine workers and strived to raise the conscience of the working class. This radical movement advocated an interesting way to work based on seeing, judging, and acting. We applied this method to training illiterate workers to be leaders in their own milieus. The idea was that either you are an adult, an intellectual, an advisor, or a priest, or you were a worker. You should not take the place of the workers. They should do the work themselves. I served behind the scenes. We trained a lot of leaders like this, and many have good positions in the new society.

By this time, I felt I had stayed too long in the Catholic Action Movement, from which developed Rev. Cardijn's service to workers. I nearly became general secretary but realized it was not a career. I stayed at the Mango Orchard until 1968 when the United Nations Development Program (UNDP) came to look for somebody to work at the National School of Social Work in Saigon.

I joined the UNDP team to build up the school. My BA was not enough, so I needed to get a master's degree. The UN designed a scholarship that could be a good fit. Everybody was eager for scholarships, but corruption abounded. The man who had a big part in making the decision probably wanted me to bribe him. I didn't, and I didn't get it.

Another opportunity arose. An organization in Geneva advertised for an Asian sociologist and invited me to work there for a year to prepare an international assembly. I looked at community development courses in Germany and Switzerland, but their courses seemed irrelevant and outdated. Instead, using the money earned in Geneva, I attended a community development course at a university in the Philippines. To cover the costs of a second year, I applied for a scholarship from a Catholic organization in Holland.

While I was away studying, the Young Christian Workers movement became radical to the point they burned U.S. trucks and participated in huge demonstrations. Father Phan Khac Thu came to the parish as a young seminarian to learn how to work with mission workers. He was already a priest and joined the garbage collectors, becoming famous as the priest garbage collector. Workers' unions had different branches, and he joined one to fight for workers at a factory. He was unaware there were revolutionary people at the factory; they met him, and toward the end, before liberation, they spoke frankly to him about their cause. Many of our young workers and students became radicalized and joined other movements inspired by the revolution, which is why many young Christian workers became members of the revolution.

During these years, I also ran a community center and taught social group work at the Caritas school of social work. I juggled projects, family case work, and community work.

Between 1963 and 1968, Ngo Ba Thanh and I were like twins. [Ed. note: Ngo Ba Thanh joined the third force: a group of urban elite seeking a middle path between Communism and the U.S.-backed regime in Saigon. With a PhD from Columbia University, she taught international law at the University of Saigon. Openly urging the Thieu government to end the war, she was arrested in 1971. She died in 2004.] We were out together all the time. When I worked and studied abroad, Ngo Ba Thanh plunged deeper and deeper into real politics. I came home to find she was in prison and tortured. My family worried so much about me after what happened to her and tried to keep me away from all that. I was torn apart by all the different movements. I felt I had to build up social work as a discipline.

Coming back in 1972, I didn't expect I would be immediately appointed dean of studies at the National School of Social Work, a school dominated by anti-Communist reactionaries and corrupt people. After a year, I couldn't stand it. I wanted to work for the people. I thought of the school as being anti the people. I left to start freelancing.

That didn't last long. Different agencies tried to employ me. I chose never to work for an agency that is not Vietnamese; I even turned down UNICEF. I wanted to work for Vietnam. I had to choose an agency that really served the people. People may think it's by chance I am in Saigon. No, it is by choice—step by step.

We had an association of several hundred social workers that needed in-service training. About fifteen of us were university graduates; many had just six months of training. Regardless, many schools and organizations requested our consulting services. I was the main one to build it up. We were a respected group and set up a research and training center for social development. It was a lot of fun.

Next, I worked on professional research and professional in-service training. At university in the Philippines, left-wing social work promoted a push for liberation before development. I was treated as the "red" social worker. When I came back from the Philippines in 1972, all sorts of activist groups were eager to involve me in their activities. Many of us came to realize just how much in essence humanitarian aid is like neocolonialism and concluded there could be no development without liberation first.

Besides government circles, social welfare activities were the most fertile ground for corruption. Especially fertile were projects related to refugees and child welfare. The number of orphanages grew rapidly, not because the number of orphans increased but because too much money was available. Thousands of tons of donated food were diverted from refugee camps and reported as stolen in attacks by the Viet Cong and then sold for profit. As always, children and war victims were used and abused during these so-called humanitarian actions. Everyone knew donors did not care as along as the money went to South Vietnamese society to revive its dying economy.

So-called humanitarian aid was really military and economic support to fight Communists. They used the "aid" label to authorize the money because U.S. taxpayers were sick of the war.

Between 1973 and 1975, the social work projects I worked on aimed to prepare people for nation building with a new regime; we tried to help young people be ready to join the new society with strong national spirit. We were idealistic. We don't mind socialism; we even want it, given we can't solve our problem of independence and poverty. Before the revolutionaries came, we closed our center on March 1, 1975. I joined a Catholic group to work on reconciliation, which preceded the Catholic Committee for Renovation and Reconciliation.

Graduates of our social workers' association are everywhere. One became president of Hoc Mon District; she plans to run in local elections. Two are at *Tuoi Tre* (Youth) newspaper, as a social issues reporter and as head of the social work section. One is at the school for party members; I find that funny. Two work in the Ministry of Social Welfare. One joined the health sector and taught health education to thousands of workers. She was elected a union leader and has a high position in worker welfare. Some are party members, good ones.

Saigon was no longer Saigon. Refugees were pushing into town, so we took on relief work while preparing people to return to their localities. At least we had come to freedom.

I let our family home be used for meetings by lots of youth groups; I didn't know all the people. I knew they were in different movements, including the Communist youth. In January 1975, I had been approached about a job by the World Council of Churches (WCC); I had just met folks in the WCC when they visited in June 1974. They had an office for the reconciliation and reconstruction of Indochina and asked me to be their program officer based in Bangkok. I was sick of the former regime, and I realized that many of the projects we had done were quickly wiped out. I accepted the job because this reconciliation fund worked for both the North and the South. I signed a contract to start in June 1975.

After Da Nang was liberated in early April, the WCC called me to go right away to start my job based in Bangkok and help provide relief in the newly liberated area in central Vietnam. Then my telephone started ringing every fifteen minutes with people asking, "Are you going?" "When are you going?" Legally speaking, I could have gone. But if I went, I worried many others would leave. I sent a telegram to WCC saying I would not be leaving.

I was not alone. Many Catholic intellectuals decided to stay to help the bishop draft letters appealing to Catholics not to take up arms against the Communists and not to leave the country. Over a hundred people signed up, swearing they would not leave; when I reviewed that list, I saw at least ten did leave. This was a very difficult period. There was also danger with the police. But we also knew they had already become weak, confused about what they should be doing. We had a lot of exciting times as we cooperated with the Catholics on reconciliation.

After Liberation, an appeal urged people to go to the New Economic Zones. The communist government relocated hundreds of thousands of people between 1975 and 1980. Intellectuals and students were invited to a collective farm to work and get the feeling for doing that. At the archbishop's house, Catholics started a temporary coordination office where we arranged for volunteers to work at that farm. I worked there a few months. I joined the Society of Patriotic Intellectuals in July 1975, where I met Nguyen Thi Me (Mme Me). People like Mme Me are one of the reasons I didn't rush out of the country. She and others made a huge impression.

Mme Me, Oanh's Friend and Guide

Oanh often said she had been greatly influenced by Mme Me, who also became a friend. Wearing loose pajamas, hair in a tight bun, and eyes shining behind thick-lensed glasses, Mme Me recounted her life dedicated to the revolution and sacrifices made. Mme Me served as vice minister of social welfare in the provisional revolutionary government. She talked about joining the revolution and shared letters from sons who died in the war, one dated a few weeks before his death in the Tet Offensive. On the wall of her living room, arranged as three points in a triangle, hang large black-and-white photos of her three boys who did not come home. In the pictures, their mouths are tight and unsmiling, while their eyes reflect lost innocence.

Mme Me

I was born in Cuu Long in 1921 and attended the Collège des Jeunes Filles Indigènes and Ecole à la Tunique Mauve (School of the Purple Tunic) from 1936 to 1940. When the North became independent on September 2, 1945, I began to be interested in politics. The French returned within weeks, though, and clung to power until losing at Dien Bien Phu and leaving in 1955.

I worked as a businesswoman to develop the economy and, in turn, support the revolution. My husband liaised with cadres in the jungle while I stayed in town with the children and made contacts. I bought all the legal papers we needed to buy things and sell them at a profit to be used for the revolution. I started a school and joined the women's association. Nobody believed I could be a revolutionary. We gave hundreds of students an education focused on loving the homeland and what had to be done to preserve it. I told the students I believed in them, and not one turned me in to the French—not even the children whose fathers worked as functionaries. I taught during the day, and each night, we had four full classes for illiterates. We also went into women's homes to teach them.

A huge storm swept through the Mekong Delta in 1956, and I mobilized the population to help victims in its path. Diem gave me a medal for my work after the storm! The next year, the school was closed: we were accused of sympathizing with Communists and being against the regime. I asked to see the minister of education and complained that it was the dictatorship of the functionaries! After that, I didn't dare stay in the province.

A director general in the ministry said, "Come to Saigon, where you can teach small classes without permission." I did until 1960, when the NLF was established and invited me to join. If I hadn't been asked, I would have been home a week later when the authorities came to get me. Luckily, a former student put my police dossier at the bottom of the pile, so it wasn't found until I was gone. I left with my four sons while my daughters stayed with an aunt in Saigon.

From 1960 to 1964, I worked with the front by mobilizing populations in western provinces against the government. We traveled to villages and met with rich families to hear their opinions and explain the goals of the revolution. False propaganda spread by radio and pamphlets dropped from planes accused revolutionaries of fighting for themselves. It was up to us to explain the revolution, explain that we had been invaded and this was our duty as citizens. I found this work came to me easily. Most people realized the revolutionaries were working for them. My job included addressing groups about the political, military, and diplomatic struggles.

The children revered their father. My four sons excelled in school, especially in math and Vietnamese. By 1967, during preparations for the general uprising, all four asked to join the army. They wrote to me, asking to be forgiven, explaining, "While we are young, we must fight for our country. We can bear death, but not dishonor to the family." My sons announced they were joining the army and wanted their parents to be proud to have children willing to give up their youth to the high revolutionary mission. One wrote that this challenge is the "best training for youth" and asked us to believe in him.

Earlier, in 1966, one of my elder sons, Nguyen Huynh Tai, wrote a series of letters to his little sister Be Sau (little sister number six). Based in Tra Vinh, he gave his address as HT 134A C 6 and his brother Tu's as HT 16 G 72. He wrote:

I got mom's and your letter. I learn that you, dear little sister, are growing up well in the revolutionary struggle. So I am happy and proud of our family because we have a girl like you. All of us have to do honor to our family.

It's impossible to express all the thinking and feelings of a brother who has been separated from his dear sister for five years but I think that I can help you make progress in your endeavor to be good.

Though I have to be away from you and Be Bay [little sister number seven] and am so busy with my work, never the image of my two sisters fades from my memory.

For the revolution, the resistance, the Party's cause, girls like boys have to do their best and devote all their energy to contribute to the great cause. Our parents and I are very pleased to know that you are actively serving the revolution.

You shouldn't forget the virtues of a Vietnamese woman. These are purity in thought and feelings, gentleness in relationships with others. All of those are not feudal morals but part of the beauty of Vietnamese women which the world admires. You've read about young heroines like Vo Thi Sau . . . good examples for young girls to follow. When facing the enemy, they never bowed but always held their head high, which frightened the enemies, but in their families they were very good daughters, kind sisters, nice neighbors, and loving friends.

Our dear mother is the typical Vietnamese woman who has all these qualities. She made sacrifices for the revolution, the great cause of the Party; she has accepted great sacrifices being separated from her children. . . . A revolutionary must be fully educated by the Party but it is a great disadvantage to lack the care and guidance of a mother such as ours. Being separated from our parents, I am clearly aware of it.

Because every revolutionary has lived in the former society which is full of evils, lies, and corruption, he is more or less influenced by it. You should learn from others but not without analysis to distinguish what is revolutionary and progressive which you will follow, from what is bad, backward, which you will avoid and fight against.

A letter dated January 20, 1968, came from my eldest and was written weeks before his death during the withdrawal after the Tet Offensive. He asks me not to worry for him. But all mothers worry about their sons going in front of bullets.

After the carpet-bombing by B-52s, I was assigned to the city and stayed among the closest of friends, disguising myself in makeup and scarves and under an umbrella when out on the street. Friends protected me and helped me get around. I also stayed at home with the family, and resistance fighters came to me there.

One week, I received a letter announcing my son's death in December 1967. He was twenty-six. Another week, I received a letter saying my son died in February 1968. He was twenty-four. A third letter disclosed that a son had died in a bombing in March 1968. He was twenty-two. I had to clench my teeth and control my tears to think about how to carry on with what they left unfinished. My fourth son was wounded in the head. Only one son was buried in a cemetery, but it was bombed, and I don't know which is his tomb. We can't find the bodies of the others. How can they be finding American bones when I can't find my sons?

In 1969, the PRG Central Committee for women to free the South made me vice minister of social welfare. My husband served as a diplomat for the South.

If all women reject war, we would not be able to have it. We have our hearts in our hands. Theory is the weapon, while the situation on the ground is the master. American women suffered too; they didn't know what their children were doing. Ho Chi Minh talked about Roosevelt like he was a good friend. Who knows what might have come of that. Now, young people are responsible to the generations to come. We must turn the country over to the youth. I agree with those who worry that dedication without education and intelligence to back it up is a brake on progress. As Oanh says, we must avoid cadres of Marxist mandarins.

After 1975, things changed. I was out of a job and out of my professional career for a long time. The great majority of Saigon University graduates were unemployed. The most painful thing was that you couldn't do anything useful for society.

By then I had become something of a political person. Not really—I had no power at all! But more people accepted me because I had positive ideas toward the country and regime. At the same time, I carried a heavy background: family in the United States, being known as a Catholic, having studied in the States.

I found myself asked to run for election to the people's council of my district. This was not easy, either. I joined for a term in what was more or less a figure-head role. As part of the association of patriots, we initiated small scientific ac-tivities. I had a lot of time, so I researched and wrote a report on U.S. humanitar-ian aid. I made the association's first census of intellectuals and college graduates of Saigon. I conducted the first study on juvenile delinquency in reeducation schools. I did these on a freelance basis with little or no money.

People began to know me, and I was one of the rare ones in the association to be invited to join the Institute of Social Sciences. I did not apply; they called me. That too was not easy because people harbored different views about people like us. In early 1980, I joined the Sociology Department in the institute. It was a chance to observe the bureaucratic machinery, to know their mentality, and to realize it really couldn't work. More and more people left the institute. When the research-and-development program took a definitive technical orientation, I knew I could not work there anymore and left in 1984. Being a government employee was a big honor and brought protection and a lot of privileges; to quit bordered on the foolish—arguably foolish and certainly dangerous. But I did. As a mem-ber of the Catholic committee and of the association of intellectuals, I had a little political protection. Little by little, I became a freelance social scientist. Agencies called me because of my ability and my experience.

I had a lot of contacts who wanted to promote social work, so I made a re-quest to open a school of social work. I can't discuss it until I have legal status. I want it to be private because as a government institution, we can't do anything. The former mayor and head of the planning commission of the city thought we could do something governmental. After meeting with the vice president of so-cial affairs and vice chairman, we had to wait a really long time. Then she said, "Oh, we will make it a government school." So I prepared a project, toured Asia to assess different schools, and came back to again advocate the opening of a school. By then the vice president of social affairs had new ideas: "Well, maybe you can make it private." I made it a private project. A few months later, the un-official answer came: "No, nonparty members cannot run training schools con-cerning human science."

I worked under the umbrella of a fund for children's well-being and applied again a different way, though friends advised, "You should wait until this lady re-signs." I am waiting. Things happen haphazardly, not through a logical process. This lady is also a vice mayor. Jealous people could attack me and say what I am doing is dangerous, that it's supported by the CIA, things like that. That is why I keep a low, low, low profile. My dealing with foreigners should be extremely care-ful. Sometimes it is not so much political as a question of power, social position, and status. People can use political and other arguments to attack you.

My dream is to train social workers. We need them badly. I don't need to work anymore to support myself, but I want to in terms of the needs. We have an office and consult others, including people working in the provinces. I don't do this officially. I have also learned, working with young people, that you must let them take over.

We need change. We have to bring about change, the kind of change that enables us to tackle any human problem using scientific approaches. We need to help our people work in teams, to change behavior, to modernize behavior and attitudes. To do that, we need to learn the behavioral sciences: sociology and psychology, including social work. We need leadership and management skills. I have tried to improve those skills in different groups. We have specific challenges, like adolescent and family problems. We lack development-oriented training where you have to work with communities. Our workers will need macro skills in policy making, but now challenges lie at the micro level. We want to provide skills to work with groups in all fields.

My training program offers two packages: one focusing on human skills, the other on social work. I do this at the request of institutions and on the basis of in-service training. The urgent need is to work with street children in communities and institutions, especially in the community. The problems we see have the same features as those I saw in Manila: unbalanced development, unequal distribution, marginalized people, poor families who don't know how to educate children who run wild, slums, people from the New Economic Zones, people coming back and sleeping in the streets. I work with an ad hoc group of trainers and researchers who deal with problems at the local level. We meet weekly, visiting their sites to identify the best approach in each setting. We hope this group will become part of the children's fund of the Women's Union. Then I will withdraw.

I had applied for a PhD at the University of the Philippines but did not pursue it. We succeed because we are compelled by the needs of society. My ability to work and handle many different situations is thanks to the fact that, in an underdeveloped country, people like me are greatly needed in every field. That is why I developed all sorts of skills. I did not follow a career-minded path, but somehow events led to a successful career. Even without a PhD, I can discuss any social issue with anyone. People know me, even outside of Vietnam, as a person with a lot of experience. If I had really looked for a career, I could have gone the other way. Like many others, I could have stayed in the United States for advanced training and assumed a high position and political status as soon as I came back. I took a different track.

When I first returned, I was on the list of people invited to important occasions at the U.S. embassy. I never went. I was even invited to meet Vice President

Nixon and his wife. We always say, "French are very nice in France and very co-lonialist in the colonies." Americans were the same, exactly the same. As soon as they came, they became master of the situation, and I was anti that attitude from the beginning. Working in social work, I was furious at the huge imposed pro-grams to spend U.S. money, though we saw that it was really to back the war.

A childhood friend who ended up working for a U.S. company came to Sai-gon for an international seminar on child welfare. She confessed, "You know, Oanh, thinking of those of us in the United States writing reports on child wel-fare issues, I realize none of them knew there were such capable people in Viet-nam." I replied, they didn't know us because we belonged to two parallel worlds.

I had American friends, like the Camdens, a couple of American officers who were distraught by the direction of events. She was a social worker. They became sickened with what they saw and left before the end. At one time, Mr. Camden urged his wife, "Please tell Oanh to be careful." We had good friends like that. But we really thought the Americans were an occupation army—a military oc-cupation. Very soon, huge social problems were created by all the prostitution and delinquency.

The street leading to Mme Tuong's house, where we go for reunions, had a parallel street that was developed more or less after the refugees came. Being pi-ous, the refugees attended church mornings and evenings and prayed at home. There was a policy to disperse GIs all over because if they concentrated in one area, they would be attacked. The military rented private houses, and a lot of people in that area became rich by building motels and homes for GIs. To com-pete, they had to offer prostitutes to attract the men. The whole area became morally spoiled. Talk of "de-Christianization" reached the bishop and made him livid. One Saturday afternoon, I came to his house and said, "Bishop, if you don't believe this is happening, I can tell you about families whose children are going into prostitution, who don't care about losing face or anything else because the dollar is much more powerful than Communism in killing the faith." Dollars killed social values.

When Barry Goldwater and his wife, Margaret, visited, they wanted to visit social projects, so the U.S. embassy contacted me. I agreed but told the embassy not to come to my place in a car; they stopped the car at a distance and walked to my house. I showed Margaret Goldwater what was happening due to the occupa-tion, and I think she went back with ideas about the need for change, saying, "Oh yes, I will tell the ambassador," who was at that time interim.

We did not welcome the U.S. presence, in spite of the fact my brother and sister were among the highest-paid U.S. government employees and had a clearance at the embassy. Most people figured I must be working with the poor because of my membership in the Inter-Cultural Association (ICA). As I found out, people in the ICA also hated the Americans; they thought Americans were stupid. I listened to this even as my brother and sister built their careers at the embassy; they were profiteers off the U.S. presence. They complained but did not do anything about it. We saw each other quite often, but they did not know what I was really doing, until 1972, when they saw my close friend Ngo Ba Thanh tortured and began to fear for me.

The last days of April were tense. My sister was scared. She talked about going, and she made everybody excited. Her husband was both British and American; they left April 7. In my office, on my table, lay one packet of papers to be signed by family who decided not to leave. Next to it lay documents for those I tried to send to the States for sponsorship; I had done everything I could to help them go. My brother was angry at me because he stayed a few years after liberation and, despite the fact there were so many problems, he saw I kept on working. He was the only one bitter toward me. I was a little fearful about seeing my sister in 1978 in Belgium, but she was happy to see me. The same happened when I met my other brother. They understand me. My elder sister was angry but also proud of me when I go to meet people. It is a mixed feeling. I didn't think this situation could last. I didn't say anything to my family. They are not political; they live their everyday lives.

I often say that it's thanks to the Americans that socialism developed. I would not have taken sides so definitively if they were not here to push me into the arms of socialism. The Americans were so stupid, so inhuman, so childish in how they imposed themselves. I can overcome my feelings toward individuals, but I never thought I would go back to the United States. However, in 1967, I did because my niece was sick with a love crisis. I was already at a meeting in Europe and continued on to see her. After that, I thought I would never to go to the United States again, until my family invited me, and I went to see them. As a human being, I had negative feelings about that period, but I turned that anger to work for my country. How can an ant fight with an elephant? Somehow I thought they would lose because they were so much beside the point; they didn't understand anything about us.

In 1967, when I visited my family in the States, I was very anti-Communist. A friend's father had just been assassinated. It was strange that year; some of my good friends still worked to motivate and support GIs, and I said, "Why do you do that? We are fighting against them." One friend replied, "But when you were here before, you told us to work against the Communists!" I was exasperated. I said, "The situation has changed!" Living inside the country, you evolve, and your ideas change.

I feel sorry for Americans and all the traumas they have to go through. But I hope only that they learn a lesson.

As one of few students to think it best to study in Asia and not in the United States, I volunteered to study in Asia. People thought I was crazy: in terms of status, studying in the United States held much more prestige. I went to visit a school of social work and community development in the Philippines to which USAID and the Vietnam Christian Service sent young women for a two-year master's degree.

My views often stood out from others. At a seminar on social work in Bangkok, I spoke up against hierarchy. This happened at a meeting of the precursor to ESCAP, the United Nations body focused on Asian and Pacific countries. The workshop explored cultural factors that influence social work. A UN advisor was appointed chair of the event convening people from twenty-one "yellow"—that is to say, Asian—nations, while thirty white observers filled the room. Participants complained privately that the training took place in what was "not an Asian setting." The first day, people introduced themselves; when it was my turn, I said the atmosphere felt funny and described complaints I had heard. From then on, others started to see a problem, and they wanted to change the chairmanship and organization of the whole seminar. Many white observers withdrew. To my surprise, halfway through the workshop, Frances Yasas, the UN regional adviser on training in social work, invited me for lunch with some experts. I explained what I saw happening. She said she didn't know their way of doing things was colonial.

I am known in the region for being like that; I tried to get people to speak up.

But things have not changed very much. I traveled to a huge meeting on psychotherapy that brought fifteen hundred people to Czechoslovakia. It was completely, completely, American dominated—while they keep talking about not dominating! I didn't dare speak because there was such a big crowd. But I commented to some people, "Teaching nondomination in a very domineering way: nothing has changed."

It's best not to let people know too much about my reputation as a revolutionary. Police of the former time kept a dossier on me, asserting I had a lot of popular backing, "a lot of potential for public upheaval." Some who knew the security people told me about it. That was my reputation.

I have an album of colleagues from the intellectual patriotic association. When I look at their pictures, I see each trying to turn dreams into reality: a Catholic lawyer who joined during the French time and became the first judge in Ho Chi Minh City and a respected director of the renowned Purple Dress school. About thirty members were asked to write a brief bio; only fifteen dared accept.

I started the Let's Come Together Café as a place where social work students and their friends come together to meet new friends, discuss social issues, organize seminars, and relax. We provide whatever a community asks of us. On weekends, we arrange classes on parenting and life skills. We introduce participatory education. I teach as I was educated, even if I am not trained as an educator!

Family violence is much worse than before, and people are highly stressed. There are no grassroots social services. Parents are preoccupied with material values; they force children to choose what they themselves think brings happiness rather than what the child is interested or talented in. Depression is widespread. Crime is up among young people. In social aspects, we remain far behind. Little is known or accepted about modern social sciences.

I write a column in a women's magazine and invite students to write in; one wrote, "I am sixteen and a prisoner in my home." In a column in February 2009 called Unchained Spring, I wrote: "People were afraid not only of speaking and working, but also of taking responsibility. They waited for instructions from their superiors to be safe. At school, teachers spoke like a machine and students listened like a mouthpiece. . . . Many teachers are anxiously calling for an unchained education so that education can escape mechanical and unrealistic thought. Unbinding education is only the initial step."

At the same time I am writing more, I still have to self-censor.

Recollections of Oanh's Mentor, Father Jacques

A mentor to Oanh, Father Jacques arranged scholarships for young leaders to study at Catholic schools abroad. He also had a front-row seat to the downfall of his onetime friend Ngo Dinh Diem. Along with his brother Ngo Dinh Thuc—only the third Vietnamese to be consecrated a bishop, in 1938—Diem alienated many Buddhists by their fervent Catholicism. Father Jacques's story captures the currents of hope and despair in 1950s South Vietnam and helps show why—when Oanh returned from the United States—she was cherished for her generous spirit.

Father Jacques

I first met Ngo Dinh Diem rather casually in Hanoi around 1944. I had met his brother Nhu, and I admired the family. [Ed. note: Ngo Dinh Nhu, 1910–1963, imported personalism to Vietnam, which deemphasized individualism and rejected Communism. He and Diem believed that by promoting personalism and nationalism, they would attract Catholics and others and be able to consolidate power.] They were independent, honest with themselves, and could not be bought for any amount of money or things. Diem had stayed with the Maryknolls in upstate New York. He was very pro-Vietnam. He showed it even in choosing a coat of arms—a tradition dating from the Middle Ages and followed by all bishops. French bishops chose French symbols: a rose, a tower. Everything had a meaning. Diem chose his coat of arms differently: he chose a dragon. For Chinese and Vietnamese, the dragon is an animal of happiness and a good omen.

In a sense, Diem's faith drove his political action. He was deeply religious, in stark contrast to the similarly ambitious Ho Chi Minh. Given his faith, Diem was not easily frightened. He was not a man to buy or intimidate. He was inspired, he had a sense of justice, he had love of his people, and he would follow his faith; in what proportions, I do not know.

But the Diem family had defects. They were stubborn. Diem was a man of great integrity, but he was suspicious of everyone outside his family and his entourage. He became so isolated that he favored and indulged those closest to him, like his sister-in-law Mme Nhu, who was contemptuous of everything that was not gorgeous and splendid. There is a telling story about her riding with her chauffeur and being stopped by a policeman: Mme Nhu made him strip to his trousers and use his uniform to wash and wipe down the car.

Diem's stubbornness was almost a defect due to his virtue; he was so forceful in his desire to seek the happiness of his people, as he saw it, that he would do almost anything. In the end, he lost the feeling of the place in which he lived.

In the early 1950s, before Dien Bien Phu, Diem arrived in Los Angeles, and I flew there from Chicago to receive him. Oanh also came. For Vietnamese living in the States, Diem was a pillar, a monument. There was something almost surreal about his name. At that time, Oanh was at Viterbo College; the easiest schools from which we were able to solicit scholarships tended to be Catholic, as in the case of Viterbo College. It might not be one of the top schools, but it was a good school with a friendly atmosphere. Plus, a school run by nuns was more hospitable for women. Oanh was welcomed and developed good relations with the nuns, who trusted her character and respected her personality. They liked that Oanh was a little different. Even small colleges giving scholarships to foreigners said, "It costs us money, but it enriches the school."

Students who went back to Vietnam worked with Diem in his administration. In Oanh's mind, whether working for Diem or not did not matter: the point was to work for Vietnam. But it was almost the same because there was no alternative. I was never in charge of Diem's student program; he never gave me instructions or paid me a salary. It is true that a good number of the students who returned worked with Diem's government. At the beginning, students who came back were enthusiastic about Diem. Little by little, that enthusiasm waned.

When I was in Saigon in 1955, it was still the beginning. Hope was possible. Diem had inherited a very bad situation, with armed gangs in control of various sections of public life. It was tough, but in the early days, he succeeded. The Saigon police, the whole police force, had been in the hands of the Binh Xuyen, an independent military force, and he had to be wildly energetic to purge cancers like that from his own administration.

After Geneva, there would be elections. From the start, Diem had decided against having them. I think he decided that because he figured the Communists would, through their means, get an enormous majority in the North, more than he could get through his means in the South. He did not want elections; that much is sure. I think he should have accepted it even if they resulted in one Communist state. The Communists would not have lasted an eternity.

When I visited Vietnam in 1955, 1958, and 1959, I met Diem in Saigon. I tried to talk to him about releasing good people he had put in jail. I told him how much he and the Vietnamese people needed those good people and how much of a loss it was to leave them sitting in jail, useless. That is one of the things I tried to get across. I did not always succeed. He answered: "But, Father Jacques, you have no idea how bad the Communists are." That would not address my argument, but he had an obsession with the evil of Communism. I understand that the Communist Party in Vietnam did awful things, but can that rationalize the awful things you do yourself? He and the Communists were using each other in that relationship.

To what extent was Diem a realistic statesman or a romantic? When I visited in 1958, his brother Khan showed me a garden behind his house. He pointed to a fawn that had been brought back by one of the patrols he had secretly sent north to spy. Diem used to say things along the lines of, "A Communist Vietnamese is not a real Vietnamese." You could never trust them.

During one of my trips, I stopped by to see Diem one afternoon. I had been reading a Greek tragedy; it might have been Sophocles. There is a king—Cleon, I believe—for whom everything turns out bad. He makes mistakes. He is like a man blindfolded walking toward a precipice. You see where he is going, and you know before-hand when he will plunge. I happened to be reading that before

FIGURE 14. Ngo Dinh Diem and Father Jacques, Oanh's mentor, at one of their early meetings in Saigon when Father Jacques saw promise in Diem as a leader of South Vietnam. Diem dated the photo—May 29, 1955—dedicating it "Affectueusement" (Affectionately) to Father Jacques. Courtesy of Father Jacques Houssard.

going to see Diem. And I thought to myself, "Poor Ngo Dinh Diem— he is like King Cleon. Right from birth, he is caught up in an unstoppable chain of events."

The last time I saw Diem, in 1959, we talked for a long time about what I thought was going on, but in terms that were prudent, not direct. He took me to the balcony overlooking Norodom Avenue. "Why are you criticizing so many things? Look at this beautiful city!" He laughed. "Look at those lights." It was a pretty sight.

As we walked inside, I said to him, knowing that I would be flying out in the next day or two, "I am afraid our views are so different on some things that this might be the last time we talk together." I didn't say it like that; it took more time to tell him, but that was the essence.

When they killed him in 1963, I was in Mexico. I can still picture myself in my room the moment I heard it on the radio. I thought, "Now maybe something can be done. Perhaps there is not much chance, but maybe." At the same time, I was sorry that he had been killed. With the whole story of Vietnam, one always faces that same problem—the ambivalence, the dilemma—and one can't get out of it.

I have a copy of my last letter from Diem. A time came when he did everything wrong. He and his brother had a great deal of pride. They were sure they were right, starting from the time of the French. He came from an old mandarin family; his father served as a minister in the Bao Dai Empire, perhaps the only Catholic to reach that rank. Having his brother Thuc as bishop added glory to the family. Then he put one of his brothers in charge of the central region. Diem didn't trust anybody, but he trusted his brother. Diem was convinced he was a man of destiny, and maybe he was.

People who are unable to criticize themselves can be dangerous. Far from his country and so sure of what he is dying for: the French did not stop to ask what they were doing and why. You had to be a hypocrite to draw so many people into the effort with you. The United States did the same. It is easy to make powerful, noble arguments. This is the curse of power. The one who is powerful tends to impose, to deceive others and himself, because he is powerful. I believe that is the curse of the French during the twentieth century, along with Britain, Spain, and maybe the United States. Power is not the blessing of God. On the contrary.

I brought about a hundred scholarship students from Vietnam to the United States. How many returned? Thirty? Forty? I don't blame people who stayed in the States; you can't expect everybody to be Francis of Assisi. While some students stayed in the United States and earned their keep, Oanh and others like her returned and set about working in their generous way.

Oanh returned to Saigon at a time when it was a hard, heavy place. Everyone hid everything and trusted no one. The future seemed stymied, without hope. It's not surprising that when a person like Oanh arrives at such a moment in time, others would notice her and want to associate themselves with her in their work. Her personality drew people to her.

19

REUNITING

Across many interviews, the Saigon sisters reveal how they were able to find each other again after the war. Several recall how, after 1975, distrust and suspicion permeated society. Families had been split, many since 1954, and communication lines were severed for decades. Two sisters, Minh and Tuyen, never left Saigon. One by one, the others trickled home. Trang administered final exams at the conservatory in Hanoi and took a train south to be reunited, twenty-one years on, with her daughter. Lien An plucked her girls from a village outside Hanoi and traveled by train to Hue, then on by truck, ultimately embarking in front of the education ministry where the student Tran Van On had been killed in 1950. Le An left her artistic troupe and took a coveted spot on the first boat south, *Thong Nhat* (Unification). Thanh gave notice to Minh she would be on her way as soon as diplomatic duties allowed.

The first time the sisters met after 1975 was at the funeral of a mutual friend, Suong, the radio announcer in Hanoi, who died of cancer in Saigon in 1981. That gathering inspired Tuyen, in particular, to find a way to bring the group of friends back together. The funeral also explains how Suong's mother, Mme Tuong, became a surrogate mother to the sisters.

As Tuyen tells it:

> I saw that we needed to reunite. At first, we were apprehensive about talking with each other since no one knew what the other was thinking. Through the years, friends might have changed; we heard accusations about those who joined the other side. I decided an effort had to be made.

Not everyone had a phone, so I went in person to scout out a venue and contact everyone to agree on a date and time to meet. I coaxed some by recalling stories from Lycée Marie Curie to make them want to get together. Minh, who ran the association of intellectuals created to bring together those who stayed in the country, did half the work. The two of us had the means, motorcycles, to travel around and be the liaisons. As soon as we saw each other, well, we realized we had not changed a lot. Family matters, especially, stay the same. With the passing of time, we understood that we had all faced the same difficulties in life. We realized we each kept the same passion to work for a new society in which, as Lien An says, there is more justice and equality. But the more we advance, the more we see there is to do. The work will not end.

Drawing on Minh's contacts, encouragement, and legwork, Tuyen planned a reunion at Le An's house in 1983. Tuyen organized it and delivered invitations while Thanh took the helm at the meeting, earning her the title of secretary-general. Thanh speculated on why it took time for the friends to reunite: "In the upheaval of events around liberation, we too—from each side—had many changes in our careers and in our lives. We did not yet think about getting back together. We assumed that, after many years, our points of view had diverged. Thanks to our education at the lycée and how our love of country deepened through the struggle for independence, we were determined to liberate our country. Thanks to that, each of us succeeded in her way, and I am not surprised by the achievements of my classmates."

Sen agreed:

> The revolution brought us back together. Even though we had lived in the same city, circumstances fostered suspicion, vigilance, and caution. Le An and I had gone to the maquis together for six months, but I returned to care for my mother. I married Nhieu, who held a high government position, and we lived in a large villa, which was considered damning. After liberation, friends from the maquis were afraid to contact me. It was only many years later that Suong told Le An I had done my part to help the cause by feeding, sheltering, and protecting people in the resistance. Suong brought Le An and me together in 1977, twenty-six years after we first became friends.

Oanh shared her own observations:

> Life pulled us apart and put us together again. Through the years, we caught glimpses of each other. I met Xuan at the Paris airport in 1951. I noticed her well-tailored overcoat as well as her surprise when she

queried me, "You are going to the United States?" I remember when
Xuan and I went to Lycée Chasseloup-Laubat for upper classes, walking from Marie Curie—two by two, in neat rows. She sat at my right. I
once saw Tuyen in a maternity ward where my sister gave birth. Lien
An and I met briefly in the early 1970s; I was walking home one evening when, out of the darkness, a voice called, "Is that you, Oanh?
Don't you recognize me?" Meeting before 1975 proved especially
tricky. Xuan invited me to visit her, but since I identified with the
working class, I feared being seen visiting someone in the aristocratic
class. We had run into each other by the cathedral in 1958: she in a
Mercedes, me on a motorcycle. I moved in student and worker circles;
she, in elite circles. In time I understood she and Lau played a political
role, and the car was one of the props Lau needed to carry out his
work. Xuan later admonished me, "Regardless of any differences, we
ought to be friends all the time." One of the reasons we are glad to reunite is that, during times of stress, it is important to be with friends
and relax. It helps to be at ease: without protocol, without complications. We came together because we desperately needed to communicate with somebody who feels the same way, without feeling like you
don't have the "right" point of view. It makes us so happy to be together, because we love the country, accept socialism, and want to
work to find how to get away from this narrow-mindedness. We regrouped in part because we lost a lot of other friends over the years. In
any event, when we came back together, we rediscovered our old affin-
ity. It is a blessing to grow old together.

Ever the joker, Oanh suggests one more reason they meet is that Xuan "likes
to show off her diamonds, and for my part, I also share diamonds—the ones that
belong to my sister."

One of the small but enduring ties binding the sisters is an appreciation for
plants and flowers. As Oanh said, "We share plants and flowers; I often go to Xuan's to admire her hanging orchids. I started a tradition of giving friends a small
potted plant at Christmas. In the future, maybe we'll all be using canes and retire
to a compound where, if someone gets mad, they just close the door."

Mme Tuong believed the women united because they had the same education
and were all very nice, adding, "Qui se ressemble, s'assemble" (birds of a feather).
Oanh had a similar view: "It is easy for us to be together. We have the same education; we have friends in common and parents who know each other. We share
the same goal. We may be old, but we love life; we are like the merry widows! We
are not like those shy Vietnamese girls who are like the flower that closes in on

itself at the touch of a finger." Thanh chimed in, "That's right! Those flowers are not like the Marie Curie girls! We are not bashful—we are bashless!"

Lien An points to the role Lycée Marie Curie played: "Perhaps it just brings joy to be reminded of our youth at Marie Curie—before the suffering. Some of us had sentimental feelings about Saigon from when we had to leave in 1954; my last souvenirs are of Marie Curie."

Tuyen reflects further on their friendship:

> We came to realize that others from our social milieu differed greatly, prompting us to see how similar we were to each other and how similar ideas and points of view bind us together. For some, discussions take place behind closed doors. For others, we talk openly now that the government encourages—actually, orders—that even newspapers talk about mistakes, the rottenness. We gather because we need to communicate with people who feel the same way—people who love the country and want to get away from narrow-mindedness, people who want to take a more intellectual approach to the revolution. We share the ideal of service to the people and remain very concerned about the future of the country.

Lien An expressed a similar view: "We want to serve and rebuild the country despite challenges. It is the flame that burns. Others from Marie Curie focus on their families and personal interests—not friends. There is nothing that separates us, nothing except that some, personally, led private lives that were easier, others that were more difficult. Minh had to take care of a large family; as the eldest, she had to care for her elderly mother."

Thanh, asked by a journalist if she had thought lycéens would meet again after many years, replied:

> I believed the city would be liberated and the country independent. That much was clear. But while participating in the resistance, I didn't think we could all find each other again. The passing of time and our different lives added to the geographic separation of the group. It was not common to reunite. One had to make an effort: find the glue, make the commitment. While going our separate ways, I think we hoped one day to find each other. If we gathered, it was to fulfill an emotional need. We found that, wherever we ended up, we all worked toward the same goal. We all wanted to serve the country. That bond ties us together. Oanh returned from the United States, Xuan from London, Lien An from Hanoi. We had been a bigger group at school and during the revolution, but some had different political views and left. I have not been privileged in

my private life. Each of these friends gave me plants that mean a lot to me. We meet to share our joys, like the wedding of Xuan's daughter, as well as to share losses. When they heard of my father's death, they attended the funeral, visited our house to console my mother, and sent a condolence card to me at the United Nations in New York. I was so grateful.

Husbands and in many cases children have cheered on the women's friendships, enjoying each other's company as they tag along to reunions. Xuan's husband, Lau, postulated: "I would like, on the basis of Xuan's life, to venture the idea that it was the mystic chords of memory, stretching from the days of Lycée Marie Curie, that kept the sisters in communion of spirit through all the trying times and kept intact their bonds of affection."

One more reason to gather, Thanh asserts, is a basic foundation stone: "We went to the jungle in 1949–1950; that was a turning point in our lives." Her words bear weight, as became clear during a reunion held in 1989.

The Saigon Sisters

On a drizzly afternoon, November 4, 1989, the Saigon sisters gather at their friend Tien's French villa on Nam Ky Khoi Nghia (General Uprising Street), two blocks from Lycée Marie Curie. Hooded figures emerge from a light rain—on foot, on bicycle, astride motorbikes. Tien helps lay out a buffet to which each contributes, starting with Xuan's spring rolls made with rice noodles, plump shrimp, slivers of pork and vegetables, with peanut and soy sauce for dipping, and ending with Lien An's dessert of donut-hole-sized coconut and chocolate cakes.

Outside, motorcycle engines growl, and horns bleep; the room's high ceiling amplifies the clatter. But nothing distracts the ladies as they greet each other and settle into a circle. In their late sixties, the sisters banter and laugh together like the schoolgirls they once were at Lycée Marie Curie in the 1940s.

As the afternoon unfolds, the Saigon sisters nudge and prod each other's memories to the surface. Each detail they recall fosters another distant memory, and soon the room hums with women's voices. Xuan teases Oanh about going to study in the United States so soon after the girls had participated in anti-U.S. protests in Saigon. Oanh reminds Thanh of the day she stood up in class and dropped anti-French leaflets to the floor. They sing a few bars from the inspiring songs composed by Tuyen's brother Luu Huu Phuoc and sung by his friend Tran Van Khe. By the time the sun sets, these friends have rekindled memories, recited beautiful songs, and even discovered what Thanh calls a revelation.

The revelation will emerge as the sisters turn to what they agree is *the* year of change, their last year together as young women at Lycée Marie Curie: 1950.

Oanh, describing herself as the least political in the group, asks her friends what instigated their rebellion in 1950. Thanh notes they were at the right age to join student associations that in turn energized and strengthened the resistance. She distributed anti-French documents aimed at changing the minds of young people, which leads Oanh to recall how, at the end of Mr. Cosserage's physics class, students filed out and a sheaf of papers fell from under Thanh's arm and fluttered to the floor for all to see: "Down with Bao Dai!" the pamphlets exhorted, referring to the last king in the Nguyen dynasty, seen by many as a puppet of the French. Thanh was reprimanded but neither expelled nor arrested. Oanh adds: "Remember when Thanh went into the bathroom and wrote a big sign, 'Down with the Puppets!'" Minh recalls making tracts (leaflets) in people's homes using flour or agar paste, to make a palette on which to pen revolutionary slogans in purple ink. Pressing thin paper on these primitive ink pads produced multiple copies before the message had to be carved into the paste again using a fountain pen and purple ink.

The sisters bring to life the events of January 9, 1950, when two thousand students from Saigon secondary schools gathered in front of the Ministry of Education of the puppet government to ask that students from the Pétrus Ky and Gia Long secondary schools be released from prison. As the crowds swelled, police cracked down. More than thirty students were wounded; one, Tran Van On, was shot and taken to Cho Ray Hospital, where he died. Students carried On's body back to his school, Pétrus Ky, and put it in a coffin. Police clubbed hundreds of students on the head, including girls from Marie Curie, and took them to Catinat prison, headquarters of the feared French Sûreté, the prison across from Notre Dame Cathedral that stretches a full city block down Rue Catinat, the heart of Saigon. Students squatted on the ground outside, and locals brought them bread. The sisters laugh as Xuan admits to having been confused, because she thought the French had provided the food. In the afternoon, police escorted those arrested into an office to take fingerprints and pictures and open their official police files. Xuan remembers being shuttled back and forth and not knowing why. Others could not remember what they did with their bicycles. At five o'clock, the Sûreté released the girls to their relieved parents. Some speculate their families had to bribe the police.

The death of the student Tran Van On, the women agree, triggered the tumult of 1950. On January 12, the girls—wearing white ao dais—joined the throng trailing Tran Van On's casket to his burial. Hundreds of thousands of people participated in the procession; as Sen recalls: "The head of the convoy entered Cholon, Chinatown, while the tail was still back in Saigon." The night before, using their own savings to buy cloth and red paint, the girls prepared the Marie Curie banner that diminutive Le An helped carry during the march. That day, rides on buses and cyclos were free. Cyclo drivers carried wreaths. People lining the streets offered water. The procession unspooled over kilometers. The sisters recall the funeral crowd, despite its size, being very silent. Students from several lycées marched, row upon row of boys and girls in white, the color of mourning. One of the French teachers at Marie Curie wanted to join in but was at odds with her superior. The huge student outpouring at the funeral shocked some upper-class families into sending their children to France to avoid political involvement. The Sûreté openly warned families: "Send your children abroad or risk seeing them jailed."

Among those sent abroad in 1950, Xuan and Oanh crossed paths at Orly Airport, where Xuan grilled Oanh, "What? You are going to the United States? Are you with the Americans now!" Decades later, they can laugh about it.

The Binh siblings did not go abroad, in part because their father did not think it appropriate for girls. This stance did not keep them from taking up activities for the resistance, which came to the notice of a member of the lycée's discipline committee: "Ah, Thanh, are you the Joan of Arc of Vietnam?" The sisters chuckle at the comparison. Thanh added: "He said it very ironically: '*Well*, are you?' I did not say yes, and I did not say no. Everyone was so serious. 'Well,' he said, 'you work hard, and you are a very good student, an excellent student—but a poor example for the lycéens.'" This was a warning. On the blackboard at the lycée, the discipline committee listed names under two categories: those to be congratulated and those to be disciplined. Only one name straddled both categories—Thanh's.

Tran Van On's death marked the start of a year of demonstrations. On March 19, students joined workers and others marching to demand the departure of two U.S. ships docked in Saigon's port. Madame Nguyen Thi Binh—an older student who had finished her baccalaureate—was a cadre designated to lead the student movement. This young woman, who would lead the National Liberation Front delegation to the Paris Peace Talks, where she worked side by side with Thanh, used a revolutionary name, Yen Sa. She attended meetings, but the students weren't supposed to know who she was. "Students found her captivating," Thanh states, "with profound eyes, so beautiful that we called her 'the beautiful sister.'" When the U.S. ships docked, Yen Sa led protests, chanting: "A bas l'impérialisme Américain!" (Down with American imperialism!) Students cheered, the sisters yelling their support in French. Oanh recalls the crowd walking toward the big marketplace, which had emptied out because shopkeepers and shoppers had joined the river of protest. Back home, Minh was scolded for losing her Peugeot bicycle that day.

To push the working population out of the city and weaken the resistance, the French started a big fire in the Bao Sen neighborhood. A commune house in

Cholon burned down, prompting a huge relief effort. Thousands joined to collect rice for the victims, arrange medical visits, reconstruct houses, and provide water. The tactic to intimidate the resistance backfired, as Thanh recalled: "The French started the fires to scare the resistance, but in bringing food and materials to the victims, students were able to show their organizing capabilities!"

The principals of Saigon's major lycées admonished the students: "Here you are attending a French school, and here you are demonstrating against the French!" Thanh exclaims: "We shocked them!" As rallies reached high pitch, schools closed; nobody could study.

Oanh asks if anyone remembers Professor Georges Boudarel, Ong (Uncle) Bou. Thanh only said hello to him at lycée but then met him again in the resistance and in Hanoi, as did Trang. He was one of the lycée professors who influenced the sisters.

The women also recall the artistic and theater activities that stoked their patriotic feelings. A French literature teacher taught Molière, and one year she asked the girls to stage the *Bourgeois Gentilhomme*, in which Thanh played Mr. Jourdain. This inspired the girls in the direction of Vietnamese patriotic plays. They became interested in a very romantic opera about a man and a girl meeting on a pilgrimage to the Trung Hung pagoda in the north. Thanh shares a few precious black-and-white photos of the staging of the opera, complete with costumes of knights from ancient times.

Turning back to her photo album, Thanh points to a scene in the Marie Curie courtyard, the girls all wearing white on May 19 in honor of Ho Chi Minh's birthday. It was done on the sly, girls huddling quickly to snap a photo before disbanding so as not to draw attention. She moves on to a small black-and-white photo of her in pigtails, sporting a white shirt and floral skirt she made herself. Wearing round glasses, she is smiling and clutching two thick tomes awarded as *prix d'honneur*. In 1949, despite having been nearly thrown out of school, Thanh received the 1932 edition of *L'Art des Origines à Nos Jours* on behalf of the French high commissioner to Indochina. The director of the school, Mme Brissaud, and the rector clashed over Thanh's behavior. At one point, the director had to tell the rector, "Either resign or take Thanh back!"

As the afternoon progresses, the women listen to each other's memories and take turns embellishing, "correcting," and reinforcing each story. At one point, everybody seems to be talking at once, and Oanh sighs, exclaiming: "We sound like a brood of hens!"

Suddenly, soft-spoken Xuan raises her voice over the others and announces she has a letter Thanh sent inviting her to a Tet party in 1950. Xuan has kept the slip of yellowed onionskin paper all this time—a revelation to Thanh, who admonishes Xuan, "You never told me!" Xuan replies: "I've carried it for nearly forty years; I guess I never mentioned it to you before." Thanh stares at the letter Xuan gently coaxes from a pocket in her wallet, along with two small black-and-white photos from that long-ago joyful Tet. These souvenirs reawaken a time of being teenagers, idealistic and determined. If not yet sure of themselves, they were sure of the goal they chose to pursue.

Peering at the letter, Thanh recognizes her handwriting, flowing script with artistic flourishes to lend pleasure to the eye. A phantom smile plays on her lips as she reads the letter that alludes to the pride two guards feel as part of General Tran Hung Dao's campaign against Mongol invaders. The guards she refers to in the following letter are her and Xuan:

> Saigon, the last day of the year Ky Suc, February 16, 1950,
> in the solar calendar
>
> Xuan,
>   New Year's Eve is here. We have only a few hours before we step into the New Year. . . .
>   Tet [Lunar New Year] will come again . . . and this Tet reminds me of last year's Tet when we were together in those youthful and sweet days under the same roof at the school. And the sound of Xuan's voice still echoes in Thanh's ears, the voice of a protesting Vietnamese guard under Tran's reign [general defeating the Mongols in 1288]:
>   "The sky is gloomy, overcast with sadness, are you aware, my friend
>   On the far horizon, smoke fills the void"
>   And in my imagination, Thanh answers,
>   "I am angry at the invading Mongol soldiers who, believing them-selves invincible, fall upon their neighbors."
>   How joyful the memory, Xuan!
>
>   But sadly, this year, Guard Number One has already left the old school, and unexpectedly Guard Number Two followed in her steps and now, the old school misses the shadow of these two friends. . . .
>   To find again the perfume, the atmosphere of those precious moments of our youth, Xuan, move your jade [precious] feet to Thanh's house at nine o'clock on the second morning of the New Year and we will welcome the arrival of Spring with cheerful singing and music. Xuan, you will please come, won't you? (After all, Xuan, "Spring," is here!) Most of the guests will be friends of Minh and Trang. Thanh didn't invite anyone but niece Autumn, and Xuan.
>
> Affectionately, Thanh

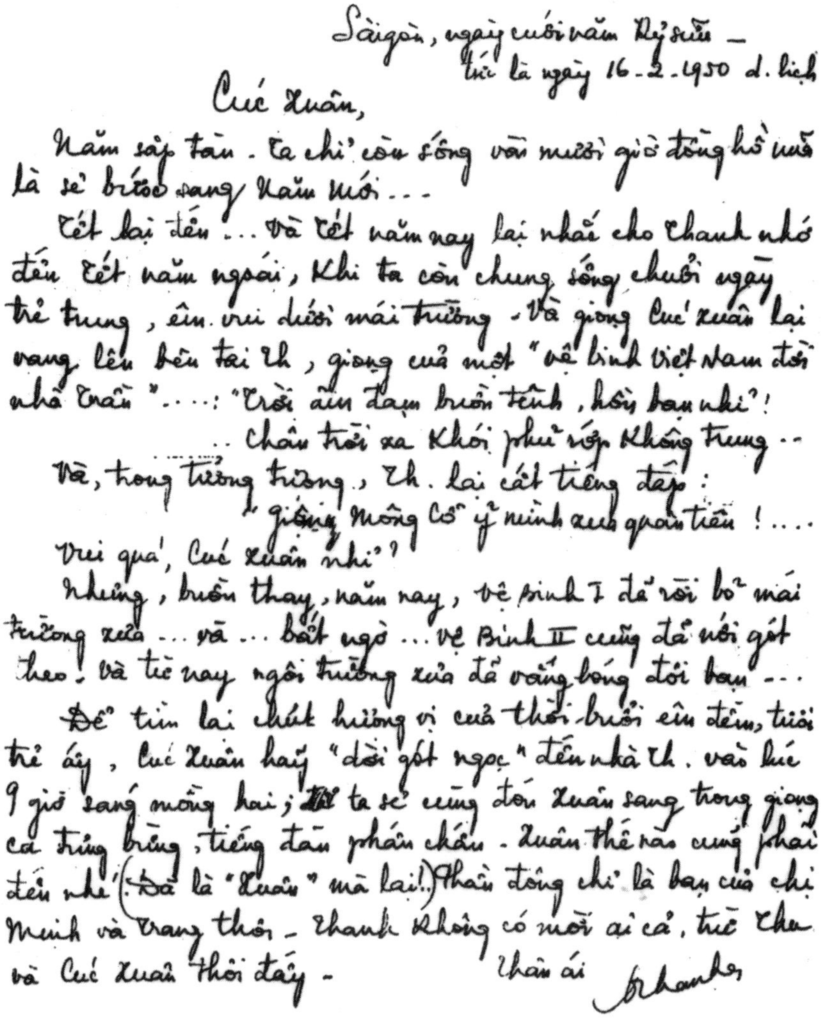

Sàigòn, ngày cuối năm Kỷ Sửu —
tức là ngày 16-2-1950 d. lịch

Cúc Xuân,

Năm sắp tàn. Ta chỉ còn sống vài mươi giờ đồng hồ nữa là sẽ bước sang Năm mới...

Tết lại đến... Và Tết năm nay lại nhắc cho Thanh nhớ đến Tết năm ngoái, khi ta còn chung sống chuỗi ngày trẻ trung, êm vui dưới mái trường — Và giọng Cúc Xuân lại vang lên bên tai Th, giọng của một "vệ binh Việt Nam tới nhà Trần"....: "Trời âm đạm buồn tênh, hỡi bạn nhỉ"!
.. Chân trời xa khói phủ rợp không trung..

Và, trong tưởng tượng, Th. lại cất tiếng đáp:
"giông mông cổ ý nình xuất quân tiến!....

Vui quá, Cúc Xuân nhỉ"?

Nhưng, buồn thay, năm nay, vệ binh I đã rời bỏ mái trường xưa... và... bất ngờ... vệ binh II cũng đã nối gót theo! Và từ nay ngôi trường xưa đã vắng bóng đôi bạn...

Để tìm lại chút hương vị của thời buổi êm đềm, tươi trẻ ấy, Cúc Xuân hãy "dời gót ngọc" đến nhà Th. vào lúc 9 giờ sáng mồng hai; ta sẽ cùng đón Xuân sang trong giọng ca trầm bổng, tiếng đàn phấn chấn. Xuân thế nào cũng phải đến nhé! (Đã là "Xuân" mà lại!) Thầy đồng chí là bạn của chị Minh và Trang thôi — Thanh không có mời ai cả, trừ Chu và Cúc Xuân thôi đấy —

Thân ái
Thanh

FIGURE 15. Thanh's letter of February 16, 1950, invited Xuan to her house for Tet. Thanh alluded to the end of their childhood shared at Lycée Marie Curie and change to come. At a reunion in 1989, Xuan surprised Thanh by gently unfolding the letter from a small pocket in her wallet. Courtesy of the author.

Guard Number One did join her friend to celebrate a Tet that, Thanh muses, marks one of the last times the sisters were together: "We dared to sing the national hymn of the North at our house in the middle of town! Had we been caught, we all would have been imprisoned."

As the afternoon reunion unfolds, the women are not yet tired. Energy and laughter are in the air. Many talk about the patriotic feelings awakened through music and song, recalling that the national anthem had to be sung out of earshot of police. The official hymn of the *écoliers*, the schoolgirls and boys, stoked patriotism. At mention of the hymn, the sisters break out in song—holding the melody when words escape them. Written by Tuyen's brother Luu Huu Phuoc, the anthem exhorts students to get on the path and march on:

> Fellow students, future of the country,
> Our hair still downy as we greet the dawn;
> Happy together, holding hands, singing as we walk
> Through wind and rain to battle for our land.
> Awaiting danger, hardship, even death
> Students, hurry, hasten forward, never backward
> Students, study think and labor,
> Hoping always to advance.
> May we inspire our countrymen
> Students, sing out with pride
> Ahead, the future lies glorious and bright.

With clouds having passed and the sun beginning to set over Ho Chi Minh City, the light of day turns soft and golden. Shadows lengthen across the room made cozy by friends reminiscing. Outside, motorbikes still sputter past on Nam Ky Khoi Nghia Street. The women collect their albums. Xuan folds and tucks the Tet letter from Thanh back into her wallet, careful not to tear it.

Minh, the eldest of the Binh girls, speaks for the group as she concludes, "Our generation was the generation at the crossroads." A crossroads offering three choices: rebel against foreign domination, collaborate, or leave their beloved country.

This reunion is almost over. On her way out, Xuan, reflecting on her study of the revolutions in France, England, and America while at Lycée Marie Curie, quietly states: "We concluded we had to have our own revolution."

EPILOGUE

The death of the first sister saddened and shocked her friends, who could not believe a freak accident killed someone who had endured so much. In 2000, in early morning darkness, Thanh balanced on the back of a motorcycle taxi to go see a close friend—a fellow diplomat at the Paris Peace Talks—who was ill. As the motorcycle gathered speed, the tail of her silk ao dai caught in the spokes of the back wheel, dragging Thanh off the bike, her head striking the ground. Rushed to hospital, the same one where the student Tran Van On had been taken in 1950, she lay in a coma and died on September 7, 2000. Thanh was cremated. Minh and Thanh's daughter took the urn with her ashes on a boat into the middle of the Saigon River, where they sprinkled them in a long thin trail across the water.

Oanh expressed the loss: "Thanh's death was a shock. I cried like I never cried for my family members." By 2001, Oanh observed, the sisters were getting together less often.

Without a clear cause, Oanh was the next to pass away on May 1, 2009. She was always private about health problems, including treatment of a possible cancer in her jawbone. A memorial took place on May 1, 2010, in a room in the diocese across from the Saigon cathedral. Former students, teachers, colleagues, and many others touched by her work on social issues gathered for a eulogy to "a model and devoted teacher who contributed to many generations of lecturers and social workers for universities." As affirmed in the program, "We will continue your concerns for the sustainable development of community and society."

In early 2017, Lien An died in her home. Two days before, Tien—the friend of the sisters with whom I stayed in 1989—had visited, and she described a remarkable scene. Always rail thin, Lien An's face looked the same, but, outlined by the sheets, her limbs looked like twigs. She weighed fourteen kilos, just over thirty pounds, "a live skeleton." Yet Tien marveled at how Lien An had talked to her for an hour, as though nothing were unusual, as though she were not about to die. She had held onto Tien's arms, happy, smiling. She had showered Tien with advice! Back home, Tien had called Xuan, who had gone to visit the following day. Lien An died a day later.

Another sister, Le An, broke her femur in early 2017, and Sen, Xuan, and Tuyen visited her for Tet. Le An was happy to see them. In June, Tuyen returned to visit Le An at her daughter's apartment in Chinatown. Her small, thin figure draped in mismatched pajama top and bottoms, Le An lay on her back—eyes closed, knees pulled up. A cerebral hemorrhage had taken away her speech. She wore a peaceful expression. Missing were her trademark round glasses.

In retirement, Minh and her sister Trang are opposites. Dressed in form-fitting ao dais of lush colors, Minh scoots around town to attend concerts and check on friends and colleagues she knows from decades of teaching and working. Sitting at the piano in the home built by her father, she launches into a spirited rendition of songs popular when the Saigon sisters were part of a generation of students "at the crossroads," as she often puts it. Trim, energetic, smiling, Minh remains youthful and open in spirit.

Trang no longer teaches music or conducts; she returned to being an emotional "turtle." She rarely leaves the family home, which is divided into sections; she shares the second story with her daughter, Autumn, a respected translator fluent in English, Russian, and French. Autumn studied at Lycée Marie Curie, in Moscow, and in the United States. While isolated, Trang is not alone. She is surrounded by evidence of her sentimental nature in cabinets of photo albums and mementos from near and far—a six-inch candle in the shape of a champagne bottle from Russia, a row of nesting dolls. One source of delight mother and daughter share is dogs, several of which patrol the courtyard.

For Xuan, the death of her husband, Lau, in 2010 left her bereft. Xuan and Lau are *the* love story among the sisters. Xuan still finds pleasure in gardening, a small joy she and Oanh shared over many years. With one son in Saigon and several children abroad, Xuan prefers to reside in the former French hill station of Da Lat. Built into the slope of a hill, her narrow house overlooks the rose-colored spires of Sainte-Marie Cathedral. Xuan transformed the front and back yards from scrubland into a cornucopia of flowers and fruit trees. Inside, a narrow table along the living room wall displays the altar to Lau. One of Lau's favorites photos shows him sporting sunglasses and a fedora. Xuan often shuffles to the churchyard across the street and peers in the direction of the place where Lau was cremated before she scattered his ashes in the sea off Nha Trang. Her children come to stay with her, and she occasionally descends to Saigon for medical appointments. Her son wants her to spend more time in Saigon. It is in listening to classical music that she continues to find peace.

Sen, too, has children all around the world who regularly visit. Knowing their children are well educated and hold steady jobs overseas is comforting. At the same time, health problems have slowed Sen, who used to host the sisters at her comfortable home, offering delicious noodle soups, crab dishes, and indulgent desserts. Now she rarely leaves her house.

For her part, Tuyen lives with her son and his wife and daughter. "Aunt" Oanh would be pleased to know Tuyen's granddaughter wants to study social work or psychology. Other offspring live overseas and visit. While Tuyen's stamina has waned, her curiosity about the world has not. She likes to travel, keeps up her French—writing it beautifully—and reads in English. Calling herself "shy," Tuyen still enjoys choreographing reunions. Just as she helped arrange the gathering of Marie Curie friends in 1981, for years she quietly continued to phone and make house visits to spread word of a reunion. Braving the hot sun in a floppy hat, flat sandals, and a flowery shirt over her slacks, Tuyen could be spotted on her motorcycle navigating the chaotic streets of Saigon. Today, she resigns herself to hailing taxis. She visits friends who are too frail or withdrawn to leave their homes.

Still, it is possible another reunion will bring together the Saigon sisters, including the spirits of those departed. It would be fitting to gather again to rekindle memories of bonds forged at Lycée Marie Curie, share stories of privileged girls who rebelled, and celebrate—across long and terrible years—the strength and the solace of enduring friendship.

Bibliography

Bass, Thomas. *The Spy Who Loved Us*. New York: Public Affairs, 2009.

Bong-Wright, Jackie. *Autumn Cloud*. Herndon, VA: Capital Books, 2001.

Borton, Lady. *After Sorrow: An American Among the Vietnamese*. New York: Viking Penguin, 1995.

Boudarel, Georges. *Autobiographie*. Paris: Jacques Bertoin, 1991.

Chanoff, David, and Doan Van Tai. *Vietnam: A Portrait of Its People at War*. London: Taurus Parke, 2009.

Dawson, Alan. *55 Days: The Fall of South Vietnam*. Bangkok: Phimphilai, 1977.

Duiker, William. *Vietnam: Nation in Revolution*. Boulder, CO: Westview, 1983.

———. *Sacred War: Nationalism and Revolution in a Divided Vietnam*. New York: McGraw-Hill, 1995.

Duras, Marguerite. *Un barrage contre le Pacifique*. Paris: Editions Gallimard, 1950.

Eisen, Arlene. *Women and Revolution in Viet Nam*. London: Zed Books, 1984.

Elliott, Duong Van Mai. *The Sacred Willow—Four Generations in the Life of a Vietnamese Family*. New York, Oxford University Press, 1999.

Fall, Bernard. *Vietnam Witness, 1953–66*. New York: Frederick A. Praeger, 1966.

Goscha, Christopher. "'So What Did You Learn from War?': Violent Decolonization and Paul Mus's Search for Humanity." *South East Asia Research* 20, no. 4 (2012): 569–93. Accessed June 21, 2019. https://cgoscha.uqam.ca/wp-content/uploads/sites/28/2017/01/So-what-did-you-learn-from-war.pdf.

———. *The Penguin History of Modern Vietnam*. London: Penguin Random House, 2016.

Hammer, Ellen. *The Struggle for Indochina, 1940–1955*. Stanford, CA: Stanford University Press, 1954.

———. *A Death in November*. New York: E. P. Dutton, 1987.

Hue-Tam, Ho Tai. *The Country of Memory*. Berkeley: University of California Press, 2001.

———. *Passion, Betrayal, and Revolution in Colonial Saigon*. Berkeley: University of California Press, 2010.

Huynh, Kim Khanh. *Vietnamese Communism, 1925–45*. Ithaca, NY: Cornell University Press, 1982.

Isaacs, Arnold R. *Vietnam Shadows: The War, Its Ghosts, and Its Legacy*. Baltimore: Johns Hopkins University Press, 1997.

Kelly, Gail Paradise. *French Colonial Education*. New York: AMS Press, 2000.

Lessard, Micheline. "The Colony Writ Small: Vietnamese Women and Political Activism in Colonial Schools during the 1920s." *Journal of the Canadian Historical Association / Revue de la Société historique du Canada* 18, no. 2 (2007): 3–23.

Mai, Thu Van. *Vietnam, un peuple, des voix*. Paris: Pierre Horay, 1983.

Marr, David. *Vietnamese Tradition on Trial (1920–1945)*. Berkeley: University of California Press, 1981.

Ngo, Vinh Long, trans. *Vietnamese Women in Society and Revolution*. Vol. 1, *The French Colonial Period*. Cambridge, MA: Vietnam Resource Center, 1974.

Nguyen, Thi Dinh. *No Other Road to Take*. Ithaca, NY: Southeast Asia Program, 1976.

Osborne, Milton E. *The French Presence in Cochinchina and Cambodia.* Ithaca, NY: Cornell University Press, 1969.

Riffaud, Madeleine. *Dans les Maquis "Vietcong."* Paris: Rene Julliard, 1965.

Shaplen, Robert. *Bitter Victory.* New York: Harper & Row, 1986.

Sheehan, Neil. *A Bright Shining Lie.* New York: Random House, 1988.

Taylor, Sandra C. *Vietnamese Women at War.* Lawrence: University Press of Kansas, 1999.

Truong, Nhu Tang. *Vietcong Memoir: An Inside Account of the Vietnam War and Its Aftermath.* New York: Harcourt Brace Jovanovich, 1985.

Turner, Karen Gottschang. *Even the Women Must Fight.* New York: John Wiley & Sons, 1988.

Woodside, Alexander B. *Community and Revolution in Modern Vietnam.* Boston: Houghton Mifflin, 1976.

Xuan, Phuong, and Daniel Mazingarbe. *My War, My Country, My Vietnam.* Great Neck, NY: EMQUAD International, 2004.

Index

Page numbers in italics refer to figures.